Open Source Intelligence Methods and Tools

A Practical Guide to Online Intelligence

Nihad A. Hassan
Rami Hijazi

Apress®

Open Source Intelligence Methods and Tools: A Practical Guide to Online Intelligence

Nihad A. Hassan
New York, USA

Rami Hijazi
Mississauga, Ontario, Canada

ISBN-13 (pbk): 978-1-4842-3212-5
https://doi.org/10.1007/978-1-4842-3213-2

ISBN-13 (electronic): 978-1-4842-3213-2

Library of Congress Control Number: 2018948821

Managing Director, Apress Media LLC: Welmoed Spahr
Acquisitions Editor: Susan McDermott
Development Editor: Laura Berendson
Coordinating Editor: Rita Fernando

Cover designed by eStudioCalamar

Cover image designed by Freepik (www.freepik.com)

Distributed to the book trade worldwide by Springer Science+Business Media New York, 233 Spring Street, 6th Floor, New York, NY 10013. Phone 1-800-SPRINGER, fax (201) 348-4505, e-mail orders-ny@springer-sbm.com, or visit www.springeronline.com. Apress Media, LLC is a California LLC and the sole member (owner) is Springer Science + Business Media Finance Inc (SSBM Finance Inc). SSBM Finance Inc is a **Delaware** corporation.

For information on translations, please e-mail rights@apress.com, or visit www.apress.com/rights-permissions.

Apress titles may be purchased in bulk for academic, corporate, or promotional use. eBook versions and licenses are also available for most titles. For more information, reference our Print and eBook Bulk Sales web page at www.apress.com/bulk-sales.

Any source code or other supplementary material referenced by the author in this book is available to readers on GitHub via the book's product page, located at www.apress.com/9781484232125. For more detailed information, please visit www.apress.com/source-code.

Printed on acid-free paper

To my mom, Samiha, thank you for everything.
Without you, I'm nothing.

—Nihad A. Hassan

Table of Contents

About the Authors

Nihad A. Hassan is an independent information security consultant, digital forensics and cybersecurity expert, online blogger, and book author. He has been actively conducting research on different areas of information security for more than a decade and has developed numerous cybersecurity education courses and technical guides. He has completed several technical security consulting engagements involving security architectures, penetration testing, computer crime investigation, and cyber open source intelligence (OSINT). Nihad has authored four books and scores of information security articles for various global publications. He also enjoys being involved in security training, education, and motivation. His current work focuses on digital forensics, anti-forensics techniques, digital privacy, and cyber OSINT. He covers different information security topics and related matters on his security blog at www.DarknessGate.com and recently launched a dedicated site for open source intelligence resources at www.OSINT. link. Nihad has a bachelor's of science honors degree in computer science from the University of Greenwich in the United Kingdom.

Nihad can be followed on Twitter (@DarknessGate), and you can connect to him via LinkedIn at https://www.linkedin.com/in/darknessgate.

Rami Hijazi has a master's degree in information technology (information security) from the University of Liverpool. He currently works at MERICLER Inc., an education and corporate training firm in Toronto, Canada. Rami is an experienced IT professional who lectures on a wide array of topics, including object-oriented programming, Java, e-commerce, agile development, database design, and data handling analysis. Rami also works as information security consultant, where he is involved in designing encryption systems and wireless networks, detecting intrusions and tracking data breaches, and giving planning and development advice for IT departments concerning contingency planning.

About the Technical Reviewer

Reem Naddar has a bachelor's of science degree in mathematics from Dalhousie University and has been in the data analytics industry since 2006. She has substantial experience in designing and executing solutions that address complex business problems involving large-scale data warehousing, real-time analytics, software architecture, and reporting solutions. She employs leading-edge tools and techniques when implementing fast and efficient data acquisition including Big Data processing used by global practitioners.

Reem has worked for major corporations and chartered banks in Canada both as a contractor and as a permanent staff member. She is fond of open source intelligence (OSINT) projects where she adopts different frameworks and processes to capture, transform, analyze, and store terabytes of structured and unstructured data gathered from publicly available sources.

Acknowledgments

I start by thanking God for giving me the gift to write and convert my ideas into something useful. Without God's blessing, I would not be able to achieve anything.

I want to thank the ladies at Apress: Susan, Rita, and Laura. I was pleased to work with you again and very much appreciate your valuable feedback and encouragement.

Specifically, to book acquisitions editor Susan McDermott, thank you for believing in my book's idea and for your honest encouragement before and during the writing process. To book project editor Rita Fernando, you were very supportive during the writing process. You made authoring this book a joyful journey. To book development editor Laura Berendson, thank you very much for your diligent and professional work in producing this book.

I also want to thank all the Apress staff who worked behind the scenes to make this book possible and ready for launch. I hope you will continue your excellent work in creating highly valued computing books. Your work is greatly appreciated.

—Nihad A. Hassan

Introduction

Open Source Intelligence Methods and Tools focuses on building a deep understanding of how to exploit open source intelligence (OSINT) techniques, methods, and tools to acquire information from publicly available online sources to support intelligence analysis. The harvested data can be used in different scenarios such as financial, crime, and terrorism investigations as well as in more regular tasks such as analyzing business competitors, running background checks, and acquiring intelligence about individuals and other entities. This book will also improve your skills in acquiring information online from the surface web, the deep web, and the darknet.

Many estimates show that 90 percent of useful information acquired by intelligence services comes from public sources (in other words, OSINT sources). Social media sites open up numerous opportunities for investigations because of the vast amount of useful information located in one place. For example, you can get a great deal of personal information about any person worldwide by just checking their Facebook page. This book will show you how to conduct advanced social media investigations to access content believed to be private, use advanced search engines queries to return accurate results, search historical deleted versions of websites, track individuals online using public record databases and people-searching tools, locate information buried in the deep web, access and navigate the dark web, collect intelligence from the dark web, view multiple historic satellite images and street views of any location, search geolocation information within popular social media sites, and more. In short, you will learn how to use a plethora of techniques, tools, and free online services to gather intelligence about any target online.

OSINT-gathering activities should be conducted secretly to avoid revealing the searcher's identity. Therefore, this book will teach you how to conceal your digital identity and become anonymous online. You will learn how to exchange data secretly across hostile environments like the Internet and how to communicate with your peers privately and anonymously. You will also learn how to check your digital footprint and discover what kind of digital traces you are leaving behind and how to delete them.

Open Source Intelligence Methods and Tools is an indispensable guide for anyone responsible for collecting online content from public data, and it is a must-have reference for any casual Internet user who wants to dig deeper into the Internet to see what information it contains.

Target Audience

The following types of people will benefit from this book:

- Penetration testers

- Digital forensics investigators

- Intelligence services

- Military personnel

- Law enforcement

- UN agencies and nonprofit organizations

- For-profit enterprises

- Risk management professionals

- Journalists

- Academic researchers

- University students

- End users who want to learn how to exploit Internet resources effectively

What the Book Is Not

This book is not about the history of open source intelligence, and it does not discuss at length the legal issues of personal reconnaissance online. We will not talk about policies and regulations that govern different countries or business organizations. Although some of these issues are discussed briefly in Chapter 1, the main aim of this book is to create a guidebook to support all types of investigations. You can read the chapters in any order because each chapter is considered an isolated unit that discusses the chapter subject's comprehensively.

Summary of Contents

Here is a brief description of each chapter's contents:

- Chapter 1, "The Evolution of Open Source Intelligence": In this chapter, we introduce you to the term OSINT and explain how it has evolved over time. We introduce the different parties interested in exploiting publicly available data and the benefits gained from doing so. We include some technical information about online gathering techniques and the challenges involved, as well as the legal aspects when harvesting data from publicly available sources.

- Chapter 2, "Introduction To Online Threats and Countermeasures": In this chapter, we teach you everything you need to know to stay safe when going online. This knowledge is essential when conducting advanced searches online to avoid being tracked since using advanced search operators and other OSINT search techniques will attract attention online and make your connection a target for interception by different outside parties.

- Chapter 3, "The Underground Internet": This chapter is devoted to uncovering the secrets of the invisible web, which contains both the darknet and the deep web. This knowledge is essential as the underground net contains a wealth of valuable information that any cybersecurity professional should know how to access.

- Chapter 4, "Search Engine Techniques": In this chapter, we show you how to use advanced search techniques using typical search engines such as Google and Bing to find anything online. We also cover other specialized search engines for images, video, news, web directories, files, and FTP.

- Chapter 5, "Social Media Intelligence": In this chapter, we show you how to use a wide array of tools and techniques to gather intelligence about a specific person or entity from social media sites. For instance, using Facebook you can gather intelligence about people worldwide. Other major tech companies like Google and Microsoft own huge databases of information about their users. A great amount of information is published publicly on these sites, and this chapter teaches you how to search for people, including their relationships, names, addresses, and communications (and interactions) with others on social sites, to formulate a complete profile about your target.

- Chapter 6, "People Search Engines and Public Records": Here we list specific search engines and other public resources to search for people's names and get details around them. You will learn to use different reverse search criteria to find people online such as birth records, mail addresses, résumés, dating websites, e-mails, phone numbers, previous breached usernames, and more. We also cover government resources such as vital records, tax records, criminal information, and other public sources you can use to gain intelligence about people and entities.

- Chapter 7, "Online Maps": This chapter covers how to use Google Maps and other free geolocation services to investigate the geolocation information acquired about target people.

- Chapter 8, "Technical Footprinting": This chapter covers how to gather technical information about a target website and network system in passive mode to support your OSINT intelligence.

- Chapter 9, "What's Next?": This chapter covers the OSINT process and its future trends.

Book Companion Website

In this book, we list hundreds of online services that help OSINT gatherers to collect and analyze information. We all know about the ever-changing nature of the Web, though; new sites launch and others close down daily, so some links might not work by the time you read this. To prevent this hassle and to avoid making part of this book useless after publishing it, we have created a dedicated website where we offer a digital list of all the links mentioned in this book in addition to many more resources that just wouldn't fit in the printed version. We will do our best to keep this site updated and continually work to add new useful OSINT content that reflects improvements in the field. Dead links will get deleted or updated, so the content of this book will remain current for many years to come.

See www.OSINT.link.

Comments and Questions

To comment or ask technical questions about this book, send an e-mail to nihad@protonmail.com. For additional references about the subject, computer security tools, tutorials, and other related matters, check out the author's blog at www.DarknessGate.com.

CHAPTER 1

The Evolution of Open Source Intelligence

Since the end of the Cold War, global societies have become more open, and the revolution of the Internet and its widespread use have turned the world into a small village. Unleashing the Internet network to billions of people worldwide to communicate and exchange digital data has shifted the entire world into what is now an information age. This transformation to the digital age brought huge benefits to our society; however, the speed and scope of the transformation have also triggered different kinds of risks. For instance, cybercriminals, terrorist groups, oppressive regimes, and all kinds of malicious actors are using the Internet effectively to conduct their crimes. Juniper Research predicts that cybercrime will cost businesses more than $2 trillion by 2019,[i] so these risks encourage governments to invest in the development of open source intelligence (OSINT) tools and techniques to counter current and future cybersecurity challenges.

OSINT refers to all the information that is publicly available. There is no specific date on when the term OSINT was first proposed; however, a relative term has probably been used for hundreds of years to describe the act of gathering intelligence through exploiting publicly available resources.

The United States is still leading the world in the intelligence arena, with vast resources dedicated by the U.S. government to its intelligence agencies that enable it to build sophisticated surveillance programs to harvest and analyze a large volume of data covering all the major spoken languages. This makes our discussion of OSINT history largely dependent on U.S. history, although during the Cold War many countries also developed OSINT capabilities to gain intelligence. Still, no other country has reached the level of the U.S. programs.

© Nihad A. Hassan, Rami Hijazi 2018
N. A. Hassan and R. Hijazi, *Open Source Intelligence Methods and Tools*,
https://doi.org/10.1007/978-1-4842-3213-2_1

The U.S. Department of Defense (DoD) defines OSINT as follows:

> "Open-source intelligence (OSINT) is an intelligence that is
> produced from publicly available information and is collected,
> exploited, and disseminated in a timely manner to an appropriate
> audience for the purpose of addressing a specific intelligence
> requirement."[ii]

In modern times, OSINT was introduced during World War II as an intelligence tool when the United States established the Foreign Broadcast Information Service (FBIS) to monitor publicly available information that related to supporting its troop operations at that time. This all happened before the U.S. intelligence community even existed.

After the end of World War II, the FBIS has continued its work in exploiting OSINT sources globally, until the September 11, 2001, terror attacks on the United States. This drew attention to the importance of creating an independent OSINT agency to intensify exploiting these resources to protect national security. This is what was suggested by the 9/11 Commission, which called for the creation of a specialized agency for gathering OSINT.[iii] In 2005, the WMD Commission, which was formed to measure the effectiveness of the intelligence community to respond to threats raised by weapons of mass destruction (WMD) and other related threats of the 21st century, suggested the creation of an Open Source Directorate within the Central Intelligence Agency (CIA).[iv]

Following these recommendations and other debates, the Director of National Intelligence (DNI) announced the creation of the National Intelligence Open Source Center (OSC). The main tasks of the OSC are to collect information available from both online and offline public sources, which was previously done by the FBIS. Later, the Intelligence Reform and Terrorism Prevention Act, which was proposed to reform the intelligence activities of the U.S. government, merged the FBIS and other related research entities into one body. This organization is now called the Open Source Enterprise and is managed by the CIA.

OSINT sources are distinguished from other forms of intelligence because they must be legally accessible by the public without breaching any copyright or privacy laws. That's why they are considered "publicly available." This distinction makes the ability to gather OSINT sources applicable to more than just security services. For example, businesses can benefit from exploiting these resources to gain intelligence about their competitors.

Note!   During the search for OSINT sources, classified information that is not protected properly can appear. This includes leaked documents, such as those published by WikiLeaks. This type of information is called NOSINT, as opposed to OSINT. Intelligence usually considers all sources regardless of their legal accessibility.

In addition to its significant importance to the intelligence community, OSINT gathering is less expensive and less risky than traditional spying activites. Unlike other intelligence sources that may require using spy satellite images or secret agents to collect information, all you need to gather OSINT online resources is a computer and an Internet connection. And, of course, you need the required searching skills.

As technology proliferates and the volume of available data increases, government departments, nongovernmental organization (NGO) organizations, and business corporations are starting to rely to a large extent on OSINT rather than private and classified information. This book will teach you how to exploit OSINT sources to search for and gather information online. In this chapter, we will describe the term OSINT, discuss the types of OSIN, and talk about different parties' benefits from using OSINT and their motivations, as well as trends and challenges for the future. In later chapters, we will cover how to use a plethora of tools and techniques to acquire data from publicly available sources.

Open Source Information Categories

There are different kinds of information that you may encounter when conducting OSINT analysis. According to the *NATO Open Source Intelligence Handbook V1.2* published in 2001, there are four categories of open information and intelligence.

- *Open source data (OSD)*: This is generic data coming from a primary source. Examples include satellite images, telephone call data and metadata, datasets, survey data, photographs, and audio or video recordings that have recorded an event.

- *Open source information (OSINF)*: This is generic data that has undergone some filtering first to meet a specific criterion or need; this data can also be called a secondary source. Examples include books about a specific subject, articles, dissertations, artworks, and interviews.

3

Note!   The set of sources legally available to the public through specific channels is called *gray literature*. These sources include books, journals, dissertations, technical reports, and internal documents of commercial enterprises, commercial imagery, and any information that is controlled by its producer. Gray literature is a major element of OSINF and can be obtained legally by acquiring the permission of its copyright holder or by paying for it (for example, through subscriptions agencies, commercial bookstores, and so on).

- *Open source intelligence (OSINT)*: This includes all the information that has been discovered, filtered, and designated to meet a specific need or purpose. This information can be used directly in any intelligence context. OSINT can be defined in a nutshell as the output of open source material processing.

- *Validated OSINT (OSINT-V)*: This is OSINT with a high degree of certainty; the data should be confirmed (verified) using a non-OSINT source or from a highly reputable OSINT source. This is essential, as some outside adversaries may spread inaccurate OSINT information with the intent to mislead OSINT analysis. A good example of this is when a TV station broadcasts live the arrival of a president to another country; such information is OSINT, but it has a large degree of certainty.

As you saw, OSD and OSINF comprise the main sources (primary and secondary) of information that OSINT uses to drive its results.

Another issue you need to understand within the OSINT context is the difference between data, information, and knowledge. The three terms are usually used interchangeably; however, each one has a different meaning, although the three do interact with each other.

- *Data*: This is a set of facts describing something without further explanation or analysis. For example, "The price of gold per ounce is $1,212."

- *Information*: This is a kind of data that has been interpreted properly to give a useful meaning within a specific context. For example, "The price of gold per ounce has fallen from $1,212 to $1,196 within one week."

- *Knowledge*: This is a combination of information, experience, and insight that has been learned or inferred after some experimentation. Knowledge describes what your brain has recorded in the past, and these records can help you to make better decisions about the future when facing similar contexts. For example, "When the price of gold falls more than 5 percent, this means the price of oil will fall too."

OSINT Types

OSINT includes all publicly accessible sources of information. This information can be found either online or offline, including in the following places:

- The Internet, which includes the following and more: forums, blogs, social networking sites, video-sharing sites like YouTube.com, wikis, Whois records of registered domain names, metadata and digital files, dark web resources, geolocation data, IP addresses, people search engines, and anything that can be found online

- Traditional mass media (e.g., television, radio, newspapers, books, magazines)

- Specialized journals, academic publications, dissertations, conference proceedings, company profiles, annual reports, company news, employee profiles, and résumés

- Photos and videos including metadata

- Geospatial information (e.g., maps and commercial imagery products)

Digital Data Volume

As you already saw, OSINT encompasses not only online sources. Paper editions of public sources must also get investigated thoroughly as part of any OSINT-gathering process; however, online sources comprise the largest segment of OSINT.

Today we live in an information age, and publishers as well as corporations, universities, and other suppliers of OSINT sources are shifting their business processes to digital formats. The number of users on social media sites will also continue to increase, and the number of Internet of Things (IoT) devices will intensify in the future, leading to a huge increase in the volume of digital data coming from the billions of sensors and machines worldwide. In other words, most OSINT sources in the future will be online sources.

Note!   Gartner estimates that 20.4 billion IoT devices will be in use by 2020.[v]

The volume of digital data is exploding rapidly. According to IDC Research,[vi] by the year 2020, the total amount of digital data created worldwide will reach 44 zettabytes, and the number will increase faster within five years to reach 180 zettabytes in 2025.

By 2020, the Gartner research group estimates that an average person will spend time interacting with automated bots more than with their spouse, and of course all these interactions will be digital. Another estimate says that in 2021, 20 percent of all activities a human do will involve using a service from at least one of the giant IT companies (Google, Apple, Facebook, Amazon). Not to mention, most people will prefer to use voice commands to interact with their computing devices over typing.

These figures should give you an idea about what the near future will look like in the digital age. The volume of digital data along with the increased number of people using the Internet to do their jobs will make online sources the primary source of OSINT for both governments and business corporations in the future.

OSINT Organizations

Some specialized organizations provide OSINT services. Some of them are government based, and others are private companies that offer their services to different parties such as government agencies and business corporations on a subscription basis. In this section, we will mention the main OSINT organizations worldwide.

Government Organizations

Government organizations working in OSINT analysis are still considered the best because of the resources available from their governments to do their jobs. The two most famous government agencies that do OSINT globally are the Open Source Center in the United States and BBC Monitoring in Great Britain.

Open Source Center

We already talked about the Open Source Center (OSC); it is the largest OSINT organization and has vast resources to do its job. OSC works closely with other local intelligence agencies in the United States and offers its services to U.S. government intelligence agencies.

BBC Monitoring

BBC Monitoring (`https://monitoring.bbc.co.uk/login`) is a department within the British Broadcasting Corporation (BBC) that monitors foreign media worldwide. It has a similar role as the Open Source Center in the United States, with the main difference being that it does not belong to British Intelligence. BBC Monitoring is funded from its stakeholders in addition to many commercial and governmental entities around the world. It was first established in 1939 and has offices in different countries around the globe. It actively monitors TV, radio broadcast, print media, Internet, and emerging trends from 150 countries in more than 70 languages. BBC Monitoring is directed by the BBC and offers its services on a subscription basis to interested parties such as commercial organizations and UK official bodies.

Private Sector

You should not underestimate the private sector when looking at who supplies OSINT information; many private corporations have developed advanced programs and techniques to gathers data from public sources for commercial gain. Indeed, most private OSINT corporations partner with government agencies to supply them with such information. In this section, we will mention the main ones around the globe.

Jane's Information Group

Jane's Information Group (http://www.janes.com) is a British company founded in 1898. Jane's is a leading provider that specializes in military, terrorism, state stability, serious and organized crime, proliferation and procurement intelligence, aerospace, and transportation subjects. It publishes many journals and books related to security matters in addition to its OSINT sources that track and predict security matters in 190 states and 30 territories.

Economist Intelligence Unit

The Economist Intelligence Unit (https://www.eiu.com/home.aspx) is the business intelligence, research, and analysis division of the British Economist Group. The main domain of the Economist Intelligence Unit is its business and financial forecasts; it offers a monthly report in addition to a country economic forecast for the coming five years with a comprehensive view about current trends on economic and political issues.

Oxford Analytica

Oxford Analytica (http://www.oxan.com) is a relatively small OSINT firm compared with the previous two. Oxford Analytica specializes in geopolitics and macroeconomics subjects. It has a global macro expert network to advise its clients on the best practices of strategy and performance when accessing complex markets. Its expert networks contain more than 1400 experts. Most of them are scholars on their subject, senior faculty members in top universities, and high-profile specialists in their sector.

Gray Literature Vendors

We already talked about gray literature as part of OSINF data. However, this type of data deserves to have its own reference when talking about the main sources of information used in OSINT gathering because of its great intelligence value.

Gray literature is mainly produced by the world's publishing companies. It includes books, journals, newspapers, and anything published publicly. However, there is another type of gray literature called *gray information* that has different acquisition requirements.

Usually the terms *gray literature* and *gray information* are used interchangeably. However, in the intelligence arena, they are slightly different. Gray literature refers to all publications that can be obtained from traditional bookstore channels, while gray information refers to other publications that cannot be obtained from traditional routes. Hence, gray information has its own channels, and it may be difficult to identify and acquire it. Gray information includes the following and more: academic papers, preprints, proceedings, conference and discussion papers, research reports, marketing reports, technical specifications and standards, dissertations, theses, trade publications, memoranda, government reports and documents not published commercially, translations, newsletters, market surveys, trip reports, and festival agendas.

Gray literature can be divided into three main kinds.

- *White*: This includes anything published publicly for sale through traditional bookstore channels. The publication should have an ISBN or ISSN and can be obtained directly from its seller. Books, journals, and newspapers fall in this category.

- *Ephemeral*: This type is short-lived. Examples include flight schedules, draft versions, copies of invoices, advertisements, posters, tickets, business cards, and anything that is self-published.

- *Gray*: This contains a mix of the previously mentioned two types.

Generally, gray literature can be obtained by paying subscription fees for such content or through buying books, journals, magazines, and other publications directly from bookstores. To acquire more hidden gray information, you have to use other specialized services. The following are some of them.

Factiva

Factiva (`http://new.dowjones.com/products/factiva`) is a global news database with licensed content. It harvests data from more than 33,000 premium sources, and many of these sources (74 percent) are licensed and cannot be found freely online. Factiva collects sources in 28 languages in addition to its unique service of being able to provide access to resources that have not been published yet by their creators.

LexisNexis

LexisNexis (`https://www.lexisnexis.com/en-us/gateway.page`) is currently owned by RELX Group (formerly Reed Elsevier). It originally focused on providing high-quality legal and journalistic documents, but it has expanded its coverage to include more services such as media monitoring tools, supply management tools, sales intelligence solutions, market intelligence tools, and risk solutions that analyze public and industry-specific content to predict risk and improve decision-making.

The following are other companies that specialize in gathering online intelligence from both public and private sources:

- InsideView (`https://www.insideview.com`)

- NewsEdge (`www.newsedge.com`)

- Semantic Visions (`www.semantic-visions.com`)

- DigitalGlobe (`www.digitalglobe.com`)

Parties Interested in OSINT Information

OSINT can be beneficial for different actors. In this section, we will list them and explain what motivates each one to search for OSINT resources.

Government

Government bodies, especially military departments, are considered the largest consumer of OSINT sources. The huge technological developments and widespread use of the Internet worldwide have made governments a huge consumer for OSINT intelligence. Governments need OSINT sources for different purposes such as national security, counterterrorism, cybertracking of terrorists, understanding domestic and foreign public views on different subjects, supplying policy makers with required information to influence their internal and external policy, and exploiting foreign media like TV to get instant translations of different events happening outside.

Intelligence agencies combine legally accessible information with their secretly acquired intelligence (for example, using spy satellite images, electronic listening stations, and spies) to answer a specific question or to predict the future. Those people have the required resources (money and equipment) to capture and analyze huge quantities of data on the Internet. The act of mining OSINT data by governments is expected to intensify as we move steadily toward what is now a digital age.

International Organizations

International organizations like the UN use OSINT sources to support peacekeeping operations around the globe. The UN balances superpowers' and emerging nation-states' concerns when creating its policy, which requires it to be as transparent as possible. To achieve this, the UN found that it is more convenient to exploit OSINT sources (including commercial satellite images) for intelligence needs instead of depending on reports from its member states, which may have conflicting policies.

Humanitarian organizations, like the International Red Cross, use OSINT sources to aid them in their relief efforts in a time of crisis or disaster. They use OSINT intelligence to protect their supply chain from terrorist groups by analyzing social media sites and Internet messaging applications to predict future terrorist actions.

NATO depends heavily on OSINT sources for intelligence purposes and for making plans for peacekeeping operations. It also benefits from commercial satellite imagery to plan operations because not all NATO member states have such facilities. NATO has published three standard references about how to exploit OSINT to the public. The first one is *NATO Open Source Intelligence Handbook* (https://archive.org/details/NATOOSINTHandbookV1.2). The second is *NATO Open Source Intelligence Reader* (http://www.au.af.mil/au/awc/awcgate/nato/osint_reader.pdf). The third one is *NATO Intelligence Exploitation of the Internet* (http://nsarchive2.gwu.edu//NSAEBB/NSAEBB436/docs/EBB-005.pdf).

Law Enforcement Agencies

Police uses OSINT sources to protect citizens from abuse, sexual violence, identity theft, and other crimes. This can be done by monitoring social media channels for interesting keywords and pictures to help prevent crimes before they escalate.

Law enforcement uses OSINT to monitor and track a criminal's networks across different countries. For example, they use OSINT tactics to compile information about people of interest to create a complete profile for each one. They also use OSINT sources for online counterfeiting and copyright violations.

Business Corporations

Information is power, and corporations use OSINT sources to investigate new markets, monitor competitors' activities, plan marketing activities, and predict anything that can affect their current operations and future growth. In the past, exploiting OSINT sources was limited to big businesses with good intelligence budgets. Nowadays, with the widespread use of the Internet, small companies with limited budgets can exploit OSINT sources effectively and merge acquired information into their business plans.

Businesses also use OSINT intelligence for other nonfinancial purposes such as the following:

- To fight against data leakage, knowing that the business exposure of confidential information and the security vulnerabilities of their networks is a cause of future cyberthreats

- To create their threat intelligence strategies through analyzing OSINT sources from both outside and inside the organization and then combining this information with other information to accomplish an effective cyber-risk management policy that helps them to protect their financial interests, reputation, and customer base

OSINT is specifically useful for companies working in the defense industry, as such companies need to be fully aware of the surrounding circumstances of their customers to develop and target them with the appropriate equipment.

Penetration Testers and Black Hat Hackers/Criminal Organizations

OSINT is used extensively by hackers and penetration testers to gather intelligence about a specific target online. It is also considered a valuable tool to assist in conducting social engineering attacks. The first phase of any penetration testing methodology begins with reconnaissance (in other words, with OSINT). Figure 1-1 details the main phases of penetration testing.

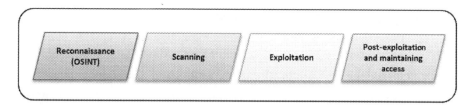

Figure 1-1. *Penetration testing methodology (source: http://www.DarknessGate.com)*

Penetration testers are paid by companies to break into internal networks to show where weaknesses lie and how to keep outsiders out. This is different from black hat hackers who exploit these vulnerabilities to gain unauthorized access to confidential data; however, both use the same reconnaissance techniques and tools to achieve their work.

Privacy-Conscious People

These are ordinary people who might want to check how outsiders can break into their computing devices and what their ISP knows about them. They also need to know their online exposure level to close any security gap and delete any private data that may have been published inadvertently. OSINT is a great tool to see how your digital identity appears to the outside world, allowing you to maintain your privacy.

Individuals can also use OSINT to fight against identity theft, for example, in case someone is impersonating you. During this book, we will teach you different techniques to search for text, images, and video, as well as digital file metadata.

Indeed, all Internet users are using OSINT techniques in one way or another, such as when searching for something online. Whether it is a company, school, university, or person you are looking for, you are collecting some form of OSINT intelligence.

Terrorist Organizations

Terrorists use OSINT sources to plan attacks, collect information about targets before attacking them (like when using satellite images such as Google Maps to investigate the target location), procure more fighters by analyzing social media sites, acquire military information revealed accidentally by governments (like how to construct bombs), and spread their propaganda across the world using different media channels.

Information Gathering Types

OSINT sources can be collected using three main methods: passive, semipassive, and active. The usage of one in favor of another is dependent on the scenario in which the gathering process operates in addition to the type of data that you are interested in. The three gathering techniques are generally used to describe the ways in which footprinting works, in other words, acquiring technical information about target IT infrastructure (types of OS, network topology, server names, and so on). However, bear in mind that this book will teach you different techniques to collect OSINT intelligence, and technical footprinting is considered a kind of information gathering.

Passive Collection

This is the most used type when collecting OSINT intelligence. Indeed, all OSINT intelligence methods should use passive collection because the main aim of OSINT gathering is to collect information about the target via publicly available resources only. In this type, your target knows nothing about your intelligence-collecting activities. This kind of search is highly anonymous and should be done secretly. From a technical perspective, this type of gathering reveals limited information about the target because you do not send any traffic (packets) to the target server—either directly or indirectly— and the main resources that you can gather are limited to archive information (mainly outdated information), unprotected files left on target servers, and content present on the target website.

Semipassive

From a technical view, this type of gathering sends limited traffic to target servers to acquire general information about them. This traffic tries to resemble typical Internet traffic to avoid drawing any attention to your reconnaissance activities. In this way, you are not implementing in-depth investigation of the target's online resources, but only investigating lightly without launching any alarm on the target's side. Although this type of gathering is considered somehow anonymous, the target can know that there is reconnaissance happening if they investigate the issue (by checking the server or networking device logs). However, they should not be able to attribute it to the attacker's machine.

Active Collection

In this type, you interact directly with the system to gather intelligence about it. The target can become aware of the reconnaissance process since the person/entity collecting information will use advanced techniques to harvest technical data about the target IT infrastructure such as accessing open ports, scanning vulnerabilities (unpatched Windows systems), scanning web server applications, and more. This traffic will look like suspicious or malicious behavior and will leave traces on the target's intrusion detection system (IDS) or intrusion prevention system (IPS). Conducting social engineering attacks on the target is also considered a type of active information gathering.

As we said earlier, active collection and semipassive collection are types of information gathering, but you usually do not use them in OSINT gathering. Passive collection is preferred because it can harvest information from public sources secretly, and this is the essence of OSINT.

Benefits of OSINT

In today's information age, no one can underestimate the vital role that OSINT plays in the different intelligence arenas. The benefits of OSINT span many areas in today's world. The following are the main ones:

- *Less risky*: Using publicly available information to collect intelligence has no risk compared with other forms of intelligence such as using spying satellites or using human sources on the ground to collect information, especially in hostile countries.

- *Cost effective*: Collecting OSINT is generally less expensive compared with other intelligence sources. For instance, using human sources or spying satellite to collect data is costly. Small businesses with limited intelligence budgets can exploit OSINT sources with minimal costs.

- *Ease of accessibility*: OSINT sources are always available, no matter where you are, and are always up-to-date. OSINT sources can be used by different parties in any intelligence context; all you need are the required skills/tools to harvest and analyze OSINT properly. For example, military departments can predict future attacks by analyzing activities on social networking sites, while corporations can use it to build their new market expansion strategies.

- *Legal issues*: OSINT resources can be shared between different parties without worrying about breaching any copyright license as these resources are already published publicly. Of course, some limitations apply when sharing gray literature; we already covered this in a previous section.

- *Aiding financial investigators*: OSINT allows specialized government agencies to detect tax evaders, for instance. Many famous celebrities and some giant companies are involved in tax evasion, and monitoring their social media accounts, vacations, and lifestyles has a great value for a government inspector who may be chasing them for undeclared income.

- *Fighting against online counterfeiting*: OSINT techniques can be used to find false products/services and direct law enforcement to close such sites or to send warnings to users to stop dealing with them. This is a great advantage of OSINT, especially when fighting against counterfeit pharmaceutical and natural health products.

- *Maintaining national security and political stability*: This might be the most important role of OSINT; it helps governments to understand their people's attitudes and act promptly to avoid any future clashes. Wise governments utilize OSINT in their future strategies, especially for their domestic policies.

Challenges of Open Source Intelligence

All intelligence gathering methodologies have some limitations, and OSINT is not exempt from this rule. In this section, we will mention some of the challenges that face OSINT gathering.

- *Sheer volume of data*: Collecting OSINT will produce a huge amount of data that must be analyzed to be considered of value. Of course, many automated tools exist for this purpose, and many governments and giant companies have developed their own set of artificial intelligence tools and techniques to filter acquired data. However, the tremendous volume of data will remain a challenge for the OSINT gatherer.

- *Reliability of sources*: Bear in mind that OSINT sources, especially when used in the intelligence context, need to be verified thoroughly by classified sources before they can be trusted. Many governments broadcast inaccurate information to mislead the OSINT-gathering process.

- *Human efforts*: As we already mentioned, the sheer volume of data is considered the greatest challenge for OSINT collection. Humans need to view the output of automated tools to know whether the collected data is reliable and trustworthy; they also need to compare it with some classified data (this is applicable for some military and commercial information) to assure its reliability and relevance. This will effectively consume time and precious human resources.

Legal and Ethical Constraints

Despite the great importance of OSINT, it has legal concerns when analyzed or captured in many cases. For example, if someone acquires OSINT sources by illegal means to justify an honest case, how should the legal system handle it? Another dilemma is when the OSINT sample is minimized or selected according to the collector's need. They could effectively discard important sources purposely in favor of bringing about a specific outcome.

Another concern is when some forms of hidden public information are collected and publicized widely as part of a scandal. As you are going to see in this book, a lot of public information cannot be viewed by the regular Internet user and needs specific techniques/methods to acquire. What is the consequence for such things? What will be the effects on some groups or individuals when revealing such information about them? What are the moral consequences?

Over the past five years, many whistleblowers have stolen classified information from well-guarded agencies and institutions and published it online (Edward Snowden is a clear example). Should we consider this information belonging to the public source? Of course, military departments around the world will be thirsty for such information, but should we use it—as individuals or companies—as a public source for our intelligence?

Many corporations (Facebook and Google are examples) harvest a large volume of online user data for commercial intelligence; most of this data belongs to the user's actions and behavior online and cannot be used to recognize the user's real identity. For instance, there are two types of data that can be collected online:

- Sensitive personal information (SPI) such as name, Social Security number, place of birth, parents' names, passport or ID number

- Anonymous information such as technical information like your OS type and version, browser version, IP address, connected device location, and anything that is shared between more than one connected user

To justify the collection, these corporations say they acquire only anonymous data, but what if this anonymous information has been combined with other sources to become SPI? How should such information be handled by the OSINT analyst?

The final legal concern that we are going to cover is the reliance on automated machines to collect and analyze OSINT information. Can we trust the outcome of automated machines and treat it just like the data collected by humans? What if there is a software flaw in the tool that produces inaccurate output that leads to harmful consequences? How we can find a balance between using automated machines, which are necessary in the OSINT-gathering process, and remaining ethical?

The limitations of OSINT in addition to its legal constraints should encourage its adopters to follow an individualized and tailored approach when using it.

Summary

In this chapter, you discovered the essence of OSINT, its types and users, and how it can be used in different contexts by different parties to gain intelligence. We distinguished between different ways to gather information online (mainly technical footprinting) and talked briefly about what things each method cares about.

We concluded by talking about the advantages and limitations of OSINT gathering. No information-gathering methodology is considered 100 percent complete; however, with the right planning and sufficient resources and expertise, exploiting OSINT will produce accurate results on a great scale.

OSINT is a great place to get intelligence about future events, but acquiring OSINT alone is not enough to produce accurate results. For instance, to achieve the best results from OSINT sources, some value-added tasks must be considered during the analysis phase, such as using an expert analyst, merging OSINT information with classified information when handling military information, and adopting the right techniques to acquire nonbiased OSINT intelligence.

This chapter was an introduction to the subject. In the following chapters, we will thoroughly cover a plethora of techniques and tools to harvest and analyze OSINT information. Before we begin diving into the world of OSINT, though, it is essential to learn how to maintain our digital privacy and obscure our online activities when conducting OSINT gathering, and this will be the subject of the next chapter.

Notes

i. Juniperresearch, "CYBERCRIME WILL COST BUSINESSES OVER $2 TRILLION BY 2019" August 25, 2017. `https://www.juniperresearch.com/press/press-releases/cybercrime-cost-businesses-over-2trillion`

ii. Gpo, "Public Law 109-163 109th Congress" August 25, 2017.`https://www.gpo.gov/fdsys/pkg/PLAW-109publ163/html/PLAW-109publ163.htm`

iii. CIA, "Intelligence in Public Literature "August 25, 2017.`https://www.cia.gov/library/center-for-the-study-of-intelligence/csi-publications/csi-studies/studies/vol.-56-no.-1/no-more-secrets-open-source-information-and-the-reshaping-of-u.s.-intelligence.html`

iv. Fas, "Final Report of the Commission on the Intelligence Capabilities of the United States Regarding Weapons of Mass Destruction" August 25, 2017. `https://fas.org/irp/offdocs/wmdcomm.html`

v.   Gartner, "Gartner Says 8.4 Billion Connected 'Things' Will Be in
Use in 2017, Up 31 Percent From 2016" August 25, 2017.
https://www.gartner.com/newsroom/id/3598917

vi.   Comsoc, "IDC Directions 2016: IoT (Internet of Things) Outlook vs
Current Market Assessment" August 25, 2017. http://techblog.
comsoc.org/2016/03/09/idc-directions-2016-iot-internet-
of-things-outlook-vs-current-market-assessment

CHAPTER 2

Introduction To Online Threats and Countermeasures

As you do your research for OSINT, you will certainly leave digital traces behind that can be used to track you. For example, consider an investigator performing an online search for drug dealers in Mexico. What if the people the investigator was searching for discovers his search? What if they could learn the source of the search (the organization or the person behind the search) and the searcher's location? If you think that criminal organizations are not technically savvy, we're afraid you are wrong. Terrorists and criminal organizations have specialized teams working in IT to gather intelligence online, and even small criminal organizations with limited budgets outsource such tasks to specialized organizations for a fee.

As you saw in Chapter 1, OSINT is beneficial to many user groups. We already gave an example for an investigator searching for drug dealers; however, the same thing applies to anyone conducting OSINT searches such as individuals, government entities, business corporations, and even NGOs and global organizations like NATO. Revealing the searcher's identity when conducting OSINT searches can have dangerous—and even legal—consequences on some user segments.

In this chapter, we will teach you how to conceal your digital identity and become anonymous online. You will learn how to exchange data secretly across hostile environments like the Internet and how to communicate with your peers privately and anonymously. You will also learn how to check your digital footprint and discover what kind of digital traces you are leaving behind. But before we begin, we will cover online

© Nihad A. Hassan, Rami Hijazi 2018
N. A. Hassan and R. Hijazi, *Open Source Intelligence Methods and Tools*,
https://doi.org/10.1007/978-1-4842-3213-2_2

threats and how outside adversaries can exploit computing devices and networks to steal confidential information. Countermeasures and best practices to maintain your online security and privacy will be thoroughly covered.

This is the longest chapter in this book; you can consider it as a mini book that teaches you how to work online privately. This knowledge is mandatory, as you cannot conduct OSINT searches with your real identity.

Note!   We cannot teach you how to become 100 percent anonymous in one chapter. However, to begin conducting your OSINT search, this chapter is enough to help you avoid attracting outside observers to your OSINT-gathering activities.

To understand all concepts in depth and learn how different actors can invade your privacy, you should read our book *Digital Privacy and Security Using Windows* (https://www.apress.com/gp/book/9781484227985), which is considered the perfect companion to this book. If you already have this book, you can skip this chapter.

Online Threats

Despite its great benefits to humanity, the Internet is still a hostile environment. Bad guys are always out there to disrupt your life. In this section, we will list the main risks that Internet users face when going online, and we will give brief advice/ countermeasures for each one.

Malware

Malware is short for "malicious software." It is the term used for any malicious software/ code that can damage to your computing device or steal your confidential information without your consent. There are different kinds of malware such as viruses, spyware, rootkits, worms, ransomware, scareware, and adware.

Note!   There are many websites that offer free samples of live malicious code (malware) for security researchers, incident responders, forensic analysts, and any interested party. Some of these sites are the following:

`https://virusshare.com`

`https://www.virustotal.com`

`http://malc0de.com/database`

`https://virusscan.jotti.org`

Black Hat Hackers

Black hat hackers are people with sophisticated computing skills. They aim to invade private networks and break into other people computing devices to steal personal information or to conduct other malicious acts. They usually exploit vulnerabilities in the OS, in application programs, or in networking devices to gain unauthorized access. After gaining access, they may install a keylogger or a Trojan horse to maintain their access, steal information, or spy on user activities.

Pharming

Pharming is a cyberattack intended to redirect users from a legitimate website to a fraudulent site without their knowledge. Pharming can be conducted either by changing the hosts file on a victim's computer or by poisoning the Domain Name System (DNS) server records with false information to lead users to unwanted destinations.

Windows users can prevent this type of attack on their local machines by preventing hosts file modifications through the following steps:

1. Navigate to the `%SYSTEMDRIVE%\Windows\Ssystem32\drivers\etc` folder (`SYSTEMDRIVE` is where you installed Windows, usually at `C:\`).

2. Right-click the hosts file, select Properties, and select the Read-only attribute; finally, click OK (see Figure 2-1).

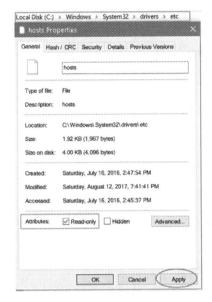

Figure 2-1. Changing the hosts file attributes to Read-only to avoid pharming attacks on Windows machines

---

Note!   You can edit the Windows hosts file using a feature-rich tool. Such tools allow you to add entries to block malware sites and enable or disable the hosts file. Check out HostsMan (www.abelhadigital.com/hostsman) and SysMate - Hosts File Walker (https://sourceforge.net/projects/sysmate-hosts-file-walker/).

Phishing

Phishing is a kind of social engineering attack where an attacker uses psychological tricks (social tricks) over the phone or uses a computing device (emails, IM chat) to convince people to hand over sensitive information about themselves or an organization and its computer systems.

Phishing emails appear as if they were sent by a legitimate company or someone you know (such as an individual on your contact list). These emails usually contain a link that the user must click to access/update an online account (for example, a bank or social site account). Upon clicking such links, the user will be directed to a fraudulent website that appears legitimate. When the user provides their credentials, the attacker will store them for later use and direct the user to the original website.

Phishing emails have some characteristics that anyone can spot. Here is a list of the main ones:

- They use threatening or urgent words in the subject line to encourage the user to act promptly. They usually ask you to update your online account or to send your personal details by replying to the email.

- Some phishing emails offer prizes, work-from-home vacancies with large salaries and no qualifications necessary, or business investments with high profits. Then they ask for your contact details for further negotiations.

- Phishing emails look unprofessional and contain many grammatical errors; they also originate from a different domain than the company they pretend to represent. For example, an email from PayPal should come from the PayPal.com domain and not from xyz.PayPal.com.

Whenever you suspect an email to be a phishing email, do not reply to it. To check whether it is a phishing email, rest your mouse (but don't click) over the links in the email to see whether the address matches the link that was typed in the message or the sender domain name. In addition, do not supply any personal information if a phishing email asks you to fill any forms (see Figure 2-2).

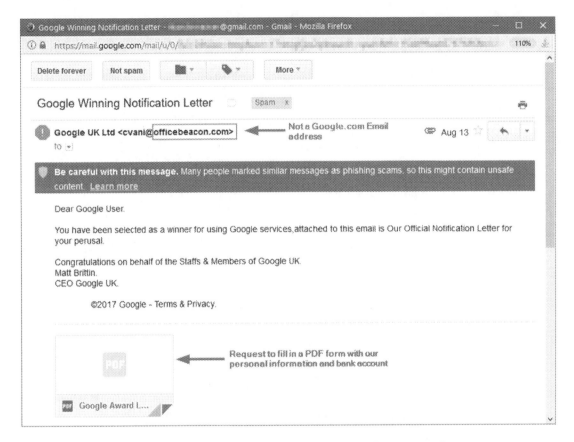

Figure 2-2. *Example phishing email pretending to be from Google*

Some attackers use URL-shortening services to mask the real phishing URL sent to the user. If you suspect that a short URL could be a scam, you can expand it using these free online services to see its destination:

- http://checkshorturl.com

- www.getlinkinfo.com

- http://wheredoesthislinkgo.com

- https://linkexpander.com

Note!   Lehigh University provides different types of phishing emails with a short description about each one (https://lts.lehigh.edu/phishing/examples). The site at www.phishing.org/phishing-examples offers sample phishing emails also.

If you suspect that you are a victim of a phishing attack, contact the Federal Trade Commission at `https://www.ftc.gov/complaint` and raise a complaint. You can report an identity theft on the same page if you suspect that someone or a company is misusing your private data. You can also file a complaint on the FBI website at `https://www.ic3.gov/complaint/default.aspx`.

Ransomware

Ransomware is malware that installs silently on the user's computer or mobile device; it works by locking the user's access to his files—or screen—by encrypting all user data on the device in addition to all the data on the attached storage devices (USB flash, external HDD, or SSD) and then requesting a ransom to remove the restriction. Some types of ransomware threaten victims to publish their data publicly if they refuse to pay the ransom. The ransom is usually paid through anonymous online payment methods like Bitcoin—which is a kind of digital currency—to get the decryption key.

Ransomware infection comes through a variety of methods. For example, a ransom could be attached to spam emails, installed upon visiting malicious websites, or installed as part of a legitimate program that has been modified by an attacker to conceal the ransomware within it. It can also get dropped by other malware such as a Trojan horse or exploit kits.

There are two main types of ransomware.

- The first type—also known as *locker-ransomware* locks the system screen in a way that is easy for an experienced computer user to unlock the restriction.

- The second type—also known as *crypto-ransomware*—encrypts whole disk drive or some files types, including all attached removable storage, and requests a ransom to remove the restriction.

A special variant of ransomware attacks the master boot record (MBR) of the vulnerable system, thus preventing the OS from booting unless the victim pays the ransom.

To counteract ransomware attacks, follow these steps:

1. Back up all necessary files regularly. All operating system types have special backup functionality. In Windows 10, you can access the backup functionality through Windows Settings (Windows + I) ➤ Update & Security ➤ Backup.

2. Regularly install all security patches for the operating system and all installed applications and keep them all up-to-date.

3. Install antivirus and anti-malware solutions if possible and keep them up-to-date.

4. Do not run macros in Microsoft Office files when receiving such files from an unknown user or when downloading them from the Internet.

If a ransom attack successfully compromises your system, follow these steps:

1. Disconnect your computer from the network/Internet.

2. Perform a full scan of all connected devices/storage media.

3. Seek advice from a specialist to find out the ransomware type as there are removal tools available for specific ransomware families.

4. Format affected devices if necessary and perform an OS reinstall.

5. Restore your data from a previous clean backup.

6. Inform law enforcement about the case and do not pay the ransom.

Tip   Crypto Sheriff (`https://www.nomoreransom.org/crypto-sheriff.php?lang=en`) helps users recover from ransomware attacks by offering a free service to check the type of ransomware affecting your device and then helping you to download the decryption solution if available.

Adware and Spyware

Adware is a kind of advertisement software that tracks users' online activities to display corresponding ads, thus generating revenue for its author. It is usually installed as part of free Internet programs such as system utilities, games, or browser toolbars. You cannot consider all adware software as being malicious because many of them are installed as part of legitimate software that declares the existence of adware as part of its end-user license agreement (EULA). However, most users simply click the "I agree" button without knowing that they are installing adware on their machine.

Spyware is another kind of tracking software; however, it is for malicious purposes only. Spyware monitors everything you type on your keyboard and sends it to its operator. Some types install other malware (like ransomware) on your machine to facilitate performing other malicious actions.

Trojan

This is a kind of malicious computer program that installs silently on the victim machine. It enables its operator to have full control over the victim machine including the camera and microphone. Most of the popular banking threats come from a Trojan family like Zeus and SpyEye.

Virus

This is what most non-computer-savvy users mean when talking about malicious computer programs. Viruses are considered one of the oldest traditional risks since the early days of personal computers. The main intent of a virus is to make the victim operating system inoperable, thus forcing the user to format it to return to its original state.

Worms

The Morris worm, or Internet worm, was one of the first to be seen in the wild. In November 1988, it was distributed via the Internet and caused significant damage to the infected systems. This is now another type of old-school attack that is still widely used. The main intent of a worm is to spread from one machine to another through internal networks or the Internet to spread malicious code. By replicating itself, worms consume a great amount of network bandwidth—for example, sending files via emails—thus causing great damage to corporate networks. Worms can also install backdoors on computers.

Scareware

Scareware is a kind of malicious software—also known as *deception software, rogue scanner software,* or *fraudware*—that tricks the victim into purchasing security software (such as antivirus and anti-malware) to remove the infection from their PC. For example, a user can see a pop-up message on their PC stating that it is infected with malware and should act promptly by purchasing a special anti-malware solution—which is fake!—to clean the PC. The idea here is to trick the user into purchasing something unnecessarily to take the user's money.

Worm infections can be mitigated through installing security software and keeping your OS and antivirus solution up-to-date.

Distributed Denial of Service

A distributed denial-of-service (DDoS) attack happens when many compromised computing devices flood a target computer—for example, a server—with many fake requests simultaneously, making it unresponsive to serve legitimate users. This attack targets a large number of entities such as banks, shopping websites, and news agencies. Unlike other attacks that aim to steal confidential data, the main aim of a DDoS attack is to make your website and servers unavailable to legitimate users.

Rootkits

A rootkit is a dangerous type of malware; it can potentially gain administrative access over the system and can prevent normal detection programs (antivirus and anti-rootkit programs) from noticing its presence. Some dangerous rootkits attack at the hardware level (firmware rootkit), and removal may require hardware replacement or specialized intervention.

Rootkit detection is difficult because there is no single security solution that can remove all known and unknown rootkits. However, there are many valuable programs that can remove a large number of rootkit types, as you'll see later in the chapter.

Juice Jacking

This is a type of cyberattack where an attacker copies data or installs malware onto a victim's smartphone/tablet when the victim connects a device—through USB cable—to a public charging station that has been modified to play a malicious role. Public charging stations can be found at airports, hotels, shopping centers, and conferences.

Wi-Fi Eavesdropping

Free Wi-Fi access points are spread almost everywhere. An attacker can exploit vulnerabilities in such devices to intercept all the communication—via phone calls, instant messages, and video conferences—that's gone through them. It is highly recommended not to use free Wi-Fi service in public places unless a strong virtual private network (VPN) has been used to protect the connection.

Security Software

It is essential to install an antivirus solution on your computer before a malicious piece of software compromises it. Having an antivirus program is considered the first line of defense against cyberattacks. New viruses are created nearly every minute. It is the job of the antivirus software to keep up with the latest threats.

Bear in mind that having an antivirus program installed on your machine does not give you 100 percent protection. With the sophistication of modern cyberattacks, you need more than one measure to protect your computing devices and network. For instance, installing a firewall solution is equally essential as the antivirus program. Many antivirus solutions come equipped with a built-in firewall. In this book, we will mention only the free products.

Antivirus

Commercial antivirus solutions are always better than their free counterparts (see Table 2-1), so we will begin by talking about the recommended features that must be existed within any antivirus solution to be considered useful.

- It should be equipped with a built-firewall.

- It should be able to scan email clients—such as Thunderbird and Outlook—and detect phishing attacks.

- It must update itself automatically and discover zero-day malware before it hits your machine.

- It should be able to detect advanced malware like rootkits and ransomware and all kinds of malicious software like adware and spyware.

- It should protect your browser from browser exploits and have DNS protection.

- It must not consume high computing resources to operate.

Table 2-1. *Free Antivirus Software (Commercial Versions of These Products Also Available with Enhanced Protection Features)*

Tool	Main Features	URL
Avast Free Antivirus	Detect and block viruses, malware, spyware, ransomware, and phishing. Protect your browser from cyberattacks, protect home Wi-Fi connection, has a built-in password manager.	`https://www.avast.com/ free-antivirus-download`
Comodo Internet Security	Many features including a personal firewall and advanced protection against zero-day malware.	`https://www.comodo.com/ home/internet-security/ free-internet-security. php`
Avira	Protection against worms, viruses, Trojans, and spyware. Has cloud protection that scans unknown files anonymously in the cloud in real time for maximum detection.	`https://www.avira.com/ en/free-antivirus- windows`

Windows 10 comes supplied with a free antivirus solution, Windows Defender. This program helps guard your PC against viruses and other advanced threats such as rootkits and bootkits; however, its main disadvantage is the lack of a personal firewall. This should not let you underestimate Windows Defender because you can install a free dedicated firewall, as we will show next.

Firewall

A firewall monitors and controls the incoming and outgoing network traffic and helps you to screen out hackers, viruses, and worms that try to reach your computer over the Internet. As we already said, not all free antivirus solutions come equipped with a personal firewall, but there are many free dedicated personal firewalls that can do the job. See Table 2-2 for the most well-known ones.

Table 2-2. *Free Firewalls*

Firewall	URL
Comodo	https://personalfirewall.comodo.com
ZoneAlarm Free Firewall	https://www.zonealarm.com/software/free-firewall/

Anti-malware

Cyberattacks are being developed continually. Every day sophisticated malicious scripts and programs are created by cybercriminals, and anti-malware solutions help to detect threats that were not previously discovered by regular antivirus solutions. To achieve maximum protection, it is necessary to have an anti-malware solution in addition to your installed antivirus program.

The free edition of Spybot (https://www.safer-networking.org/dl/) has an anti-malware and anti-spyware functionality that can be installed along with your antivirus solution.

Another famous program for detecting malware is Malwarebytes (https://www.malwarebytes.com). The free version has the basic anti-malware and spyware protection in addition to its ability to remove rootkits and repairs the files that are damaged. It can also work with any antivirus program already installed.

Securing the Operating System

No matter what kinds of security software you have already installed on your OS, securing the OS itself is still the first task you should do before installing any programs or accessing the local network or the Internet.

There are two types of risks that threaten the security of your OS.

- Logical threats originating from malware and other malicious programs.

- Physical threats. These happen when an attacker gains physical access to your machine (for example, through USB or other ports) to perform a crafted, malicious action.

We already covered how to secure the first part of the logical side of the OS through installing security software. In this section, we will continue to cover other parts of OS logical security—which is related to OS configuration—in addition to physical security.

We will not delve into the OS security as that requires a book of its own. For this book, we will cover the main security configuration that you should do to enhance OS security and privacy. The focus will be on the Windows OS because it is the most widely used OS on earth.

Hardening the Windows OS

The Windows OS is not intended to be a secure, anonymous OS. When conducting OSINT searches, you should avoid revealing your real identity online. Windows can be configured to be more private following a simple steps. Besides, the software and techniques that we are going to demonstrate later will allow you to conduct your OSINT searches anonymously in addition to hiding/masking your digital fingerprint.

Note!   There are many different operating systems, like macOS, Linux, and Windows in addition to mobile OSs like iOS from Apple and Android from Google. Whatever OS you use, it has not been created to be completely anonymous and private. There are special distributions—usually based on Linux—that provide maximum security and anonymity when going online like Tails OS, as you are going to see later in this chapter.

Warning!   Create a new system restore point before implementing the tweaks in this chapter so you can safely revert your changes in case something goes wrong.

For now, let's begin our list of recommendations to harden your Windows box.

Updating Windows

The Automatic Update feature for the Windows OS should always be turned on. Windows 10 Update is set to automatic by default.

Updating All Installed Programs

Windows usually updates Microsoft programs—such as the Microsoft Office suite and the Edge (IE) browser—as part of Windows Update, but you should make sure that other programs (Adobe Reader, VPN clients, Firefox, and Opera) are also updated regularly.

Locking Your PC Using a USB Drive

The default Windows login authentication does not offer the necessary security for its users. Many black hat hackers have successfully compromised this functionality to gain unauthorized access to Windows. To add an additional layer of security, you can lock your PC with a USB drive in addition to the default login. This procedure is necessary for older versions of Windows (7, XP) that cannot be protected using enhanced Windows 10 features.

USB Raptor allows you to lock your PC using a USB flash card. It is a free program with many advanced features. You can find it at `https://sourceforge.net/projects/usbraptor/?source=typ_redirect`.

Using a Less-Privileged User Account

When conducting OSINT searches, there is no need to use an administrator account; it is always advisable that you use a limited user account for your daily tasks. This will effectively protect your computer from malware installed inadvertently and prevent outside hackers from invading your system and installing malicious software. You can configure Windows (all versions) accounts by going to Control Panel ➤ User Accounts.

Using a Strong Password for Windows

Use a strong password to protect your Windows login and make sure to change it once every three months. Later in this chapter, we will give tips on how to create strong passwords and store them within a password manager.

To enforce a password policy under Windows 10 (all editions), follow these steps:

1. Go to Control Panel ➤ Administrative Tools ➤ Local Security Policy ➤ Security Settings ➤ Account Polices ➤ Password Policy.

2. On the right side, double-click the "Maximum password age" policy.

3. Set the number of days a password can be used before Windows 10 requires users to change it to 90 days.

Keeping Your User Account Control Turned On

User Account Control (UAC) monitors what changes are going to be made to your computer by showing a pop-up window when you try to perform actions that require administrative access, like installing/uninstalling a program. Turning on UAC will help you to deter malware from making changes to your computer. You can adjust UAC for each user account through Control Panel ➤ User Accounts; then click "Change User Account Control settings" (see Figure 2-3).

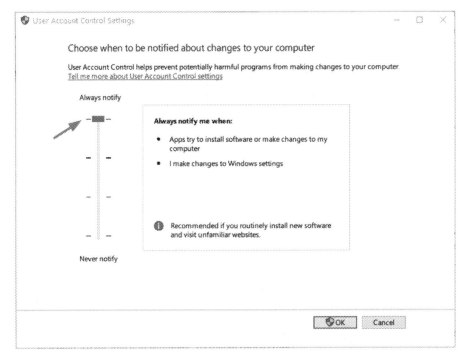

Figure 2-3. *Adjust the UAC settings under Windows 10 to notify the user of any changes to Windows and other applications*

Disabling Remote Assistance

This feature allows a remote user to access your machine over a network connection. If you are not using this feature, you can disable it to prevent hackers from exploiting it to gain unauthorized access your machine. To disable it in Windows 10, follow these steps (see Figure 2-4):

1. Enter **remote settings** into the Cortana search box and select "Allow remote access to your computer."

2. Make sure that the option "Don't allow remote connections to this computer" is selected.

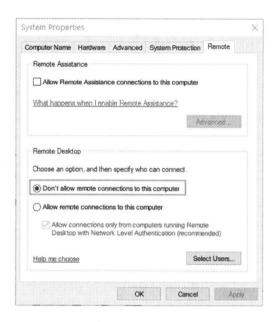

Figure 2-4. *Disabling remote connections in Windows 10*

Making Hidden Files Visible

Some malware and other malicious programs come hidden using the same attribute that Windows uses to hide its system files. To display hidden files and folders under Windows 10, select Control Panel ➤ File Explorer Options and then go to the View tab and select the option "Show hidden files, folders, and drives." Also, make sure to uncheck the option "Hide Protected operating systems files." It is advisable to view file extensions by unchecking the option "Hide extensions for known file types."

Freezing the Hard Disk

The freezing software allows a Windows user to restore their OS to a previous stable state within seconds each time the computer restarts. For example, consider a situation when a piece of malware hits your OS if you already have a freezing program and it is activated. All you need to do is to restart your machine and everything will return to its previous state.

RollBack Rx Home Edition (free for personal use) is a program for freezing Windows machines. You can find it at `http://horizondatasys.com/rollback-rx-time-machine/rollback-rx-home/`.

Setting a Password for BIOS/UEFI

Many cyberattacks against operating systems and encryption software (full disk encryption) rely on booting the victim's machine using a USB or CD/DVD to crack the encryption keys or to find a way to steal the victim's sensitive data. By a setting a password for the BIOS/UEFI, each time the user boots the machine, he needs to provide some sort of credentials—hence a password—before the computer loads the OS. This trick will also prevent an attacker from changing your BIOS settings or damaging your computer by wiping your hard drive clean. Each motherboard manufacturer has its own menu to set this password, usually in a Security section. You should first boot to BOIS/UEFI and then activate this option.

Disabling Unnecessary Ports/Protocols and Services

Each open port is considered a security risk. Hackers usually scan open ports to try to get access to a victim's machine. Monitoring traffic going through ports is a firewall task; when you configure your personal firewall properly, it will prevent attackers from exploiting open ports for malicious purposes. The best secure configuration is the "interactive mode" (in Comodo firewall, this rule is called Custom Ruleset) where the firewall asks you to grant or deny access to any connection going through OS ports (see Figure 2-5).

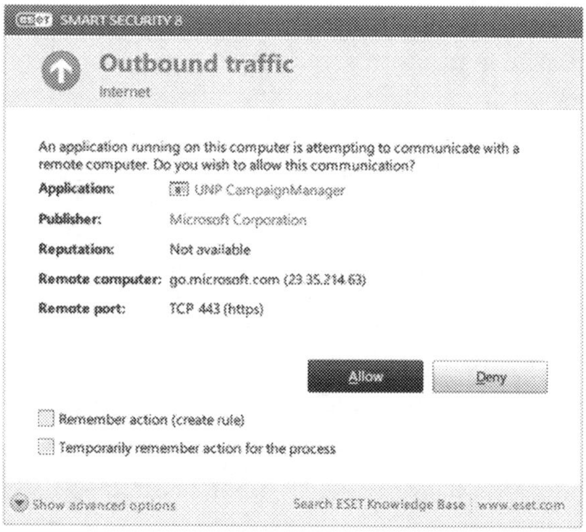

Figure 2-5. *Sample warning dialog issued by the ESET firewall when a service or application is trying to establish an ongoing connection with a remote host*

Like ports, unnecessary services should be disabled. Windows load essential services upon starting, but other unused services should be disabled.

To disable a service under Windows, do the following:

1. Go to Control Panel ➤ Administrative Tools ➤ Services.

2. Locate a service to disable.

3. Double-click it to open its Properties dialog box.

4. Choose Disabled as the startup type.

Staying Private in Windows 10

Compared with the previous Windows versions, Windows 10 comes equipped with enhanced security features for encryption and authentication. Windows 10 is also more robust against bootkits and rootkit attacks. To use the modern security features offered by Windows 10, your computer must have certain hardware components.

- *Trusted Platform Module (TPM) version 2.0*: This is used to store the cryptographic keys of BitLocker. This is a full disk encryption feature offered by some editions of Windows 10 (Windows 10 supports BitLocker on Pro, Enterprise, and Education editions).

- *Unified Extensible Firmware Interface (UEFI)*: This is the BIOS replacement used in modern certified Windows computers.

- *Fingerprint scanner*: This enhances the traditional Windows authentication schema.

A retinal scanner and a 3D camera for facial recognition are highly recommended so you can activate the advanced biometric authentication scheme of the Windows 10 Hello feature. However, their existence in modern computers is still limited because they increase a computer's price significantly.

As we already said, Windows 10 enhances the regular Windows authentication by introducing a modern authentication mechanism called Hello. This app allows a user to log in to a machine using a fingerprint, face, or even iris. User biometric data will not be stored anywhere online—according to Microsoft—for this feature to work.

It is highly recommended not to use the Hello feature on the computer where you are going to conduct your OSINT search. It is always advisable to use the local Windows account when signing into Windows as no one can guarantee what might happen when you send your credentials or other sensitive information over an unsecured medium like the Internet.

Windows 10 comes equipped with many new features to personalize the user experience when using it. For instance, Cortana is a Windows digital assistance that allows a user to navigate Windows using voice commands; it also monitors user actions on Windows—such as what the user types and searches for—and personalizes future events according to this. To control Cortana's collection and use of your data, check `https://privacy.microsoft.com/en-us/windows-10-cortana-and-privacy`, which contains instructions on how to disable it on different Windows devices.

Several privacy configurations of Windows 10 are stored in one location. Windows 10 created a privacy dashboard that is accessed by pressing Windows key + i to access the Settings page and then selecting Privacy (see Figure 2-6).

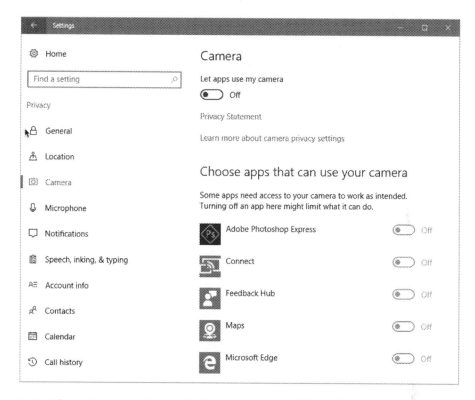

Figure 2-6. *The privacy settings in Windows 10 are all bundled together in one location*

Everything in the Privacy dashboard is self-explanatory; it is advisable to disable everything you do not need and not to use the Microsoft Edge browser for conducting online searches. Skype, Dropbox, and Microsoft OneDrive are also not recommended for exchanging important files. Secure alternatives to these programs will be given later in the chapter.

Destroying Digital Traces

Data destruction is an important step in covering your digital traces when conducting OSINT searches. Digital traces—previous usage—on the computer remain even after formatting it many times. There are three ways in which data—and remnants of it—can be destroyed securely: physical, degaussing and logical destruction (sanitizing). We will briefly describe each technique, but let's first talk about the different types of hard drives in use today.

There are two types of hard drives currently used in computing devices.

- *Hard disk drive (HDD):* This is the old type that has been used since the early days of personal computers. It is a mechanical device that mainly consists of a metal platter (could be more than one) made of glass or aluminum coated with magnetic material to store data. HDDs are usually used for mass storage and cost less than SSDs.

- *Solid-state drive (SSD)*: This is a more advanced version of a drive. It does not contain any moving parts and has no platters. Instead, it stores data on small microchip units (like USB flash drives). SSD is faster and smaller than HDD but has a limited lifespan compared to HDD.

Modern computers—and all smartphones and tablets—use SSD as the only storage unit type; however, this does not mean that HDD is going to fade away. HDD is a mature technology, and it will remain in use for a long time according to many studies.

For this book, let us see the difference between SSD and HDD in terms of data recovery.

Recovering data from an HDD is relatively easy and can be conducted by any user with the appropriate tools. When you delete a file on an HDD, the file is not deleted directly; instead, only the pointer to this file on disk is deleted. This operation helps to speed up the deletion process, saving valuable time. Recovering data from an SSD drive is quite difficult and impossible in many cases. For instance, an SSD uses a different mechanism when handling deleted files. All modern SSDs utilize the TRIM command when enabled. This command will remove deleted file data blocks instantly, allowing for another file to take up that space. This speeds up the writing process the next time the OS needs to write data onto the drive. There are many approaches to implementing TRIM on SSD devices, depending on the OS in use. Some operating systems will execute TRIM instantly after each file deletion, while others will execute TRIM at regular intervals.

Now, let's see how data can be destroyed completely when using both types of hard drive. The following techniques are used to achieve this:

- *Physical destruction*: This is the most secure and usually preferred method used by intelligence services and giant corporations to destroy classified and high-grade data assets. This technique works by physically destroying the storage medium—whether it is HDD, SSD, CD/DVD, or flash drive—so that it is no longer can be used.

- *Degaussing*: This is another secure technique to prevent antirecovery techniques from recovering your data from the storage medium; it works by exposing the storage medium to the powerful magnetic field of a degausser to destroy the stored data magnetically. This technique works well with HDD. SSD devices are better destroyed physically to avoid the ability to recover top-secret data.

- *Logical destruction*: This is the most widely used technique to destroy data while maintaining storage medium for future use. This technique works by using specialized software to cover the old data and remnants of data with random characters written by the wiping tool. There are many wiping algorithms already used to destroy data digitally in this way; some are more secure than others. However, what you should know when using such a technique to destroy data is that it cannot guarantee 100 percent removal of all data on your drive. Some advanced recovery techniques that are hardware based are still able to capture your old data, or at least parts of it (but doing so is costly and time-consuming). Logical data destruction techniques have some disadvantages too; they need time to finish because they must write random data multiple times (several passes) over all the available sectors on the hard drive. In addition, this technique assumes your hard drive is working and writable to write the random data into it. Another challenge to wiping software comes when using it to wipe data stored using the RAID technology. This technology offers fault tolerance by mirroring data onto multiple disk drives in different physical locations. In such a situation, the wiping tool should track all mirrored data across all enterprise storage servers.

Different standards have been developed to wipe data (logical data destruction) on hard drives. Table 2-3 shows the most popular ones.

Table 2-3. *Data-Erasing Algorithms*

Erasing Technique	Security Level	Overwriting Passes
HMG Infosec Standard 5	High	3
DoD 5220.22-M	High	3
Bruce Schneier's algorithm	High	7
German standard BSI/VSITR	High	7

Different programs exist to wipe your hard drives, and the majority support more than one wiping standard. Table 2-4 lists the most popular ones (free tools only).

Table 2-4. *Data Destruction Tools*

Program	URL	Comments
DBAN	`https://dban.org`	The free version supports HDD only.
Eraser	`www.heidi.ie/eraser/`	Open source; supports SSD.
CCleaner	`www.piriform.com/ccleaner`	Drive wiper and Windows trace cleaner.
SDelete	`https://technet.microsoft.com/en-us/sysinternals/sdelete.aspx`	Erases data according to DOD 5220.22-M.

For SSD drives, the majority of SSD manufacturers offer utilities to erase data securely from their drives. You can check your SSD drive manufacturer's website for such utilities. Table 2-5 gives direct links to some of them.

Table 2-5. *SSD Data-Erasing Tools*

Tool	URL
Intel Solid State Drive Toolbox	`https://downloadcenter.intel.com/download/26574?v=t`
Corsair SSD Toolbox	`www.corsair.com/en-eu/support/downloads`
Samsung Magician	`www.samsung.com/semiconductor/minisite/ssd/download/tools.html`
SanDisk SSD	`https://kb.sandisk.com/app/answers/detail/a_id/16678/~/secure-erase-and-sanitize`

Destroying your digital traces is important when conducting OSINT searches. Bear in mind that browsers, image-viewing software, Microsoft Office programs, and anything you do on your computer will leave digital traces. By using the advice in this section, you will make tracking your traces difficult and even impossible.

Warning!   For people (law enforcement and military officials) conducting top-secret OSINT searches who need the maximum anonymity possible, it is highly advisable to use an anonymous OS like Tails OS, covered later in the chapter.

General Privacy Settings

In this section, we list some recommendations to maintain your privacy when going online. Some of these tips can be considered trivial at first; however, it is important to implement them because not doing so can cause serious damage to your privacy if exploited by outside adversaries.

Covering Your Laptop Camera

Hackers and intelligence services go after computer cameras and microphones when targeting specific people. So, it is advisable to cover your webcams with tape for security reasons.

Avoiding Pirated Software

Pirated software can include malicious payload—like a Trojan or keylogger—that can invade user privacy and spy on the computing device. It is strongly advised not to access pirated websites that distribute illegal contents such as Torrent websites.

If you prefer to use freeware programs downloaded from the Internet, it is highly advisable to use your antivirus solution to scan them before executing them. To become more confident, you can scan the downloaded program with free scan services, which comes in handy when you want to scan a specific file/program using multiple antivirus engines.

VirusTotal (`https://www.virustotal.com`) is a free service that analyzes suspicious files and URLs and facilitates the quick detection of viruses, worms, Trojans, and all kinds of malware. All you need to do is enter the website URL you want to check or upload the file/program to see whether it is clear from malware threats.

Handling Digital Files Metadata

Metadata is data about data; it contains descriptive—usually hidden—information about the file it belongs to. Digital file metadata includes the author name, file size, location, creation date/time, and comments.

Conceptually, all digital file types can include metadata. From a privacy perspective, users are mainly concerned about the metadata that exists in digital images, audio files, and video files. Microsoft Office—and other digital text document creation software— also contains a wealth of metadata. Metadata usually comes stored in the digital file; however, some file types store it in a separate file.

One metadata type existing within images files is EXIF. This is a standard that specifies the format for images, sound, and ancillary tags used by digital cameras (including smartphones), scanners, and other systems handling image and sound files recorded by digital cameras. EXIF data is embedded within the image file and works with JPEG images only. EXIF metadata can contain geolocation metadata in addition to a wide array of technical information.

Other types include Extensible Metadata Platform (XMP), which supports different digital file types and is not limited to images, and the International Press Telecommunications Council (IPTC), which is considered an older meta-information format.

It is advisable to check the metadata of all digital files before uploading them to the Internet or sharing them with colleagues to avoid leaking private information about yourself and the device. There are many freeware tools that can view and edit a digital file's metadata; we'll begin with digital images.

Exif Pilot (`www.colorpilot.com/exif.html`) is a free EXIF editor that allows you to view, edit, and remove EXIF, EXIF GPS, IPTC, and XMP data in addition to adding new tags and importing and exporting EXIF and IPTC to/from text and Microsoft Excel files.

Other free tools that can be used to view image metadata are GIMP (`https://www.gimp.org`) and XnView (`www.xnview.com/en/`), which comes free for private and educational use (see Figure 2-7).

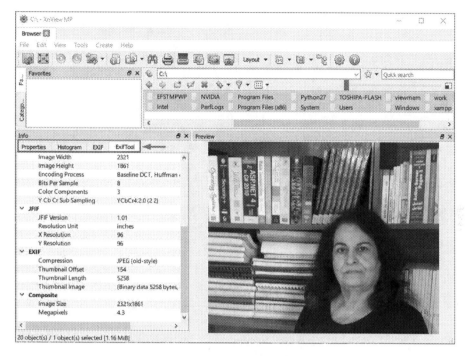

Figure 2-7. *Using the XnView tool to view EXIF tags*

Windows comes with a built-in function that allows you to view and remove some
metadata associated with documents and digital images. However, keep in mind that
Windows may not be able to remove all EXIF tags, so if you intend on sharing important
files, always use the suggested third-party tools already mentioned.

To remove EXIF using Windows, right-click the image, select Properties, and go to
the Details tab. At the bottom, click Remove Properties and Personal Information to
open the EXIF removal tool. The tool lets you either create a copy of the image with all
the metadata removed or pick and choose which properties to erase from the selected
file (see Figure 2-8).

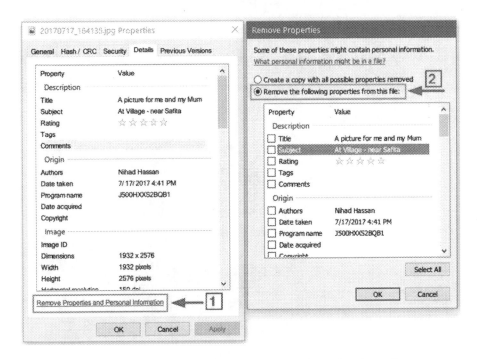

Figure 2-8. *Remove EXIF metadata using the Windows built-in function*

As we already said, metadata also exists within PDFs, Microsoft Office files, and audio and video files. In this section, we will briefly cover some useful tools to clear metadata from such file types.

To clear metadata from PDF files, Adobe has a feature called Sanitize Document. After clicking it, you can remove all the hidden metadata from the intended PDF file (see Figure 2-9).

Figure 2-9. *Clearing PDF file metadata*

Note!   Not all versions of Adobe Reader support the sanitization feature. If your current version does not have this feature, you can use third-party tools to remove metadata from your PDF files such as BeCyPDFMetaEdit (`www.becyhome.de/becypdfmetaedit/description_eng.htm`) or PDF Metadata Editor (`http://broken-by.me/pdf-metadata-editor`).

To view/edit and remove audio file metadata, use Mp3tag (`www.mp3tag.de/en`). For the video file's metadata, use MediaInfo (`https://mediaarea.net/en/MediaInfo`).

To remove metadata from Microsoft Office 2010, 2013, and 2016 documents, you can check the document metadata by selecting File and then going to the Info tab. The Properties panel will be on the right side; from here you can remove document metadata by clicking the Properties button and selecting Advanced Properties (see Figure 2-10).

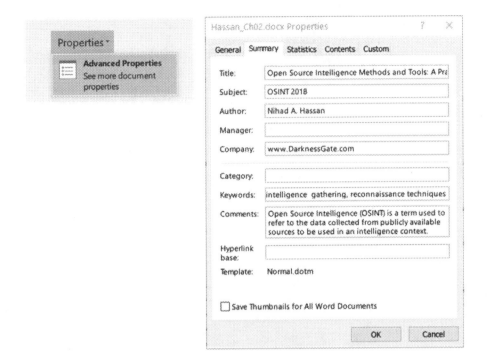

Figure 2-10. *Removing Microsoft Office document metadata*

In Microsoft Office 2007, you need to click the Microsoft Office button and then select Prepare ➤ Properties to edit the document metadata.

Another issue you need to consider when sending Microsoft Office documents to outside parties is deleting other hidden metadata. Fortunately, Microsoft Office provides functionality for deleting hidden metadata. You can access this feature in Microsoft Word 2010, 2013, and 2016 by selecting File ➤ Info ➤ Check for Issues ➤ Inspect Document. In Microsoft Word 2007, you can access this feature by clicking the Office button and selecting Prepare ➤ Inspect Document.

Physically Securing Computing Devices

We already covered different precautionary steps to maintain your privacy, but everything is useless if your computing device or hardware (or portable storage units) gets stolen or unauthorized physical access takes place while it's unattended. People working to collect OSINT information to investigate crimes and other official issues should take extra care to avoid revealing any information about the cases they are working on and losing their hardware containing confidential information.

Corporations and government agencies have special policies to quantify the risks to IT infrastructure and the possible consequences, in addition to protection measures that should be taken to mitigate such risks. Users should follow these guidelines where applicable.

Individuals also suffer from physical threats. Theft and hardware defects can prevent them from accessing data stored on computing devices in addition to revealing this data to unauthorized users. For example, laptops that are left unattended without being secured by a cable lock can be quickly stolen. To secure mobile devices, use these tips:

- When using your laptop in public places, secure it by using a cable lock attached to a heavy object (e.g., desk, table, column in a garden).

- Do not leave your office without locking it when you have portable devices in it.

- Do not store your work's sensitive files on your computing device without proper permission, and make sure to encrypt everything if you store such data on your device.

- Do not store your sensitive/personal data on mobile devices without proper encryption.

- Use a password to protect your mobile device from unauthorized access.

- Do not turn your Bluetooth connection on in public places, and if necessary, run it for a short period of time to receive or send urgent files.

- Turn off Wi-Fi when you are not using it. Be careful when using public hotspots and encrypt your connection using a VPN when using insecure Internet connections.

- Keep a written record of the make, model, serial number, MAC address, and other pertinent information about your portable device in case it gets stolen.

Online Tracking Techniques

Web tracking is used to record the web browsing behavior of users when going online. This activity is conducted by different parties for different purposes. For instance, social sites can track their users across many websites. This information can be later associated with each user social account—for example, a Facebook account—to show personalized advertisements and services.

In this section, we will introduce you to how online tracking technologies work. This knowledge is essential to understanding how you should conceal your identity later to avoid being tracked when conducting OSINT searches.

Tracking Through IP Address

The first technical thing you need to understand is the concept of Internet Protocol (IP). It is essential to understand this concept and how devices are connected to the Internet because most of the anonymizing techniques work by obscuring your real IP address to avoid tracking. Besides, you cannot protect your digital privacy without knowing how Internet devices are connected in today's digital world.

What Is an IP Address?

An IP address is a unique address that computing devices use to connect to the Internet and to identify themselves and communicate with other devices in the IP network. This address is unique for each device in the IP network; hence, no two devices can have the same address within each network.

There are two standards of IP addressing already in use. The IPv4 standard is the most widely used one; it can accommodate up to 4.3 billion addresses. Apparently, this number is not enough, especially with the explosion use of Internet of Things (IoT) devices. This fact has resulted in another standard named IPv6, which can accommodate more than 7.9×1028 times as many addresses as IPv4.

When connecting to the Internet, you either use the same IP address each time (known as static IP) or use a different number each time (known as dynamic IP).

A static IP address is an address that is assigned by your Internet service provider (ISP) and does not change over time. This kind of address is usually used by business corporations, the public sector, and other IT providers such as email service providers.

A dynamic IP address, on the other hand, is assigned dynamically by your ISP each time you connect to the Internet. It uses a protocol called Dynamic Host Configuration Protocol (DHCP) to assign new IP addresses whenever you disconnect from the Internet or your router gets rebooted.

Note!   To determine whether you are assigned a dynamic or static IP address, open a command-line prompt. In Windows 10, press Windows + X and then click Command Prompt (Admin). Type *ipconfig /all* and then press the Enter key. Locate the line containing "DHCP Enabled" under your current network connection. If DHCP Enabled is set to Yes (see Figure 2-11), then you most likely have a dynamic internal IP address.

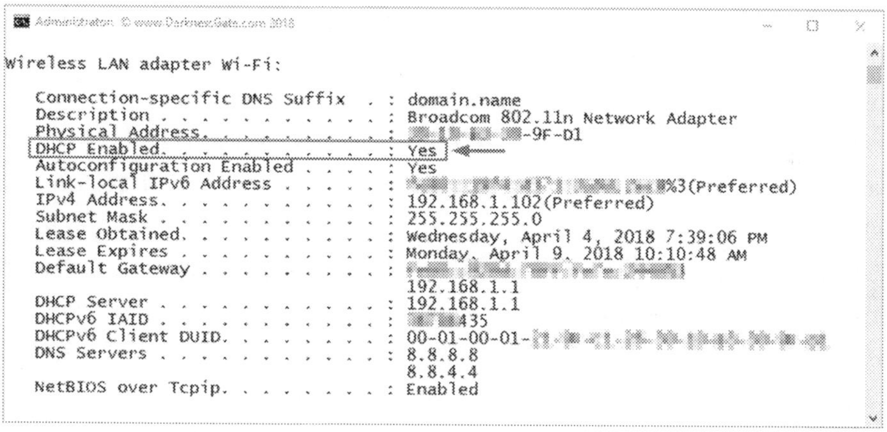

Figure 2-11. *Determine whether your PC is using a dynamic or static IP address. In this case, we're using a dynamic IP address.*

IP addresses come in two types: public and private IP addresses. A public IP address allows direct access to the Internet. A private IP address is a non-Internet-facing IP address on an internal network and is used to assign a private number to your computing devices in your home or office network to avoid exposing them directly online. For example, you can have one public IP address assigned to your router on your office network, and each of the computers, tablets, smartphones, and peripherals connected to your router (via a wired connection or Wi-Fi) get a private IP address from your router via DHCP.

Note!   DHCP is a network protocol used on IP networks. It works by dynamically allocating IP addresses to a set of connected hosts based on a preconfigured pool of addresses.

How Is an IP Address Used to Track You Online?

Whenever you visit a website, conduct a search online, or access your social site account, your connection IP address will be made available to the connected site. Nearly all websites record their visitors' IP addresses among other details such as date/time of the visit, pages visited and duration, user actions on the website, and much more. Knowing the IP address is also—almost—enough to figure out approximately your current geographical location.

Your ISP will also record your IP address. ISPs usually record the browsing history of their users and connect it with each user's real identity (ISPs usually request a valid government ID to provide Internet connections for their customers).

Social sites—like Facebook and Twitter—track their users' browsing history across many websites. For instance, Facebook's Like and Share buttons and Twitter's Tweet buttons are used to track a user's online activities even if the user does not click them. All this information is stored in a separate log attached with each user's social account ID—Facebook, Instagram, or Twitter—to better target the user with customized ads. Storing such logs is dangerous because all your web searches and web history get connected to your real name. Many WikiLeaks revelations mention that intelligence agencies have different facilities to access giant IT providers' user. Giant corporations are also interested in such data to exploit it for commercial gain. This means all your sensitive details will be exposed in one way or another.

Although tracking online users through their IP addresses is still the most prevalent method used by different actors, there are other advanced technical techniques that allow an outside observer to track a user's online activities even without knowing the user's IP address, and this what we will talk about in the coming section.

Cookies

Cookies are small text files usually stored on the client computer's browser. A cookie file contains information that is specific to a client computer in addition to the website name, expiry date, and a user ID number to distinguish the user from other visitors. Cookies allow a website owner to be able to recognize the visitor's browser the next time, effectively allowing the website to offer a customized experience for its visitors.

Mainly there are two types of cookies already in use: session cookies and persistent cookies.

Session cookies are stored in a temporary location in the client browser and are removed when the user closes the web browser or logs out of the current session. Such cookies are usually used to remember user shopping cart information or to store data between multiple pages.

Note!   Most websites plant HTTP cookies to track site visitors or to remember a user's credentials. This kind is less risky than persistent cookies and can be removed safely by using the standard browser function Remove Cookies.

Persistent cookies come in two main types: flash cookies and ever cookies. Persistent cookies are more persistent than HTTP cookies and contain information from other websites that is used to track a user's online activities across multiple websites. With flash cookies, a cookie is stored within a specific folder on a client hard drive (not within the client browser like HTTP cookies). In other words, such cookies will not get removed when you use the standard Remove Cookies browser function. For security reasons, it is highly advisable to deactivate this kind of cookie and delete the currently installed one. You can achieve this by going to Control Panel ➤ Flash Player and selecting the option "Block all sites from storing information on this computer" (see Figure 2-12).

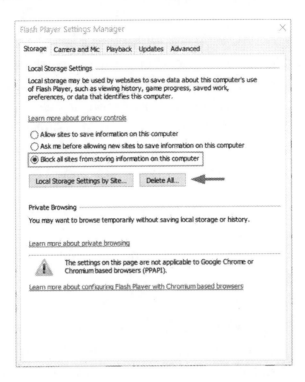

Figure 2-12. *Disabling Flash cookies through Flash Player Settings Manager*

Note!   FlashCookiesView (www.nirsoft.net/utils/flash_cookies_view.html) is a small utility created by NirSoft that allows you to display a list of Flash cookies that exist on your system and delete them.

An ever cookie is another type of persistent cookies. This type of cookie is a JavaScript-based cookie that can survive even after the user deletes HTTP and Flash cookies from their machine. Fortunately, the browsers and anti-malware software applications that exist today are now able to detect and block ever cookies.

Note!   You should disable Java plug-ins or at least to set their security settings to a high level. To do so, select Control Panel ➤ Java; then go to the Security tab and select the option "Very high."

Digital Fingerprinting

A browser fingerprint is the set of technical information about the client OS and browser that can be used to distinguish a client machine online. Such technical information includes browser type, add-on installed, user agent, fonts installed, language settings, time zone, screen size, operating system (OS) version, and color depth, among other things.

Fingerprinting allows trackers to track a user's machine even though cookies and JavaScript are disabled, and it allows them to distinguish a client machine among millions of connected devices. You may think that such technical information is generic and cannot be used to recognize a specific computing device. We're afraid you are wrong because when such information is combined, you can draw a comprehensive unique picture about each user machine, and later, this information can be linked to a real identity if combined with other sensitive personal information (SPI) such as name, Social Security number, or phone number. This should effectively allow different outside parties to easily profile people without using traditional tracking techniques such as computer IP addresses and cookies.

There are two main types of device fingerprinting: script-based techniques and canvas.

Script-Based Fingerprinting

This type works by loading a script—usually a JavaScript (Flash, Silverlight, and Java applets are also used)—into the user's browser. This script will execute and collect technical information about user browsers and machine technical specifications such as screen resolution, CPU type, and other details about the targeted system. A hash is then made based on the collected information that is later used to identify and track your computer like an IP address.

The main defense against this technique is to disable JavaScript in your browser. However, this approach is not practical and may result in breaking many websites (the majority of web design frameworks are based on JavaScript to deliver functionality).

Canvas Fingerprinting

Canvas is an HTML element used to draw graphics (lines, shapes, text, images) and animation on web pages using the JavaScript API. This technique is exploited by different actors—especially advertisers—to fingerprint browsers to profile people and track them online.

Canvas fingerprinting works by drawing an invisible image on the user's client browser. Once drawn on the client browser, the image will collect different technical information about the user's browser and OS. A hash is then created based on the collected information. This enables online trackers to track user online activities across different websites based on this hash, which is unique for each user's client machine.

Browser fingerprinting is a powerful tool for tracking users across many websites. This type of tracking (also known as *stateless tracking*) raises serious privacy concerns since it is hard to detect and non-computer-savvy users may find it difficult to counter such techniques.

HTML5

HTML5 is the latest version of HTML. It comes with new features that can be exploited to track users online. For instance, the HTML5 Web Storage feature—which is used to store offline contents on user machines—can be used to store tracking code like cookies do.

Checking Your Digital Footprint

Fingerprinting is currently considered the greatest risk that faces users when surfing online. We cannot conduct secure OSINT searches without fully understanding this risk and working to avoid it. In the following section, we will show what your current digital fingerprint shows to the public by using two free services.

Browserleaks

Browserleaks (`https://browserleaks.com`) is a web security testing tool that shows you what personal identity data may be leaked without your permissions when you surf the Internet.

Panopticlick

Panopticlick (`https://panopticlick.eff.org`) is a research project created by the Electronic Frontier Foundation (`https://www.eff.org/`). It will analyze how well your browser and add-ons protect you against online tracking techniques.

Secure Online Browsing

Earlier you learned how browsers can leak personal identifying information about you and your machine. In this section, we will cover how to configure your browser to become more private in addition and offer advice and tools to conceal your real digital fingerprint.

There are many desktop browsers; the market share is mainly divided between Microsoft Internet Explorer (IE), Mozilla Firefox, Safari, Opera, and Google Chrome. IE and its successor Edge come preinstalled on the Windows OS; however, we always encourage users to use open source software to assure maximum security when working online. Mozilla Firefox is still considered the only true open source browser of the main browsers mentioned, so in this book, we will cover how to make this browser more private.

Note!   The Epic browser is developed by a group called Hidden Reflex and promotes privacy worldwide; this browser is based on Chromium (like Google's Chrome browser) and comes with enhanced security features to eliminate online tracking. It also comes with a free built-in VPN to conceal your IP address and protect your online communications. You can give it try at `https://epicbrowser.com/index.html`.

Configuring Firefox to Become More Private

In this section, we will give basic tips to secure your online browsing when using Firefox.

Turning On Private Browsing

When you enable private browsing in Firefox, the browser will not record your visited pages, cookies, temporary files, and searches. Firefox will also activate tracking protection, which will block online trackers from monitoring your browsing history across multiple websites. To enable private browsing in Firefox, open the Firefox browser, and press Ctrl+Shift+ P. A new private browsing window will appear (see Figure 2-13).

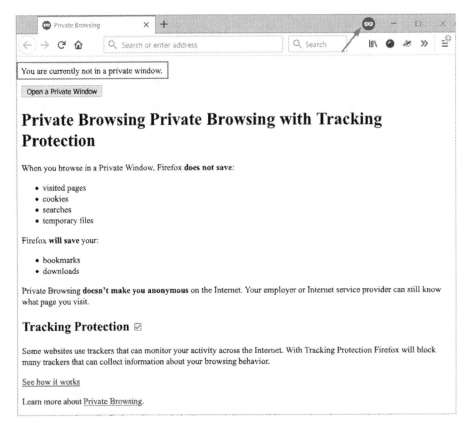

Figure 2-13. *A new private session window opened in the Firefox browser*

Changing the Firefox Settings to Become More Private

There are many tweaks to make your Firefox browser more private. In this section, we cover the main one.

Access the Firefox options by clicking the menu in the upper-right corner of your browser and selecting Options (see Figure 2-14).

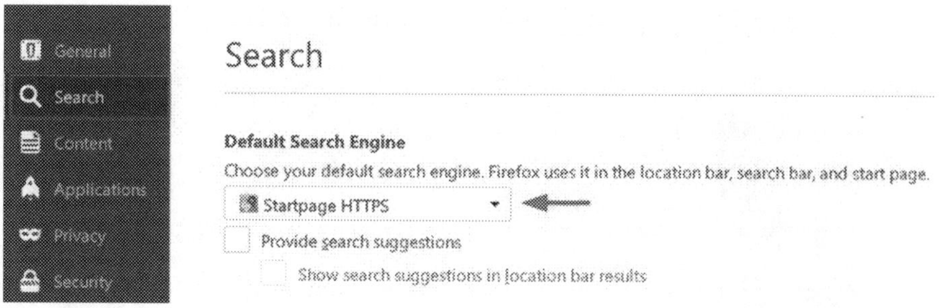

Figure 2-14. *Use an anonymous secure search engine that does not track your online activities*

Move to the Privacy tab. You need to turn on the option Use Tracking Protection in Private Windows. Now, go to the History section on the same page and select the option "Never remember history" so that Firefox will delete all your history every time you close it. Finally, go to the Location Bar section and disable all the suggestions in the search bar because the suggestion process can leak excessive data about you. Your Privacy tab should look like Figure 2-15.

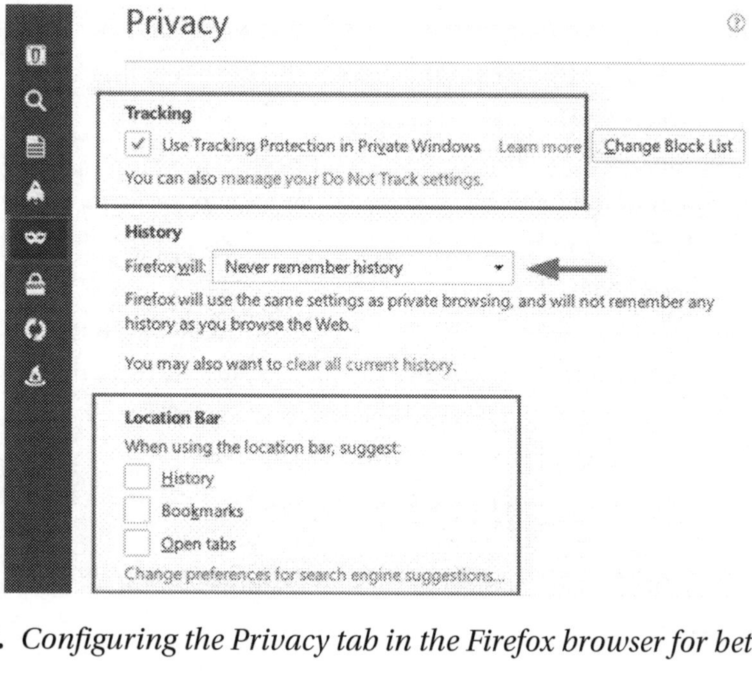

Figure 2-15. *Configuring the Privacy tab in the Firefox browser for better privacy*

Move to the Security tab and configure it like in Figure 2-16.

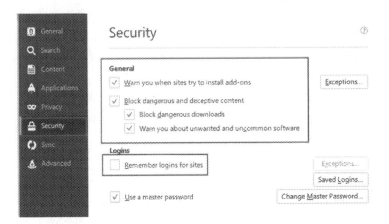

Figure 2-16. *Configuring the Security tab to stop phishing and dangerous websites*

Go to "Privacy & Security" tab ➤ "Firefox Data Collection and Use" pane and disable the following options: Allow Firefox to send technical and interaction data to Mozilla and Allow Firefox to send backlogged crash reports on your behalf. We are using for this step Firefox Quantum edition—version number 61. Crash reports can contain valuable data about your computer status that can make you vulnerable if it falls into the wrong hands, so it is better to disable them.

While you are still on the Advanced tab, go to the Network subtab, and make sure that the option "Tell me when a website asks to store data for offline use" is selected. This prevents websites from planting a tracking code on your computer.

Now that you have finished configuring the basic settings of Firefox to make it more privacy-friendly, you need to move to the advanced settings to continue your work. Access the Firefox advanced settings page by typing **about:config** in the URL address bar of your browser. A warning message will appear; hit the button "I accept the risk!" to access the advanced settings panel.

To access a specific setting, you need to type its name in the Search box that appears at the top of the page. To begin, let's change the first setting named browser.formfill. enable to false (double-click to change the settings value). This forces Firefox to forget form information (see Figure 2-17).

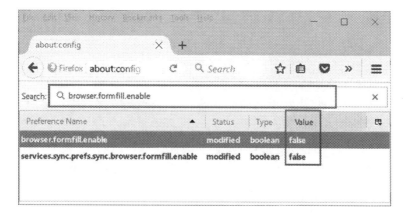

Figure 2-17. *Accessing the advanced settings page in Firefox and disabling form history in Firefox*

Now, in the same way, you need to change the following settings:

- Change browser.cache.disk.enable to false.

- Change browser.cache.disk_cache_ssl to false.

- Change browser.cache.offline.enable to false.

- Change dom.event.clipboardevents.enabled to false.

- Change geo.enabled to false.

- Change network.cookie.lifetimePolicys value to 2.

- Change plugin.scan.plid.all to false.

These advanced configurations will "harden" Firefox and make it more difficult for outside parties to track your activities. In the next section, we will cover privacy add-ons that can further secure Firefox and fight against online tracking and user profiling.

Firefox Privacy Extensions

A selection of the best Firefox extensions (see Table 2-6) that help you to maintain your online privacy will be mentioned here. Please note that some add-on providers may fool users and collect private data about browsing habits and even personal information without their consent, so it is advisable to avoid installing any add-on except the ones mentioned in this section. Also, if a new reliable add-on appears later (say after publishing this book), ensure that it comes from a reputable trusted developer and install it from https://addons.mozilla.org exclusively.

Table 2-6. *Firefox Privacy Add-on*

Add-on	Work	URL
HTTPS Everywhere	Encrypts your communications with many major websites, making your browsing more secure.	`https://www.eff.org/HTTPS-EVERYWHERE`
Privacy Badger	Blocks spying ads and invisible trackers.	`https://www.eff.org/privacybadger`
uBlock Origin	General-purpose blocker with custom rules set by the user.	`https://addons.mozilla.org/en-US/firefox/addon/ublock-origin/`
Random Agent Spoofer	Rotates complete browser profiles (from real browsers /devices) at a user-defined time interval.	`https://addons.mozilla.org/nn-no/firefox/addon/random-agent-spoofer/`

Fighting Against Digital Fingerprinting and Browser Leak

We've already covered a good amount of information on how to make your web browser more resistant to fingerprinting. Despite all these techniques, we cannot guarantee a 100 percent technical solution to stop this privacy invasion. The best solution is to access the Internet using a freshly installed of the Firefox browser. This will effectively make your browser look like most browsers' fingerprint! To make things more hidden, install your web browser within a virtual machine. This will also conceal your current machine—hardware and software—configurations. Of course, you still need to use a VPN to encrypt your connection and conceal your IP address.

Secure Online Communication

In this section, we will show you how to use different techniques to conceal your real IP address and to make your connection encrypted so it is hard to intercept. Please note that the term *privacy* is different from anonymity, although they are interrelated in many ways. So, in this context, VPN and proxy servers will help to mask your traffic; outside observers will see that there is traffic originating from your computer, but they cannot see what is passing (for example, ISPs and governments cannot see which websites you are visiting). In addition, all the websites you are visiting—and the applications you are using—will not see your real IP address. In anonymity, an outside observer should not be able to know the source of the connection; hence, they cannot attribute your online activities to you. Both privacy and anonymity are important for any OSINT analyst and should be fully understood before you begin your OSINT work in the rest of the book.

VPN

A VPN allows a user to establish a secure connection from one site to another across the Internet (see Figure 2-18). It is widely used in corporations to access remote sites while assuring the confidentiality of sensitive data. The VPN also gives users anonymous IP addresses, making them appear as if in another location so they can avoid censorship, share files with other people privately, and more. Nowadays a VPN is a necessity for anyone who cares about their privacy when going online.

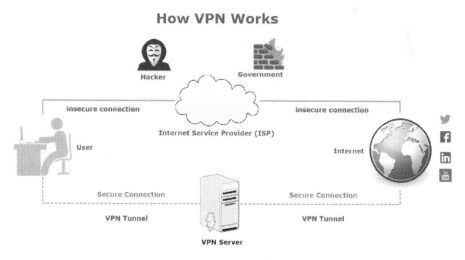

Figure 2-18. How a VPN works (source: www.DarknessGate.com)

VPN vendors offer varying features. You should care about the following features when selecting your VPN provider:

- Do not subscribe to VPN service providers that are based in one of the following countries: United States, United Kingdom, Australia, New Zealand, Canada, Denmark, France, Netherlands, Norway,

Belgium, Germany, Italy, Spain, Israel, Sweden, and of course countries such as Russia, China, Iran, and all Arab states. The best providers are based in Switzerland and follow its jurisdiction.

- A VPN provider must have its own DNS server; it must also support DNS leak protection (more on this next).

- It is preferred that the VPN software support the OpenVPN software. This is an open source program that can be audited by anyone to assure it's vacant from any backdoors.

- It should accept anonymous payments such as bitcoin, gift cards, debit cards, and cash.

- It is better to support multiple devices at the same time so you can protect your tablet and smartphone data in addition to your laptop or PC.

- It should not require many details to set up; a username and a password should be enough.

Note!   If your ultimate purpose is anonymity and plausible deniability, use the Tor Browser instead of a VPN.

Proxies

A proxy server is an intermediary computer that sits between your computing device and the Internet. Corporations use proxies to filter content and to offer a level of security by separating a corporate local network from the Internet. There are different kinds of proxies; the main type is the web proxy that most Internet users mean when using the term *proxy*. Its main function is to fetch online resources—whether it is a page or a file—from the Internet and then send them to your computer. They also provide anonymity by changing the real IP address of the user's computer into the IP address of the proxy server (see Figure 2-19).

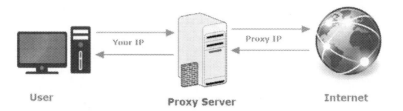

Figure 2-19. *How a proxy server works (source:* www.GarknessGate.com)

Numerous free proxy servers are available online. However, we strongly recommend that such services are not used. A free proxy usually shows advertisements in your browser, which may introduce malicious software or other tracking scripts that could infect or compromise your machine if you click a malicious link. In addition, most free proxies are not secure enough to trust to process and communicate your critical data, such as credit card details and account passwords.

DNS Leak Test

Using a VPN—and other anonymity services—does not guarantee that your web browsing history will not get revealed. Sometimes even though you are protecting your connection using a VPN, a connection leak can occur and reveal the real IP address without you being aware. Such a leak occurs when part of your computing device traffic (DNS traffic) is not routed through the secure channel of the anonymity service you are using and hence the VPN. Instead, it gets directed to your ISP's Internet servers (see Figure 2-20), allowing them to potentially monitor and log the complete web browsing history, even though you're using a VPN.

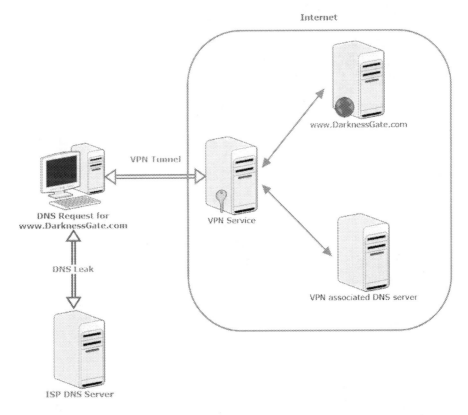

Figure 2-20. *How a DNS leak occurs (source:* www.darknessgate.com*)*

To ensure that your VPN provider is not vulnerable to this risk, you are strongly advised to test your connection directly after connecting to your VPN provider, as follows:

1. Go to https://www.dnsleaktest.com.

2. You will see two buttons along with your current IP address. The first button is labeled "Standard test," and the second is "Extended test." Click the second button for detailed results.

3. The detailed results page will show you a list of all the DNS servers (along with their locations) that are used to resolve your typed website URLs into IP addresses. If any of these servers are not related to your VPN provider company, this means your connection is leaking information about you.

Reputable VPN providers have a connection leak prevention mechanism. However, you need to make sure that your VPN provider has this feature enabled automatically for your connection.

Warning!   Always do DNS leak testing, as explained, to assure that your DNS traffic is tunneled through your VPN-encrypted tunnel and not through your ISP.

Online Anonymity

When working online to collect OSINT sources, it is vital to remain completely anonymous. VPN allows you to mask your IP address and scramble the transferred contents to and from your PC. However, the VPN provider can intercept all your communications in plain sight. For mission-critical tasks, it highly advisable to use anonymous networks (e.g., Tor, I2P, and Freenet). This allows you to conceal your identity when surfing or publishing information online. In the following section, we will cover the Tor Network, which is considered the most used anonymous network today.

Using the TOR Network

Tor is the most popular anonymous network currently used online; it is mainly composed of these two parts:

- The piece of software you run on your machine to access the Internet anonymously

- The Tor Network of volunteer computers that direct your online traffic

Tor enables users to achieve a high level of online anonymity by encrypting both the data and the destination IP addresses prior to sending them through a virtual circuit, which consists of many nodes (no fewer than three nodes at any given time). Each node then decrypts part of the data to reveal only the next node in the circuit to direct the remaining encrypted data to it. The next node performs the same function until the message reaches the final node, called the *exit relay*. The exit relay decrypts the data without revealing the source IP address, sending it on to its destination (see Figure 2-21).

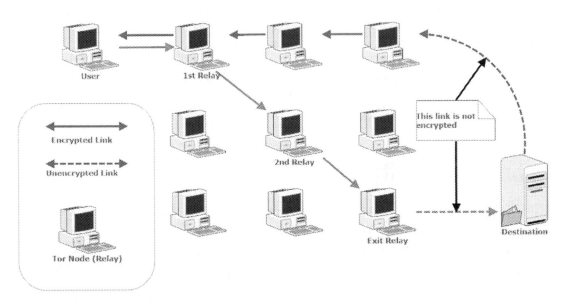

Figure 2-21. *How the Tor Network works*

Note!   The term *node* is used to describe any server working as part of the Tor Network of relays. Sometimes people use different terms for the node such as *server*, *relay*, or *router*.

When using Tor to anonymize your location, it will use the exit relay IP address instead of your real IP address as the source IP address. This will effectively conceal your identity online.

To use the Tor Network to begin your OSINT searches, all you need to do is to download and use the Tor Browser.

Tor Browser

To access the Tor Network, download the Tor Browser from | https://www.torproject.org/ projects/torbrowser.html.en. The Tor Browser is a security-hardened Firefox browser that requires no installation on the client machine; you can safely run it from your USB drive. It comes with the Tor software that allows you to access the Tor Network transparently upon launching this browser without any extra configuration (see Figure 2-22).

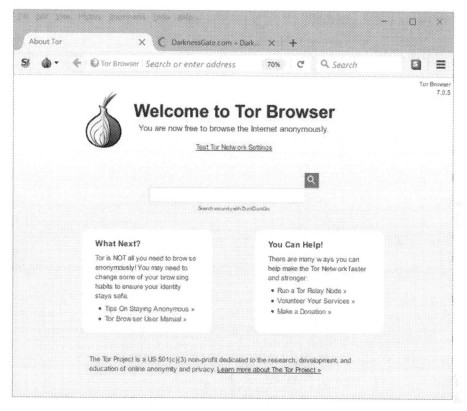

Figure 2-22. *Successful launch of the Tor Browser*

Please note that only websites visited through the Tor Browser will get routed through the Tor Network anonymously; other browsers and applications already installed on your device will not use the Tor Network.

Hiding Tor Usage

An important point that should be carefully considered is hiding the usage of the Tor Browser from your ISP. This step is essential because using Tor Browser could be considered suspicious and even illegal in some countries. Other countries—and ISPs—may forbid access to the Tor Network. This will make using the Tor Browser more difficult for novice users.

Detecting Tor usage is feasible using a variety of technical methods. However, in this section, we will introduce some techniques to conceal your Tor usage to a large extent, which makes detecting it difficult.

Using a VPN

You can hide Tor usage from your ISP by using a virtual private network service. The VPN will create an encrypted tunnel between your machine and the VPN server. Once that's initiated, you can launch the Tor Browser, which will be hidden from your ISP to a large extent.

Using Tor Bridges

Bridge relays (or *bridges* for short) are Tor relays that aren't listed in the main Tor directory. Bridges are considered entry points to the Tor Network. Since there is no complete public list of them, even if your ISP is filtering connections to all the known Tor relays, it probably won't be able to block all the bridges.

Please remember that this method may not fully guarantee that your ISP will not detect your Tor usage, but it will make discovering this fact difficult and will require sophisticated techniques to uncover. To get Tor bridges, do one of the following:

- Go to `https://bridges.torproject.org/bridges` and get your bridges.

- Send an email to `bridges@torproject.org` with the line "get bridges" by itself in the body of the email. You must send this email from one of the following email providers: Riseup, Gmail, or Yahoo.

Now, you need to configure the Tor Browser to use these bridges. To do so, follow these steps:

1. To enter bridges into the Tor Browser, launch the Tor Browser, and before the Tor Browser connects, click the Open Settings button (see Figure 2-23).

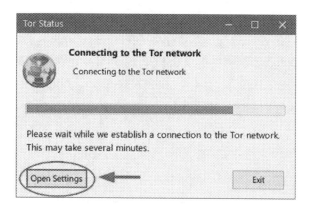

Figure 2-23. *Accessing Tor Network settings before launching the Tor Browser*

2. A Tor Network Settings window appears; click the Configure button.

3. Tor asks you whether your ISP is blocking or otherwise censoring connections to the Tor Network; click Yes and click Next to continue.

4. In the next wizard window, select the option "Enter custom bridges" (see Figure 2-24). Copy the bridges you have from step 1 or step 2 and paste them in the box; click Next to continue.

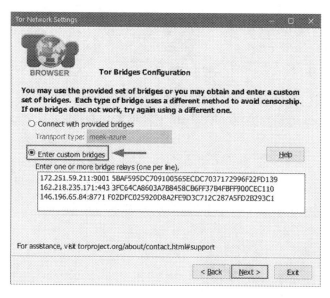

Figure 2-24. *Entering custom bridges into the Tor Browser*

5. The next wizard asks you whether your computer sits behind a
    proxy server; in our case, you don't need one (which is the most
    common). Select No and click the Connect button to continue. If
    you are sitting behind a proxy server, select Yes, then enter your
    proxy settings, and finally click Connect.

If everything works as expected, the Tor Browser will open using the customized
bridges.

As we have already introduced, using customized Tor bridges may not fully mask
your entry to the Tor Network. Some countries use a deep packet inspection (DPI)
technique to analyze Internet traffic flows by protocol to examine whether they contain
Tor traffic. However, using customized bridges is still a good way to circumvent Tor
censorship and conceal its usage in many countries.

Using Pluggable Transports

To work around the DPI censorship technique, Tor has introduced the pluggable
transport (PT). This technique transforms the traffic between your computer and the
bridge into typical Internet traffic, thus hiding your Tor usage from your ISP. To use a
pluggable transport, do the following:

1. Launch the Tor Browser and click the Open Settings button before
    Tor starts.

2. Click the Configure button, select the Yes option when asked
    whether your ISP blocks or censors connections to the Tor
    Network, and click Next to continue.

3. Select the option "Connect with provided bridges" and select a
    bridge from the Transport Type drop-down menu (see Figure 2-25).

Figure 2-25. *Connecting to the Tor Network using a pluggable transport to conceal your Tor usage*

4. The final wizard window will ask you whether this computer sits behind a proxy server. In our case, it does not, so you can select the No option and click the Connect button. If you are sitting behind a proxy server, select Yes, enter your proxy settings, and click the Connect button.

If everything goes well, the Tor Browser should now be able to load successfully.

Warning!   What should you do to stay anonymous when using the Tor Browser?

1. Do not install add-ons in your Tor Browser such as Flash Player, Adobe Reader, and QuickTime Player. Such extensions tend to open independent connections outside the Tor circuit, and this will leak your real IP address.

2. Do not open PDF files or play Flash video within your Tor Browser.

3. If you are exchanging sensitive data through the Tor Network, make sure to encrypt it first. The Tor exit relay—which is used to establish the connection with the destination—is not encrypted. If an intruder sits at that location, he can intercept your connection.

4. Make sure when using the Tor Browser to not use your real identity to register or post comments on websites. Of course, as an OSINT analyzer, keeping your identity secret is the main reason to use the Tor Network.

Using the Tails OS and Other Security OSs

Sometimes you may want to achieve the highest anonymity possible through using a specialized OS that directs all Internet traffic through the Tor Network. The Tor Browser is more than enough for concealing your identity when conducting regular OSINT searches; however, when working on sensitive cases or exchanging information with other parties, it is necessary to use an anonymous OS.

Tails is a Linux security-hardened OS that uses Tor as its default networking application. It is considered the best anonymous OS currently available, and for the record, this is the OS that Edward Snowden used to help stay anonymous during the initial NSA spying leaks. You can use Tails to communicate privately with confidence in extremely hostile environments.

Tails is portable. Hence, you can execute it from within your USB stick drive, and it is fully independent of the host machine. Tails runs using the host machine's RAM and does not copy any files to the resident host machine's hard disk.

Tails achieves its anonymity by forcing all network connections to go through the Tor Network. If an application tries to connect to the Internet directly, the connection is automatically blocked. Tails leaves no traces on the host machine's hard disk. Upon shutdown, Tails will delete all user files, unless explicitly asked not to (persistent storage). Tails comes with many cryptographic tools that allow you to send encrypted emails and have secure IM chats.

We will cover installing and using Tails in Chapter 3.

Sharing Files Securely

Sometimes you may want to share files privately with other parties located in another location. This is especially important for any OSINT analyst who may need to request and share information with colleagues to support a case. There are numerous file-sharing services, but the majority are not built to be completely anonymous. They usually require an account to share files and store some information (also called *transaction metadata*, which includes uploader and downloader IP addresses among other things) about each transaction happening through them. Such a thing is not suitable for investigators working on sensitive legal cases. In this section, we will introduce a secure file-sharing service through the Tor Network; it is considered the most anonymous solution to exchange private files online.

OnionShare

OnionShare is an open source tool that uses the Tor Network to share files anonymously. You can share any type and size of files. Your shared files will not get uploaded to the Internet. Instead, they will remain on your computer, which plays the role of a hosting service. All you need to do to share files is to share the URL given by the tool to the person you are corresponding with who should access it using the Tor Browser.

To use OnionShare, follow these steps:

1. Download and install the program from `https://onionshare.org`.

2. Launch the tool and select the files/folders you want to share. Make sure your Tor Browser is launched and connected to the Tor Network.

3. After selecting which files/folders you want to share, click the Start Sharing button. OnionShare will create a hidden Tor service for your shared files hosted on the Tor Network and will give you a URL to send to your correspondent. You can get this URL by clicking the Copy URL button (see Figure 2-26).

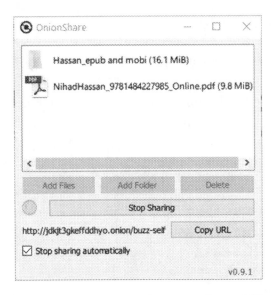

Figure 2-26. *OnionShare provides a URL for your shared files, sends it to the recipient, and keeps it private*

4. Your correspondent must access the shared URL through the Tor Browser.

5. Your OnionShare program and the Tor Browser should remain open until your correspondent finishes downloading your shared files. When the recipient receives your file successfully, OnionShare will stop the sharing process automatically. (To stop sharing automatically after the recipient receives the file, you must enable the option "Stop sharing automatically" in the OnionShare program before sharing files.)

Note!   For security-conscious people who want to share sensitive files, we advise you to use the Tails OS when sharing files through the OnionShare program.

Making Anonymous Payments

As an OSINT analyzer, during your search for OSINT sources, you may encounter websites that request you pay a fee to see some resources (mainly gray literature). This frequently happens when requesting academic papers or a corporation's internal documents. The same thing applies when buying anonymity services online (e.g., paying for a VPN provider anonymously). As you know, you may be part of a legal investigation and do not want to reveal your real identity when investigating some types of resources. In such cases, it is necessary to pay for such services anonymously.

In ordinary cases, when you purchase something online, your name, credit card information, and other transaction details will be available to the online merchant. Your credit card issuer and the bank will also know about your transaction details, and no one can guarantee how long these details will remain stored and whether any third party (e.g., advertisement agency) may have access to it. To purchase digital goods and services online anonymously, you can either use a gift credit card or pay using cryptocurrency.

Prepaid Gift Card

Major credit card providers offer prepaid cards for their customers. Such cards do not require any personal information to set up; they also do not require the existence of a bank account to work. Such cards are available in drugstores and supermarkets and are used specifically to purchase digital goods like VPNs and other anonymity services (although please note that not all websites accept such cards).

There are different types of prepaid cards. What we care about for this book is the anonymous type, which is the "nonreloadable" card. This card comes preloaded with a specific amount of cash—usually less than $500. You can purchase them with cash (which is untraceable) without revealing any personal information; even your e-mail address is not required.

Warning!   Do not buy prepaid credit cards online. If you buy a prepaid credit card online, you need to pay for it using some form of nonanonymous payment like an ordinary credit card, a bank check, or PayPal. In addition, you need to supply your postal address to receive the card (if it is a physical plastic card). This will link the purchased credit card to your real identity.

Cryptocurrency

Cryptocurrency is a type of digital currency that is designed to work as a medium of exchange using cryptography to secure the transaction and to control the creation of additional units of currency. There are hundreds of cryptocurrency types already in use; the most famous is still the bitcoin system. You can find a list of currently available cryptocurrency at https://coinmarketcap.com.

Bitcoin (https://bitcoin.org) is a decentralized and unregulated peer-to-peer payment network (like the Torrent network) that is powered by its users with no central authority or middleman. Bitcoin is a digital system; it is not printed like ordinary currency (dollars and euros) and is created by people and companies using a specialized open source software program called a bitcoin wallet (the wallet can be an online service; hence, it is called an *e-wallet*). Bitcoin does not charge fees on transactions, and it is nonrefundable (once you send bitcoin to a recipient, it will be gone forever unless the recipient returns the bitcoin to you).

We will not delve deeply into the technical side of the bitcoin digital currency and how to set up an account to buy products using it because it is out of the book's scope. What you should know about bitcoin is that you can make anonymous purchases using this currency that are near impossible to uncover. In the following list, we will give you some reputable online sources to understand how this currency works.

- *Getting started with Bitcoin*: https://bitcoin.org/en/getting-started

- *Bitcoin wallets*: https://blockchain.info/wallet

- *Bitcoin wallet programs*: https://en.bitcoin.it/wiki/Clients

- *Buy bitcoin anonymously with cash using ATM machines*: https://coinatmradar.com

Bitcoin payments are extremely anonymous; however, there is a bit of a learning curve for buying and exchanging bitcoin.

Before moving on, consider the following when conducting anonymous purchases online:

- Encrypt your online connection before making an anonymous payment. When paying anonymously online, make sure to anonymize your connection using an anonymizing network like Tor or I2P. Paying anonymously without masking your IP address will expose your technical connection details to different parties, and this may lead to revealing your identity.

- Registering for anonymity services, like a VPN, and even conducting some online purchases using an anonymous payment method may require users to supply their e-mail address as part of the transaction. Make sure not to use your primary email address; instead, use a temporary email address for such tasks.

Encryption Techniques

Encryption provides a robust set of techniques to ensure secure transactional sensitive data flows online, thus preventing hackers and cybercriminals from accessing sensitive content, even if they succeed in capturing the transmitted encrypted data. The mathematical formulas involved in today's cryptographic standards are enough to prevent most attackers from decrypting stolen data. In this section, we will present some tools and advice that helps you to keep your confidential data private by encrypting it.

Securing Your Passwords

Make sure to secure your online accounts using strong, complex passwords. It is also highly recommended to change your password every three months. There are many free tools to aid you in the password generation process. Such tools will produce highly secure passwords that contain a combination of letters, numbers, and symbols. Here is a list of some of these tools:

- Free Password Generator (`https://www.securesafepro.com/pasgen.html`)

- PWGen (`http://pwgen-win.sourceforge.net`)

Many websites offer online password generation services. However, we prefer not to use such services because your password can be intercepted while traveling to your PC.

To store your passwords, you should use a security program to keep them safe; using a password manager program is essential to keep all your passwords in a safe location. A password manager encrypts the database that contains your credentials and protects it with a master password. This is the only password you must remember.

- KeePass Password Safe (`http://keepass.info`)

- Master Password (`https://ssl.masterpasswordapp.com`)

- Password Safe (`https://www.pwsafe.org`)

Encrypting Your Hard Drive/USB Sticks

Encrypting data becomes essential in today's digital age as it considered the last line of defense if an attacker successfully gains access to your confidential data. In other words, encryption will be your last hope to prevent the compromise, use, or disclosure of your sensitive information to the public or to your enemies.

Keeping stored information on a hard drive secure is easy when using encryption software. For instance, Windows provides a built-in encryption utility that is available for most of its versions (Windows 7 and beyond) called BitLocker. Using this utility is easy; all you need to do is to right-click the drive you want to encrypt and select Turn on BitLocker (see Figure 2-27). A wizard will appear that walks you through all the steps to configure your drive encryption (setting a password and storing a recovery key).

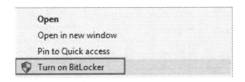

Figure 2-27.   *Activate BitLocker on a Windows box*

There are many reputable disk encryption software applications that provide disk and even OS partition encryption.

VeraCrypt (`https://www.veracrypt.fr/en/Home.html`) is supported on all major OSs. It can encrypt hard drives including OS partitions and USB stick drives. VeraCrypt also creates encrypted vaults that can be used to store data and then transfer it into a USB stick or send it over the Internet securely. You can check the documentation section for how to use this tool in different scenarios.

DiskCryptor (`https://diskcryptor.net/wiki/Main_Page`) offers encryption of all disk partitions, including the system partition. It is supported only on Windows OS.

Cloud Storage Security

Most people are using cloud storage to back up and store their sensitive data (such as documents, personal pictures, contact lists, address books, and the like). The many security incidents that have taken place lately with major cloud service providers shows that their security measures alone may not be enough to stop such compromises. To counter such risks, don't rely on the cloud service provider to secure your data. Always encrypt your data before uploading it to the cloud and make sure to have a backup copy stored somewhere else when dealing with sensitive data. Here are two programs that can be used to secure your data before uploading it to the cloud:

1. Duplicati (`https://www.duplicati.com`) uses AES-256 or GPG to encrypt your data before sending it to the cloud.

2. Cryptomator (`https://cryptomator.org`) uses AES-256 to encrypt your data and uses SCRYPT to protect against brute-force attacks. It works by creating an encrypted vault—a virtual hard drive—on your local machine that encrypts everything inside it before uploading it to the cloud provider.

Please note that compression programs like 7-Zip (`www.7-zip.org`) and PeaZip (`www.peazip.org`) also offer encryption features, so you can compress and protect your files with a password before uploading it to the cloud.

Secure E-mail Communications

Whenever an e-mail is sent, it should be encrypted to assure the integrity and confidentiality of its contents. In today's digital age, e-mail becomes the main means of communications for both individuals and public/private organizations, and breaching this communication medium would have a serious consequence. E-mail data breaches occur daily to assure that the contents of your emails are secure, so you should use encryption software.

Detailing how to incorporate encryption in your e-mails is beyond this book's scope. However, in this context, you should understand that when sharing information with colleagues (e.g., as part of your OSINT investigation) through e-mails, you should take care to encrypt it first. In this section, we will give you resources and tools to learn how to do this. However, if you want to understand the ins and outs of e-mail encryption, you should check out our book *Digital Privacy and Security Using Windows: A Practical Guide* (Apress, 2017).

- Gpg4win (GNU Privacy Guard for Windows) allows you to create cryptographic keys (public and private keys), encrypt files and folders, and sign your e-mails before sending (digital signature). Gpg4win is the official GnuPG distribution for Windows and can be found at `https://www.gpg4win.org`.

- Another implementation of the GnuPG project to be used on other platforms can be found at `https://www.gnupg.org/download/index.html`.

- Mozilla Thunderbird can be configured to use GnuPG on all major platforms through installing the Enigma add-on, which adds OpenPGP message encryption and authentication to the Thunderbird e-mail client. It features automatic encryption, decryption, and integrated key management functionality.

Note!   You can direct your Thunderbird e-mails through the Tor Network by using an extension for Mozilla Thunderbird called TorBirdy. According to its creators (it belongs to the Tor project), TorBirdy is still in beta release and should not be used to secure communications in extremely hostile environments. You can find information on how to install and use this extension at `https://trac.torproject.org/projects/tor/wiki/torbirdy`.

A browser extension is available for both Firefox and Google Chrome called Mailvelope that can be used with most web e-mail services. It allows its users to exchange encrypted e-mails using the OpenPGP encryption schema. You can either generate your key pair or import existing one (for example, from Kleopatra). You can use this extension without installing any tools except the extension on your browser. It is open source and available at `https://www.mailvelope.com/en`. However, we do not recommend encrypting messages within web browsers because this will make them more vulnerable to cyberattacks that regularly hit browsers.

Secure E-mail Providers

If you prefer to use a webmail for some of your tasks, it is advisable to use a secure end-to-end e-mail provider that offers extended security features for your e-mail account. For instance, ProtonMail (`https://protonmail.com`) is different from other regular e-mail providers in many ways. It is based in Switzerland and follows its jurisdiction, which is considered the best one in the world in terms of protecting user privacy. ProtonMail uses two passwords to protect your e-mail account. The first one authenticates your account credentials on the server, and the second decrypts your inbox within your web browser or app, meaning that it never goes online to the ProtonMail server. If you are exchanging e-mails with another ProtonMail user, you can safely set your emails to destroy itself within a time limit in addition to sending encrypted e-mails to other ProtonMail users. It is especially useful to destroy sensitive e-mails automatically on both sides of the communications.

Finally, if you want to use an e-mail for only one time (for example, to activate some services anonymously), you can go with any of the following two services:

- `https://hidester.com/temporary-email`

- `https://www.guerrillamail.com`

Secure IM and Online Calling Services

IM conversations are another form of communications that you may need to protect. No one can guarantee that giant IT providers that offer free IM, voiceover IP, and video conference services do not log your chat—or at least the metadata of the conversation such as date/time and login IP address—for some period. We cannot discuss the security features of each available application in this book. However, we will focus on the security feature that makes one application more secure than the rest. For instance, most VoIP and chatting applications work the same way. They encrypt the messages exchanged between the people involved in the conversation, but they do not encrypt the message metadata.

The best secure VoIP/IM application is one that has the following technical characteristics: it should be open source so its code can be audited by independent security experts, it should not offer/show ads or any type of commercial advertisements, the provider and hence the app should not store the decryption key on its server so no one can request the key to decrypt user data, it should not store any metadata about the user connection, and the user contact list should not be stored on the app server and if necessary it should be saved encrypted. It should offer clear options to choose what you want to backup before sending it to the cloud provider.

The following are some popular secure and well-supported messaging apps:

- *Tor Messenger* (`https://trac.torproject.org/projects/tor/wiki/doc/TorMessenger`): Although it still in beta version, this is considered the best secure IM chat. Traffic is directed through the Tor Network for maximum anonymity.

- *Cryptocat* (`https://crypto.cat/security.html`): This is an open source secure messaging application, it encrypt all communication by default and allows for secure sharing of files online.

- *Signal* (`https://whispersystems.org`): This is a secure messaging and VoIP app; it is easy to use and offers similar functions as WhatsApp and Viber Apps. This app runs on Android and iPhone devices only.

- *Ghost Call* (`https://ghostcall.io`): This is an end-to-end encrypted calling service.

- *ChatSecure* (`https://chatsecure.org`): This IM program works only on iOS when it is configured to use OTR over XMPP.

Virtualization Technology

Use virtualization technology to enhance your privacy and protect your host machine from malware and other security threats. A virtual machine allows you to have a virtual operating system that behaves like a full, separate computer. You can use virtual machines to execute programs, open e-mail attachments, test programs, and visit dangerous websites safely without being afraid of malware affecting your operating system because the virtual machine will run in a sandbox isolated entirely from its host machine's operating system. Online investigators can use virtual machines to conduct their online investigations securely, and they can use freshly installed browsers to mask their digital fingerprint, making it appear like millions of similar browsers. Finally, they can delete the entire virtual machine to clear any digital traces that may be left on the host machine!

These are the most popular two virtual machines:

- VMware Player (see Figure 2-28) (`www.vmware.com/products/player/playerpro-evaluation.htm`)

- Virtual Box (`https://www.virtualbox.org`)

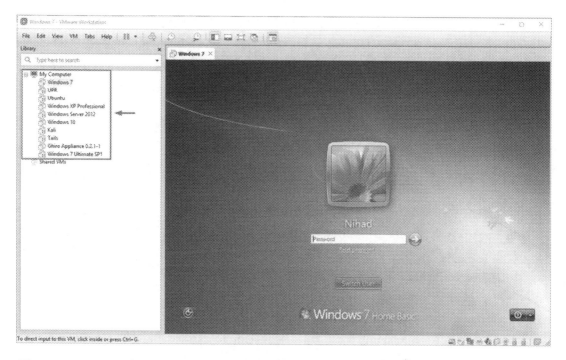

Figure 2-28. *Multiple OSs can be installed on each virtual machine; this image shows seven OSs installed within one instance of the VMware program*

You can also use portable programs that do not need to be installed to run. Such programs will usually leave a little trace on the host machine, but it is still considered a way to minimize your digital footprint online.

Using a bootable USB token or live CD/DVD when working on sensitive documents is also a great practice to hide your digital traces. Running the Tails OS (`https://tails.boum.org`) in offline mode is a great practice. There are many tools that can help you to create a bootable USB/CD drive. The following are some of them:

- Windows USB/DVD download tool (`https://wudt.codeplex.com`)

- Rufus (`https://rufus.akeo.ie`)

- WinBuilder (`http://winbuilder.net`)

Windows To Go is a new feature available in Windows 10 (Enterprise and Education editions only). It allows you to run the complete Windows 10 Live feature from a USB drive without needing to install it on your computer's hard drive. You can access this feature from Control Panel ➤ Windows To Go. This feature allows you to take your Windows box with you wherever you go, but bear in mind that some Windows 10 features may not work when using the Windows To Go operating system.

Android and iOS Emulator

An emulator allows you to run the Android application on your computer as if it were on your smartphone. There are numerous reasons why an online investigator may want this to happen; maybe he wants to test the functionality of a specific app or simply wants to gather some information using a feature that is available only for smartphone apps. The protective measures to stay anonymous can be implemented more easily when running such applications—using an emulator—on your computer rather than on your smartphone. For instance, using a VPN and accessing resources using Tor anonymously is more convenient using a computer with a mouse. The same can be achieved with smartphone apps when running on a computer using emulators. Here is a list of the most popular emulators for both Android and Apple OS:

- Andy (`https://www.andyroid.net`)

- ARChon (`https://github.com/vladikoff/chromeos-apk/blob/master/archon.md`), Google Chrome

- MEmu (`www.memuplay.com`)

- MOBIONE STUDIO (`http://download.cnet.com/MobiOne-Design-Center/3001-2247_4-75910775.html`), Apple apps

Essential Prerequisites

In this section, we will list some of the supporting software and methods that can aid an investigator for preparing the gathered OSINT data into usable formats for further analysis.

Drawing Software and Data Visualization

Drawing software—including mind mapping—and other data visualization tools help online investigators visualize their findings, make search plans, and avoid forgetting something during the gathering process; they also present the final results in a clear manner. In this section, we will focus on the best free programs/services available for aiding OSINT investigators in completing their mission.

Mind Mapping and Idea Generation Tools

When conducting OSINT gathering, it is better to use some tools to organize your findings. The following are some popular tools for drawing diagrams and charts, taking notes, and creating mind maps to visualize your results.

FreeMind

FreeMind (`http://freemind.sourceforge.net/wiki/index.php/Main_Page`) is the most popular free mind-mapping software. Using this tool, you can draw different diagrams that visually organize information.

Storytelling Tools

These tools help you to create a timeline for your OSINT gathering. Here are some popular free solutions:

- Story Map (`https://storymap.knightlab.com`)
- Visual Investigative Scenarios (`https://vis.occrp.org`)

Diagramming Software

The following are some tools for diagramming.

Apache OpenOffice Draw

Apache OpenOffice Draw (`https://www.openoffice.org/product/draw.html`) allows you to draw different technical and business process diagrams.

Google Drawings

Google Drawings (`https://docs.google.com/drawings/create`) is a free cloud-based diagramming tool developed by Google.

Note Management

Here are some tools for note management.

TagSpaces

TagSpaces (`https://www.tagspaces.org`) is an offline, open source, personal data manager that helps you organize files on your OS—Windows, Linux, Android, or Mac—using tags and notes to files/folders.

KeepNote

KeepNote (`http://keepnote.org`) is an open source cross-platform program for organizing your notes and to-do list. You can attach different media—like such as and videos—to your note making it more informative.

Data Visualization

Here are some tools for data visualization.

Microsoft Excel

This helps you to summarize large amounts of data and present it in charts/tables and other graphical visualizations. Microsoft Excel is proprietary software by Microsoft.

Business Intelligence and Reporting Tools

Business Intelligence and Reporting Tools (`https://www.eclipse.org/birt/about`) is open source software that helps you to visualize data and create reports based on it.

Dradis CE

Dradis CE (`https://dradisframework.com/ce/`) is an open source reporting and collaboration tool for InfoSec professionals; it allows you to combine the output of different tools like Burp, Nessus, Nmap, and Qualys to create a single report for a specific case.

Bookmarking

When working on collecting OSINT sources, you will encounter a large sum of useful online resources. To handle this large volume of data, you need a method or tool to organize your favorite web pages. All web browsers have a built-in feature to organize favorites; we already recommended Firefox as a preferred web browser for conducting OSINT searches. The built-in bookmarking organizer associated with Firefox is enough to organize your work. However, it is preferable to use it efficiently by associating your bookmarks (see Figure 2-29) with tags and grouping related bookmarks in one folder. Firefox also gives you the ability to export your bookmarks to an HTML file so that you can import this HTML file into another browser later. To export your bookmarks in Firefox, select Bookmarks ➤ Show All Bookmarks ➤ Import and Backup ➤ Export Bookmarks to HTML.

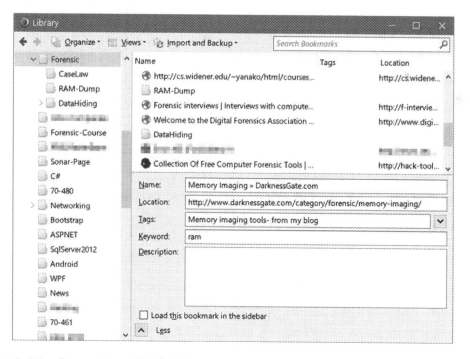

Figure 2-29. *Organizing Firefox favorites*

There are plenty of online bookmarking managers; however, we found storing bookmarks using online services is not a good thing for the secrecy of the OSINT investigation.

Free Translation Services

During your OSINT searches, you will encounter useful resources in other languages that you do not understand—for example, Arabic. Online instant translation services offer a great aid to understand these foreign resources to add them to your case data. The following are some free translation services:

- Google Translate (`https://translate.google.com`)

- Bing Translator (`https://www.bing.com/translator`)

- Babylon's Free Online Translation (`http://translation.babylon-software.com`)

- Systranet (`www.systranet.com/web`)

Final Tips

Finally, we want to give you some tips for you to follow before you begin your online OSINT research.

Use a False Identity to Register on Some Websites

While you are conducting your OSINT searches, some websites may require you to register or create a free account to use its service or to access some sections. Make sure not to use your real personal information; you should also have a specialized e-mail address (preferably on Gmail) for this issue with fake information. The same thing applies when opening fake accounts on Facebook, Twitter, Instagram, and other social networks to conduct your OSINT searches.

Warning!   Some social sites prohibit creating fake accounts; it is always advisable to read the rules before you sign up. However, for people working in the intelligence arena, it is unlikely that they will obey such terms!

A fake identity generator can generate everything you need to become a new digital citizen. This includes phone, website, e-mail, username, password, account security questions, fake credit card and Social Security numbers, occupation, company, physical traits, and more. Here is a list of the most popular identity generation websites:

- `www.fakenamegenerator.com`

- `https://names.igopaygo.com/people/fake-person`

- `www.elfqrin.com/fakeid.php`

Be Anonymous

Enable your VPN service—or simply use the Tor Browser—before you begin your OSINT search. If you are not using Tor, make sure to use a virtual machine that has a freshly installed web browser within it to collect online resources. Make sure that your VPN connection is enabled for all applications installed on your machine including your virtual machine instance.

Destroy Your Digital Traces Upon Finishing

Use virtual machines and browse the Web using Firefox incognito mode. Make sure to use tools such as BleachBit (`https://www.bleachbit.org`) to wipe clean your applications' digital traces in addition to any remnants left on hard drive.

Use Linux

Many powerful OSINT tools work on Linux-based systems. These tools are available on Kali Linux (the successor of Backtrack), although many of these tools have been imported into Windows. You can download Kali from `https://www.kali.org` and install it on a virtual machine. Mastering the Kali Linux distribution is essential for any penetration tester and digital forensic investigator. Kali comes equipped with a plethora of out-of-the-box security tools.

Summary

In this chapter, we prepared the stage before you begin your OSINT search. We talked about different online threats and how you can counter them through security software as well as best practices when using computing devices. We covered some OS-hardening tips focusing on Windows as it is still considered to have the largest user base worldwide.

We talked about how online tracking works technically by listing its types and gave countermeasures to prevent outsiders from tracking your online activities. Then we moved on to talking about secure online browsing; we gave hardening tips for the Firefox browser as well as useful privacy add-ons. Using VPN to encrypt online traffic is important for any Internet user; we briefly described the concept of a VPN and proxy server and then gave important hints on how to use them safely to avoid leaking your real IP address without your knowledge even though you are using a VPN service. The anonymity section is essential before conducting OSINT searches; you should not do any OSINT search without activating an anonymity service or a VPN. We talked about using the Tor Browser to surf the Web anonymously. For people who live in extremely hostile environments, using the Tails OS—which directs all your Internet traffic through the Tor anonymity network—is strongly advisable.

Virtualization technology comes in handy when you want to test other applications or you want simply to cover your digital traces on the host machine. Virtual machines also help you to lower your digital footprint when conducting your research online as you can use a standard OS and web browser installation to make your search and finally delete the entire OS in one click.

This was a long chapter full of advice on how to deal with today's online threats. Understanding online threats, countermeasures, and how to become anonymous online is essential before beginning your work to harvest OSINT resources online. The rest of the chapters in this book are dedicated to OSINT search techniques. In the next chapter, we will delve beneath the surface of the ordinary Internet to explore the hidden underground Internet, known as the deep web.

CHAPTER 3

The Underground Internet

How well do you know the Internet? Being a regular Facebook, Twitter, and Instagram user and knowing how to use Google to find stuff online will not make you a super Internet user because you are just scratching the surface of the Web. Most web content is hidden and needs special methods to access it.

According to Internet World Stats, the number of Internet users in the world on June 30, 2017, has reached 3,885,567,619. (The world's population is 7,519,028,970 people.[i]) This is a huge number, and it is predicted to increase to 4 billion Internet users by 2020. Most Internet users worldwide are using the surface web—also known as the ordinary Internet. Only a tiny percentage of Internet users use the other hidden layers of the Internet on a daily basis or have even heard about them!

In August 2017, the total number of live websites belonging to the surface web was 1,800,566,882,[ii] while the estimated number of Tor websites on the darknet from March 2016 to March 2017 was about 50,000 to 60,000. Despite the huge number of websites within the surface web, Their contents -which can be indexed by typical search engines- constitutes only 4 percent of the whole Web, while the rest belongs to the deep web portion (which includes the darknet).

In this chapter, we will introduce you to the terms *deep web* and *dark web*. Both terms are used to point to the part of Internet that is hidden from an ordinary Internet user's sight and cannot be indexed by typical search engines. Deep web contents can be accessed using the regular HTTP/HTTPS protocol and typical web browsers; however, this is not the same for the darknet, which needs special software to access its contents. Before beginning our discussion, let's first differentiate between the three terms— surface, deep, and dark Internet.

© Nihad A. Hassan, Rami Hijazi 2018
N. A. Hassan and R. Hijazi, *Open Source Intelligence Methods and Tools*,
https://doi.org/10.1007/978-1-4842-3213-2_3

Layers of the Internet

Let's begin with the ordinary Internet or the surface web. This is the portion of the Web that includes all the contents that are readily available to the public. Websites on the surface web can be indexed using regular search engines such as Google so a user can find them easily.

Search engine providers use software known as *web crawlers* to discover publicly available web pages. Crawlers work by clicking hyperlinks inside pages and then sending these pages (results) to search engine servers that organize the results in a search index. The search index contains hundreds of billions of indexed pages. Finally, a user submits a search query, and the search engine responds by ranking pages that match the user query and returning an ordered list (see Figure 3-1).

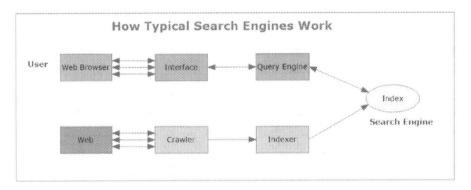

Figure 3-1. *How search engines index websites (source:* www.darknessgate.com*)*

Note!   If you want to understand how search engines index websites, Google offers a simple tutorial describing this issue. You can find it at `https://www.google.com/search/howsearchworks/`.

As of November 2017, Google is aware of about 130 trillion pages. The numbers change continually because of the fast-changing nature of the Web.

As mentioned, search engine web crawlers discover new pages through clicking links. However, this method is not perfect, and a vast volume of data will remain unindexed as search engines crawlers cannot reach them through web crawlers.

As an example, say you want to know the Canadian dollar exchange rate in the year 2000. There are many websites that offer currency exchange rates over time. So, for this example, you go to the `www.xe.com` website to see the Canadian exchange rate in the year 2000. But wait, there is a problem here. If you want to act as a regular search engine crawler, you can only click hyperlinks! But this will not give you the result you need. However, if you act as a human and went to the search form at `www.xe.com/currencytables` and entered the specific search date (2000/01/01) and clicked the Submit button, then the website would retrieve the historical result from its database and present it to you (see Figure 3-2). This result cannot be fetched using conventional search engines because it requires you to use a search box on the website and enter a search query to retrieve it. The fetched result is a clear example of deep web content.

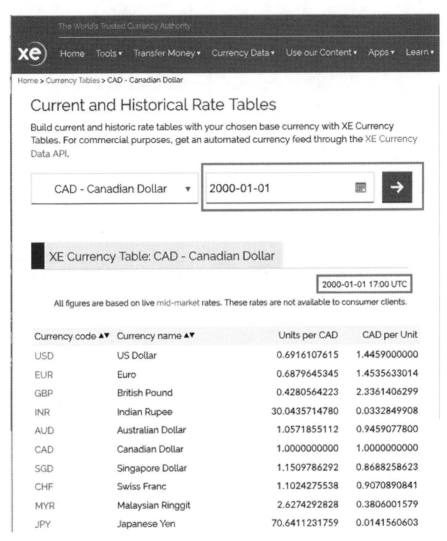

Figure 3-2. Historical data extracted from a website's database is an example of deep web data

Many Internet users—and even some experts—use the terms *deep web* and *darknet* synonymously, but there is a difference between them. The term *deep web* describes all the online resources that are not indexed using conventional search engines such as Google, Bing, or Yahoo, but the deep web can still be accessed like any regular website using the standard HTTP/HTTPS web protocol and typical web browsers without using any special software. Any Internet user has certainly used some type of deep web while browsing the Internet; however, most users may not know that such resources belong to the deep web.

Deep web resources are usually buried within databases accessible to online public view, but the user needs to type a query (for example, into a web search form) or use a drop-down menu to set some search values to retrieve the contents of these databases. This is what makes its contents hidden; it cannot be seen by typical search engines because it cannot be accessed through hyperlinks. The same thing applies to websites that require registration (username and password) to access content and websites that are purposefully designed to keep search crawlers out. Encrypted networks and websites that require payment to view content also fall under the category of the deep web. No one can know the accurate volume of deep web websites because of the ever-changing nature of web content, but many studies suggest that it is approximately 500 times that of the surface web.

Here are some examples of major deep web websites:

- The Library of Congress (`https://www.loc.gov`) This is the largest national library in the world, it includes a huge collections of resources -like books, photographs, newspapers archive, maps and manuscripts- in different topics.

- Vital Records (`www.vitalrec.com`) gives access to U.S. birth certificates, death records, and marriage licenses.

- Science.gov (`https://www.science.gov`) gives access to more than 200 million pages of authoritative federal science information.

- Alexa (`https://www.alexa.com`) gives detailed analytical information about websites.

- Directory of Open Access Journals (`https://doaj.org`) gives access to high-quality, open-access, peer-reviewed journals.

- The Online Books Page (`http://onlinebooks.library.upenn.edu`) gives free access to more than two million books that are accessible (and readable) on the Internet.

As you already saw, finding content on the deep web is not a straightforward task for a typical user, and most of the valuable deep web contents must be extracted manually. However, there are many approaches to simplifying this task:

- *Specialized search engines*: This includes any search engine that helps you locate deep web content within one subject or more. The following are some examples:

  a. `https://www.doi.org` helps you to resolve the digital object identifier (DOI) of any publication.

b. `https://www.100searchengines.com` contains specialized
    search engines for almost any topic online. It allows you to
    search multiple search engines at the same time (although
    searching multiple search engines at the same time may omit
    some results because not all search engines use the same
    mechanism to fetch data from their index).

c. `https://books.google.com/?hl=en` is one of the biggest deep
    web databases that contains millions of books. Google includes
    results from this database when conducting regular searches.

d. `www.academicindex.net` is a scholarly academic search
    engine accessing only a selected set of websites that are
    specialized in academic and research papers.

e. `https://www.truthfinder.com` searches social media, photos,
    police records, background checks, contact information, and
    more. The result will be fetched from TruthFinder's database
    of deep web sources.

- *Web directories*: A directory is a website that shows a list of websites
  organized into categories. A user enters a search query, and the
  directory gives the user the relative subjects to the entered query.
  Each subject may contain hundreds and even thousands of websites
  that fall into that category. To browse a directory, a user selects the
  topic and then moves down from the broadest to the narrowest.
  Some directories are paid, while others are free and maintained by
  a community of volunteer editors. Web directories are smaller than
  search engines as they are maintained by humans, unlike search
  engines, which are mainly maintained by spiders (web crawlers). The
  following arc some famous web directories:

  a. `https://www.hotfrog.com.au` is the largest online business
      directory; it lists 120 million businesses in 38 countries.

  b. `www.akama.com` is a U.S. business directory.

  c. `http://vlib.org` is the WWW Virtual Library.

  d. `http://dmoztools.net` closed in March 2017. It is still
      considered the largest web directory online.

- *Internet of Things (IoT) search engines*: The term Internet of Things
  is used to describe any device that can connect to the Internet and
  can collect and exchange data. The list of devices includes routers,
  servers, traffic lights, cell phones, coffee makers, washing machines,
  headphones, lamps, wearable devices such as watches, security systems
  including alarms, Wi-Fi cameras, baby monitors, smart refrigerators,
  smart TV sets, smart air-conditioning systems that can adjust the
  heat remotely, and almost anything else you can imagine that can be
  connected to the Internet and controlled remotely. Shodan (`https://
  www.shodan.io`) is a sophisticated search engine that specializes in
  searching Internet-connected devices through finding where they are
  located and who is using them. Shodan collects data mostly on these
  ports: HTTP (80), FTP (21), SSH (22), Telnet (23), and SNMP (161).
  Shodan allows both individuals and corporations to secure their IoT
  devices by discovering which one is vulnerable to outside attack or
  misconfiguration (for example, still uses the default manufacturer
  username and password). This search engine can be used effectively to
  find information about active IoT devices worldwide.

Now, we have reached to the third layer of the Web. This is the deepest one and called the *darknet*. The darknet—or dark web—is an online resource that has been designed purposefully to be hidden and anonymous. The darknet forms a small part of the deep web, but unlike the deep web, this one cannot be accessed using typical web browsers. It needs special software to access it such as Tor (short for The Onion Router).

Darknet—or anonymity—networks are composed of collections of computers spread all over the world that form a decentralized web. These anonymity networks form collectively what is known as the darknet. Users can access these networks to surf the Web anonymously or to visit the anonymous hidden websites within these networks.

Individuals get to the darknet for various purposes, and a significant number of them are unlawful. While there are no accurate statistics on the quantity of illicit sites (called *Tor services* or *hidden services* on the Tor Network), the Intelliagg group in 2015 reviewed more than 1,000 samples of Tor hidden services and found that 68 percent of Tor darknet contents are unlawful.[iii] Criminals are not only visiting the darknet to look for illegal products but are utilizing it as a medium to anonymize their online correspondences and keep others from following them when utilizing the surface web. Still, even though most darknet websites are associated with illegal activities, many people utilize it for legitimate purposes (for example, using a Tor Browser to conceal a user IP and machine digital footprint when surfing the ordinary Internet).

There are different anonymity networks. The following are the most popular:

- Tor Network (`https://www.torproject.org/index.html.en`)

- I2P network (`https://geti2p.net/en/`)

- Freenet (`https://freenetproject.org/index.html`)

As you already saw, deep web resources can be found by searching for them within target websites or by using specialized search engines, directories, and other online paid services that offer access to nonfree contents (such as gray literature). The same thing does not apply to the darknet. As an OSINT analyst, you need to understand where to start your darknet investigations and how to access and search within the darknet. OSINT investigators usually use darknet networks—especially the Tor Network—to browse the surface web anonymously. This will effectively help them to conceal their online activities from outside observers (see Figure 3-3). The rest of this chapter will explore what the darknet is and how to access and exploit its resources.

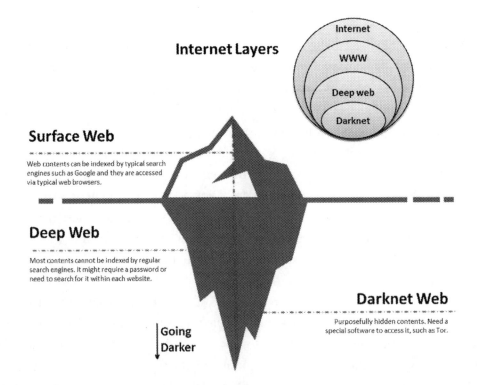

Figure 3-3. *Internet layers (source: www.DarknessGate.com)*

Darknet Users

Darknet has a bad reputation for being the preferred place for malicious actors to conduct their criminal activities online. The following are some bad actors:

- Drug dealers exploit the anonymity feature of the darknet to conduct their illegal sales safely.

- Arm dealers use the darknet for illegal buying and selling of weapons.

- People buy false government papers (such as passports and national IDs).

- Black hat hackers use it to download and share exploit tools; sell ready-to-launch distributed denial-of-service (DDoS) attacks, ransomware, and security exploits; and offer espionage services to customers.

- Terrorists use the darknet to share information and trade unlawful goods in addition to concealing their activities on the surface web.

- Gambling and betting websites are on the darknet.

- Sellers of stolen information—such as corporate secrets, credit card numbers, and the personal information of people obtained during fraudulent activities—use the darknet to sell their stolen information to interested parties.

Even though many darknet sites are directed toward criminal activities, there are many legal uses for the darknet. Some of these include the following:

- Human rights activists, journalists, and whistleblowers use it to reveal secret contents to the public without uncovering their identity.

- Privacy advocates use the darknet anonymously away from governments and corporate surveillance.

- Law enforcement uses the darknet for different purposes (e.g., tracking criminals and collecting information about them).

- Individuals, governments, and corporations use anonymity networks as a secure medium to exchange top-secret information.

- Intelligence services and military organizations use the darknet to gather open source intelligence information and to counter terrorism activities.

- Business corporations may monitor darknet forums and blogs to see their own leaked proprietary information.

Maybe you wonder how traders do their business anonymously on the darknet. The answer is simple. Every dark website accepts payment via bitcoins. We already covered the concept of cryptocurrency in Chapter 2; bitcoin (`https://www.bitcoin.com`) is the most popular one and can be used to conduct online money transactions anonymously.

Accessing the Darknet

The Tor Network is the most popular anonymous network in the world, so we will focus on it in this chapter to describe the darknet. However, before we begin, remember the essential precautionary steps upon accessing the darknet.

Note!   Although accessing the Tor Network is considered legal in most countries, its usage can arouse suspicion with the law. And some countries consider accessing the Tor Network as an illegal practice that can lead to questions by authorities. A rule by the U.S. Supreme Court gives permission to the FBI to search and seize any computer around the world that is found using the Tor Network or even a VPN service.[iv] Make sure to read the section on how to conceal your Tor usage in the previous chapter.

Security Checks When Accessing the Darknet

Chapter 2 was dedicated entirely to personal cybersecurity; however, it is worth remembering the following main points before accessing the darknet (detailed descriptions on how each precaution works technically are available in the previous chapter):

- Make your entry to the Tor Network hidden by using pluggable transports, custom bridges, or a VPN before starting your Tor Browser.

- Cover your webcam and microphone.

- Prepare your anonymous e-mail (like the Protonmail.com service) or use a free disposal e-mail service.

- Generate a false digital identity in case you need to register at some websites to access some locked contents. Make sure not to use any personal details that relate to you.

- Make sure that your Tor Browser is up-to-date to avoid leaking your real IP address—the Tor Browser will warn users to update it upon launch in case it becomes outdated.

- Make sure that your OS and antivirus software are up-to-date. The presence of a dedicated anti-malware software is highly recommended.

- Disable JavaScript on your Tor Browser by activating the NoScript add-on that comes preinstalled with the Tor Browser (see Figure 3-4).

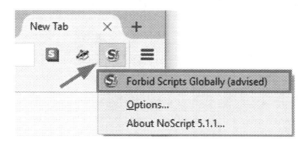

Figure 3-4. *Disabling JavaScript on all websites before accessing the dark web*

- It is advisable to change your online identity and hence the IP address for each visited site on the dark web, as in Figure 3-5. Selecting the New Identity option will require restarting the Tor Browser and lose the current session.

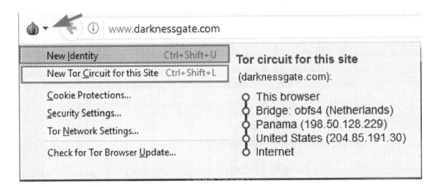

Figure 3-5. *Changing the Tor Browser identity for each visited site on the darknet*

- Do not download anything from the darknet to your computer, especially software and pirated media such as songs and movies.

- Be suspicious before clicking any hyperlink because you do not know who operates darknet websites and the destination that such links will take you to.

Accessing the Darknet from Within the Surface Web

Some websites offer a functionality to access the Tor hidden websites (hidden services) from within the surface web—using regular browsers—without using the Tor Browser or Tor software. The following list shows some websites that connect Internet users to content hosted inside the Tor Network. Bear in mind that accessing the darknet in this way does not guarantee that you can surf it as you would do with the Tor Browser. This method is more convenient—for a casual user—to surf the Tor Network easily. However, you will lose the anonymity that Internet users seek when using the Tor Browser in addition to making your browsing history susceptible to interception.

- Not Evil (`https://hss3uro2hsxfogfq.onion.to`)

- Tor2web (`https://tor2web.org`)

- Torchtorsearch (`www.torchtorsearch.com`)

Warning!   If you want to access the darknet (Tor Network) from within regular web browsers using proxy websites, make sure to encrypt your connection first using a VPN.

Using Tor

We already covered how the Tor Network works in Chapter 2; however, we will give you a brief description of how data flow works within this network.

Tor sends user requests across many relays (also known as a *server* or *router*); usually, at least three relays are used. The entire connection within these relays is encrypted. The first relay establishes the user connection to the Tor Network. This relay knows your current location, so it is advisable to use a VPN connection first to mask this or to use custom bridges/pluggable transports to mask your entry to the Tor Network from your ISP/government or any other outside adversary.

The second relay knows that the data is coming from the first relay, the third relay knows that the data is coming from the second rely, and so on. The last relay—also known as the *exit relay*—cannot know the origin of the data.

Tor relays do not record any activity pass through them, and all connections within these relays are totally encrypted. However, the weakest link resides on the last relay— the exit relay—as this relay can intercept data flowing through it if it is not already encrypted. There are some cases when this relay got comprised by intruders to unmask Tor users and to sniff their unencrypted traffic.

To mitigate the risk of someone intercepting your data at the exit relay, you should encrypt everything before sending it across the Tor Network. The Tor Browser comes with an add-on named HTTPS Everywhere (`https://www.eff.org/https-everywhere`) that forces your browser to encrypt your communication transparently—with major websites using the SSL protocol.

Websites hosted on the Tor Network end with the `.onion` extension. Unlike normal web addresses that end with `.com` or `.net`, Tor websites can be accessed only through the Tor Browser.

To access the Tor Network, all you need to do is to download and use the Tor Browser; you can always download the latest version from `https://www.torproject.org/download/download`. Download the version that matches your current OS and then launch the browser. The Tor Browser is a hardened version of Firefox that comes occupied with the Tor software to enable transparent access to the Tor Network. The Tor Browser can also be used to browse the public Internet.

If you do not know where to start after launching the Tor Browser, go to the hidden wiki (see Figure 3-6) at `http://zqktlwi4fecvo6ri.onion/wiki/index.php/Main_Page`. This site provides a directory of the most active darknet websites organized into categories. Bear in mind that some websites may not work instantly; however, this does not mean the darknet is offline. Many websites run for specific number of hours daily, so return and visit later.

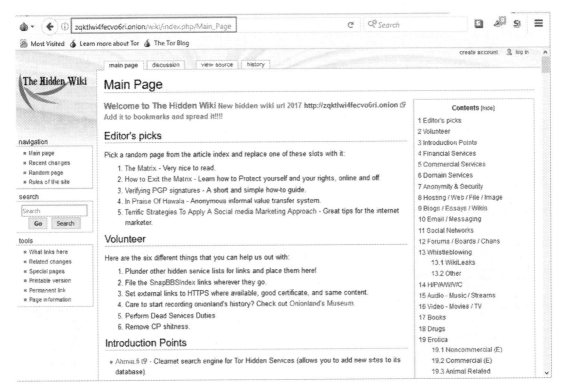

Figure 3-6. *The hidden wiki—beginner entry to the darknet*

Tor was primarily created to allow users to access regular (surface) Internet anonymously. This fact is considered a disadvantage for it when compared with other anonymity networks (like I2P, which was created as a stand-alone network within the ordinary Internet). For instance, the ability of a global adversary—with good resources—to monitor Tor exit relays (where data leaves Tor to the surface Internet) can reveal the identity of Tor users if their activities have been successfully correlated to their entrance to the Tor Network (the first relay). To overcome this shortcut, Tor allows its users to have their own hidden websites that no one can track. As mentioned, websites hosted on the

Tor Network are known as *Tor services* or *hidden services* and have the `.onion` extension. These sites are accessible only from within the Tor Network. Actually, you can run your own using your home computer, but you must know how to avoid revealing your true identity. Tor offers instruction on how to configure your hidden website at `https://www.torproject.org/docs/tor-hidden-service.html.en`. The collection of Tor hidden websites is part of what is known as the darknet; indeed, the most popular sites within the darknet belong to the Tor Network.

Finally, a major drawback with the Tor Network is speed. Tor is notoriously slow. This because the traffic needs to go through no less than three relays before reaching the destination. Tor will slow down even more when a large number of users are using it simultaneously.

Using the Tails OS

In extremely hostile environments where there is a high risk of intercepting communications by outside adversaries, it is highly recommended to use the Tails OS for your top-secret communication and offline work. In this section, we will cover how to use this OS in some detail, showing you how to use it in both online mode and offline mode (offline mode allows you to create and read documents in a secure environment).

As we said in the previous chapter, Tails is a Debian GNU/Linux security-hardened OS that routes all network connections through the Tor Network. It comes equipped with many applications that are preconfigured with security in mind like the Tor Browser, secure IM chat, encrypted e-mail client, and encryption software in addition to its productivity applications like the Office suite. Tails is a portable OS that runs from within a USB or CD/DVD and loads directly into the host machine's RAM memory; it leaves no traces on the host machine's hard disk. Upon shutdown, Tails will delete all user files, unless explicitly asked not to. Tails can be configured to allow a user to store personal documents and program settings (persistent storage).

To install the Tails OS on your USB drive, follow these steps:

1. Download Tails from `https://tails.boum.org`.

Warning!   Before you create the live Tails DVD/USB/SD card, you should check the integrity of the ISO image you have downloaded to ensure your copy of the Tails file is genuine. Always download Tails from its official website (`https://tails.boum.org/install/index.en.html`). Do not download the Tails ISO image from any other mirrored location.

2. Download the Universal USB Installer from `https://www.pendrivelinux.com/universal-usb-installer-easy-as-1-2-3`. This tool is used to install Tails into a USB stick drive.

3. Configure the Universal USB Installer as shown in Figure 3-7. You should have a USB drive with 8GB of free storage. Finally, click the Create button.

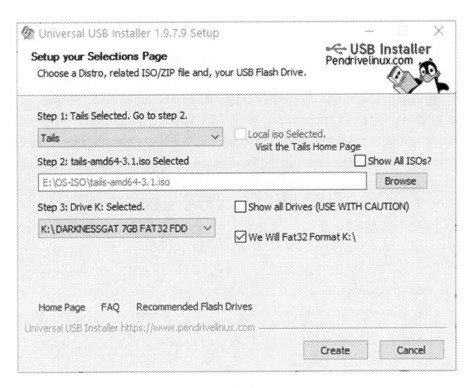

Figure 3-7. *Installing Tails on a USB stick drive*

4. Change the boot sequence of the host computer to start from the USB zip drive. Each computer manufacturer has its own method to access the BIOS/UEFI; consult its website or computer manual.

5. Plug in your Tails USB stick and restart your host machine to start Tails. If Tails boots successfully, select the first option from the menu Tails to boot into the system (see Figure 3-8).

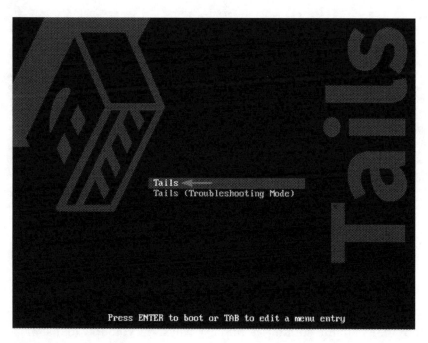

Figure 3-8. *Tails boot screen*

6. When the Tails Greeter screen appears (this window allows you to select your language preference and keyboard layout), click the Start Tails button to access the Tails desktop.

Upon starting, Tails needs little configurations because everything is already set to work through the Tor Network (see Figure 3-9). All you need to do is to configure your Wi-Fi by entering the access point password; if you are connecting through a cable, no configuration is needed.

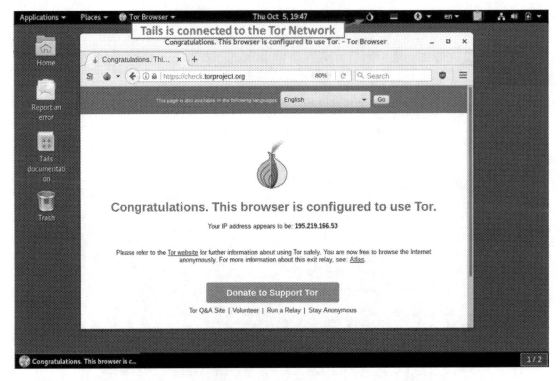

Figure 3-9. *Tails desktop showing the Tor Browser launched*

You just installed Tails in read-only mode—also known as an *intermediary*. In this mode of installation, you will not benefit from important features such as automatic security upgrades or the ability to store some of your documents and configurations in encrypted storage. In the coming section, we will show you how to install Tails in a persistent storage mode so you can keep your program settings, bookmarks, stored documents, and notes while conducting your OSINT search activities.

To install Tails as persistent storage, you will need another USB stick with 8GB of free storage. Of course, if you are planning to store large files, use a higher-capacity USB drive.

1. Plug the second USB stick into the computer while the Tails OS is still running.

2. Go to Applications ➤ Tails ➤ Tails Installer to start the Tails Installer.

3. When Tails Installer launches, select the "Install by cloning" option.

4. Select the second USB drive in the Target Device drop-down list and then click Install Tails (see Figure 3-10).

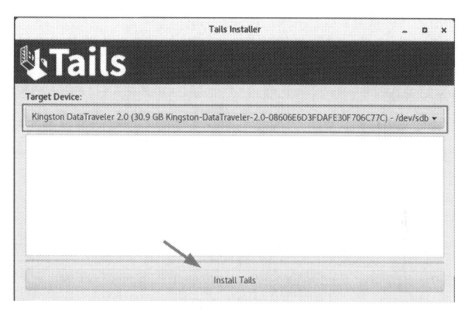

Figure 3-10. *Select the target USB stick where you want to install Tails with persistent storage*

5. A warning message appears informing you that all data on the selected drive will get lost. Confirm your action, and Tails will begin the installation process, which may last for about three minutes.

Now, to access the new Tails, restart your machine while leaving the second USB stick plugged in—you should remove the first one. Start Tails as you did before.

To save some of your documents and configurations in an encrypted storage on the final Tails USB stick, you need to create an encrypted persistent storage. Follow these steps to create such storage. This storage will occupy the remaining space on your Tails stick drive.

1. Go to Application ➤ Tails ➤ Configure persistent volume. Select a passphrase to protect your encrypted data within the persistent storage.

2. Click the Create button to begin.

3. Upon finishing, Tails will ask what kind of files you want to store on the persistent volume. We recommend selecting Personal Data, Network Connection, GnuPG, and Browser Bookmarks.

4. Click the Save button, and Tails will reboot.

5. This time, the Tails Greeter screen will ask you whether you want to use persistent storage. Click Yes and then enter your passphrase.

6. You can now save your working documents in the Persistent folder. To open the Persistent folder, go to Places ➤ Persistent.

Warning!   Remember two points when working on persistent storage.

- Persistent storage is not hidden; if someone captures your Tails USB stick, they will be able to read it.

- The persistent storage folder can be opened in another OS; make sure to open it on a trusted secure computer to avoid compromising the Tails security.

Tails can be used in offline mode without an Internet connection if you want to read or create sensitive documents. To start Tails in offline mode, launch Tails. When you reach the Tails Greeter screen, in the Welcome to Tails window, click the Yes button. Then click the Forward button to enter advanced startup. The advanced startup window appears. Go to the bottom of the window and click the "Disable all networking" button. Then click the Login button.

Warning When Using the Tails OS

Tails is an excellent anonymous OS that uses the Tor anonymity network by default, but to stay completely anonymous when using this OS, you must be aware of any threats or attacks against the Tails OS that may result in your privacy being invaded while using it.

- *Tails does not protect you against hardware-based attacks*: Hardware keyloggers and other malicious software that infect the host computer firmware can intercept your communications stealthily even though you are using Tails.

- *Encrypt everything before sending it through Tor*: As we mentioned previously, the Tor Network is an anonymous network. The link between Tor relays —within the network—is encrypted. However, once your data leaves the Tor Network, nothing is encrypted. Tails also does not encrypt your data by default before sending it through the Tor Network, but it offers ready tools for this task, and you should consider using them.

- *Tails does not clear a digital file's metadata by default*: As mentioned in Chapter 2, metadata exists within most digital file types. Make sure to clear the metadata of digital files—images, Office files, videos— before sending them online to avoid revealing your identity.

- *If you are using Tails and live in an extremely hostile environment, you should take extra care when working online by separating your online identity into many identities*: For example, use separate identities when you want to perform multiple actions online such as uploading a post to your blog, checking your e-mail, and replying to comments on a specific blog or website. To remain anonymous in such cases, you should restart Tails after doing each task previously mentioned. This will effectively make tracking you by a global adversary with great resources extremely difficult.

As an OSINT investigator, it is highly recommended to practice using the Tails OS and the Tor Browser before conducting your online investigations.

Searching the Tor Network

You will not find much useful information—similar to the surface Internet—when searching the darknet (Tor Network). This network is mostly directed toward illegal activities, and some websites may not always be available. However, it can still contain useful resources that can aid you in your online investigation. In this section, we will mention popular useful hidden services that can help you to find useful resources in the Tor Network.

Here are some search engines:

- Ahmia (`http://msydqstlz2kzerdg.onion/`)

- Candle (`http://gjobqjj7wyczbqie.onion/`)

- Torch (http://xmh57jrzrnw6insl.onion/)

- Grams (http://grams7enufi7jmdl.onion/)

- not Evil (http://hss3uro2hsxfogfq.onion/)

- DuckDuckGo (https://3g2upl4pq6kufc4m.onion/)

- Searx (http://lqdnpadpys4snom2.onion)

These sites are bitcoin-related:

- EasyCoin (http://easycoinsayj7p5l.onion/)

- WeBuyBitcoins (http://jzn5w5pac26sqef4.onion/)

- OnionWallet (http://ow24et3tetp6tvmk.onion/)

Here are some social networks:

- Atlayo (http://atlayofke5rqhsma.onion/)

- BlackBook (http://blkbook3fxhcsn3u.onion/)

- Daniel's Chat (http://danschatjr7qbwip.onion)

Here are some Tor e-mail services:

- Onion Mail (http://p6x47b547s2fkmj3.onion/)

- RetroShare chat server (http://chat7zlxojqcf3nv.onion/)

- TorBox (http://torbox3uiot6wchz.onion/)

- Mail2Tor (http://mail2tor2zyjdctd.onion/)

Other Anonymity Networks

Other anonymity networks perform similar roles as the Tor Network. The second most popular anonymity network is I2P, covered next.

I2P

I2P stands for the Invisible Internet Project; it was first released in 2003. It is an anonymity network like Tor, but it differs from it in many aspects, as you are going to see next. Before explaining how to use this network to access the darknet, we'll first explain briefly the technical side of this network.

I2P is a decentralized peer-to-peer (also called *client, node,* or *router*) network built using the Java programming language. I2P allows you to host websites and access the darknet of I2P websites (also known as *deepsites,* which have an .i2P extension). It offers a wide range of applications such as anonymous web hosting, BitTorrent, e-mail, file sharing, and much more. In the I2P network, the communication between sender and destination—within the I2P network—is completely encrypted. Traffic usually passes through four layers of encryption before reaching the destination.

Using I2P

Now, we'll begin explaining how to access the I2P network.

Note!   To run I2P on your computer, you must have Java already installed on your machine because I2P is written using the Java programming language. You can download Java from `https://www.java.com/en/download/index.jsp`.

---

1. Go to `https://geti2p.net` and download the software version that matches your current OS.

2. After installing the software (I2P router), click the "Start I2P (restartable)" icon, which will bring up the router console using your default browser, which has further instructions to configure this network. If the router console does not pop up automatically, go to `http://127.0.0.1:7657/home` to view it.

3. It may take several minutes before I2P connects successfully to the network; a message labeled "Network OK" (see Figure 3-11) should appear on the router console. If another error message appears instead of it (such as "Network: Firewalled"), you need to check your firewall settings to allow a connection to I2P ports. We cannot

describe the reasons /proposed solutions for all possible problems. You can always copy the error message and Google it to find the appropriate solution. Running I2P inside a virtual machine without installing a firewall is another option for non-tech-savvy users.

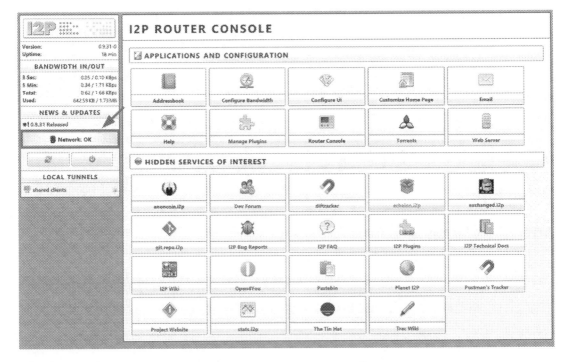

Figure 3-11. *I2P router console view—"Network OK"*

4. Now you need to configure your web browser to use the I2P network. We will describe how to do this for Firefox; other browsers use similar configurations.

5. Open Firefox Options ➤ General ➤ Network Proxy (located at the bottom of the page) and click the Settings button.

6. In the Connection Settings window, click the circle next to "Manual proxy configuration." Then enter **127.0.0.1** in the HTTP Proxy field and **4444** in the Port field. Enter **127.0.0.1** in the SSL Proxy field and **4445** in the Port field. Be sure to enter **localhost, 127.0.0.1** into the "No Proxy for" box. Finally, click the OK button to accept the new settings (see Figure 3-12).

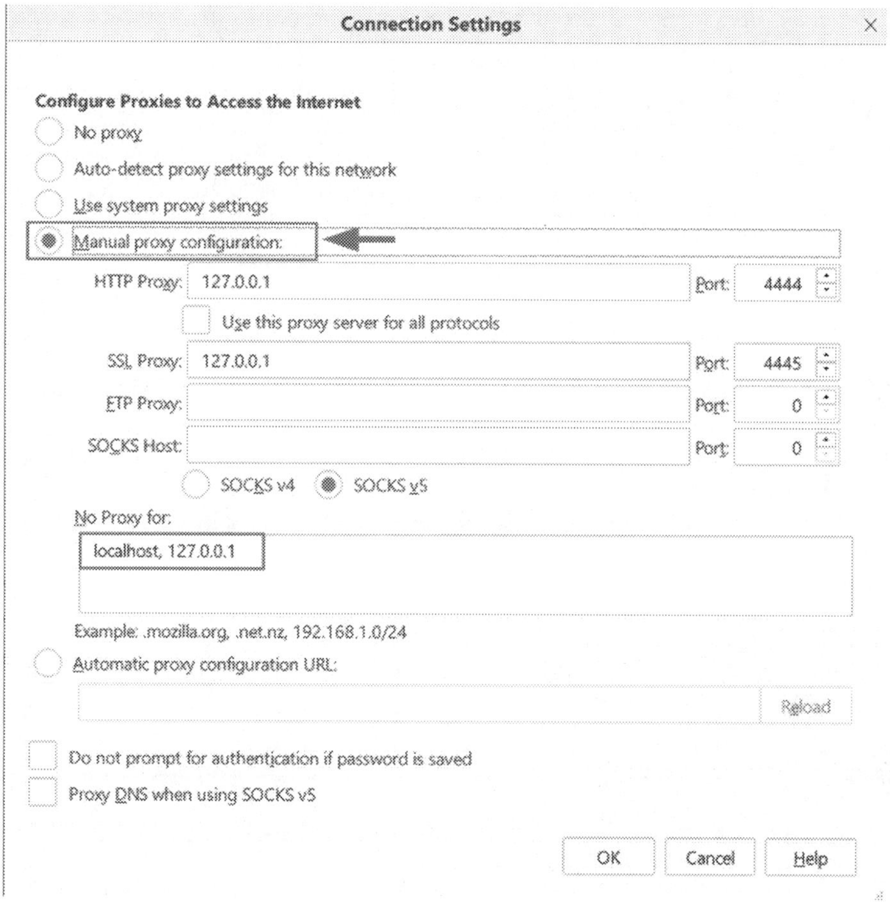

Figure 3-12. *Configure Firefox to use the I2P anonymity network*

Warning!   Unlike Tor, I2P does not provide a mechanism to hide your entry to the I2P network from your ISP and government. However, once the connection is established, everything will become completely encrypted and anonymous.

I2P doesn't go through Tor.

The previous configuration of Firefox allows you to use the normal Internet anonymously. In the same way, you can access any website hosted on the I2P anonymous network (such websites have a `.i2p` extension instead of `.com` or `.org`).

After successfully connecting to the I2P network and configuring your browser properly to use it, you can begin discovering this network. If you are stuck and do not know where to start, point your browser to the I2P wiki at `http://i2pwiki.i2p`.

When you first visit an I2P website, you may receive an error message stating "Website Not Found in Addressbook" because you do not have any I2P website addresses in your router address book. To solve this problem, you need to click one of the jump service links at the end of the page (see Figure 3-13).

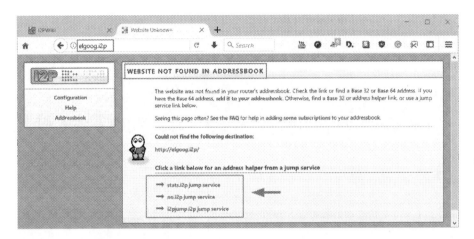

Figure 3-13.   *Accessing an I2P website for the first time—the visited website was not found in your router's address book*

Try to click each jump service link (boxed in Figure 3-13) until you find one that takes you to the page that allows you to add this website to the I2P router address book (see Figure 3-14).

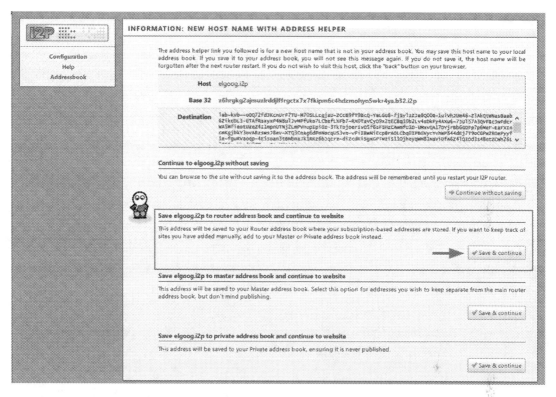

Figure 3-14. *Adding a new I2P website that has not been visited before to your router address book. The next time you visit this website, you will not see this message.*

After clicking "Save & continue" in the section "Save {Website Name} to router address book and continue to website," the page shown in Figure 3-15 will redirect you to the intended website (ELGOOG.I2P in this example).

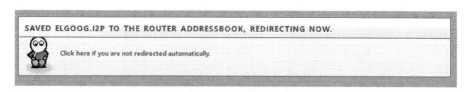

Figure 3-15. *Redirecting you automatically to the requested website after adding the website hostname to your router address book*

I2P vs. Tor

The main difference between Tor and I2P is how their designers perceived the threat model. For instance, Tor was primarily created to allow users to surf the surface web anonymously. I2P was created as a stand-alone anonymity network that enables fully anonymous communication between two parties within its network.

Tor uses a circuit-switching method to drive its data through the Tor Network, while I2P uses the packet-switching model. Circuit switching was originally invented for voice communication, and it was less suitable for data transmission. Tor uses a single path for data transmission, while I2P uses packet switching, which makes all peers participate in forwarding packets across the network. Unlike Tor, I2P uses two routes (tunnel) to direct inbound and outbound traffic. This will effectively improve the overall anonymity of the system and will make data delivery more flexible as each packet will take different routes to reach the destination, unlike Tor packets, which need to travel using a single path in both directions (the lifetime of each Tor circuit is ten minutes). I2P is faster when moving big files within its network than the Tor Network, which suffers from network congestion and service interruptions, as it uses only one route for data delivery.

Tor uses a directory structure to view the overall performance of the entire network, as well as gather and report statistics. Tor directories maintain a list of all Tor nodes and hosted hidden services on the Tor Network and are placed in the United States and Europe. The I2P approach is to use a decentralized peer-to-peer network where there is no single point to view the entire network, and each peer (router) locally maintains a list of all known routers (relays).

I2P uses Garlic encryption—which is a variant of Onion encryption—where multiple messages to different recipients are bundled together. This makes it harder for outside adversaries to analyze the traffic flow through the network and will also speed data transfer and make it more reliable.

Tor has more exit relays compared to I2P. I2P uses the term *outproxy* to name its own exit relay routers. The number of I2P users is smaller than Tor. This makes the number of I2P outproxies considerably smaller than Tor exit relays. This will effectively make I2P more susceptible to outside traffic analysis compared with the Tor Network, which owns a large number of exit relays.

Tor acts as a proxy server by using Secure Sockets (SOCKS), so any application (e.g., web browser, IM chat, or e-mail client) able to use SOCKS can be configured to use the Tor software directly. I2P uses its own API that must be implemented by any applications wanting to communicate through the I2P network. This makes I2P more secure and anonymous than Tor as its API is designed specifically for anonymity. However, applications should be adjusted to use it, and this is somehow costly and limits the number of applications that are ready to use the I2P network.

Finally, Tor is well funded. It has a large user base and more supporters from the academic and hacker communities compared with I2P network. This clearly appears from its website, documentation, and the other projects currently underway. Tor also has an advantage in being written in the C language, making it faster when running on client machines than I2P, which is written using Java and consumes more RAM memory.

To conclude, both I2P and Tor are excellent anonymous networks, but the context in which they are used determines which one is best in terms of performance and anonymity. For instance, I2P is preferred over Tor for hosting anonymous sites and for making communications within the I2P darknet as it is faster and gives stronger anonymity. Tor is preferred to anonymize your traffic when accessing the surface Internet, unlike I2P, which is almost unusable—and risky—for this task.

Freenet

Freenet is another anonymous network. It is a fully distributed, peer-to-peer anonymous publishing network. We will not cover how to use this network like we did with the previous ones. However, you can check out `http://freesocial.draketo.de` for a complete tutorial on how to use this anonymous network. Tor, I2P, and Freenet are the most popular anonymous networks currently available. Tor surpasses the other two in being more widely used and more mature. We recommend using the Tor Network for all your online work that requires anonymity.

Going Forward

As you saw during this chapter, searching for deep and dark resources is not straightforward. Current search engines are optimized to search the surface web and cannot search—and index contents—below it, even though some commercial companies that have developed some advanced search tools try to harvest data from the deep web (including dark web). The effectiveness of such tools is still limited in terms of retrieving accurate, linked, and complete results.

Now, with the advance of computing technology and the widespread use of Internet services around the globe, more criminals are shifting their activities online. Black hat hackers, terrorist organizations, and countries controlled by oppressive regimes are also using the Internet—especially the darknet—to conduct illegal activities. Governments and law enforcement entities around the globe must utilize all resources possible to capture and prevent bad actors from using Internet technology to facilitate their crimes.

To help overcome these challenges, the Defense Advanced Research Projects Agency (DARPA) in the United States has created the Memex program to help fight against human trafficking activity across the world. Memex is a next-generation search engine that focuses on helping law enforcement investigators find online perpetrators engaged in human trafficking in the cyberspace. Memex has the ability to search within the darknet and deep web in addition to the surface Internet to find linked information spread everywhere online to support investigators in their mission.

Although the key mission of the Memex is to fight against global human trafficking, it can be used by intelligence services and other military organizations to collect and correlate useful OSINT information from the deep/dark web about anything they want.

Summary

The deep web and dark web have gained increased attention by researchers, law enforcement, and government entities. However, both terms are still unclear for most web users. In addition, the nature and technical architecture of darknet networks still lack clarity for many people.

In this chapter, we shed light on the concept of Internet layers and demonstrated by example the contents of each layer and how they can be accessed to retrieve information from them.

Two darknet networks were presented and compared. While Tor is a mature anonymity network with a wide user base and mostly used to browse the surface web anonymously because of its many exit nodes, I2P is beginning to get more attention as a preferred solution to host hidden websites inside the I2P darknet network because of its speed and stronger anonymity for both users and website operators.

As we already said, many darknet websites are dedicated to illegal activities; it is not the purpose of this chapter to introduce you to such illegal services and teach you how to access them. We highly encourage a typical Internet user not to visit the darknet at all. The main point here is to introduce you, especially OSINT investigators, to how to use online anonymity tools like the Tor Browser and the Tails OS to conduct your online investigations safely and anonymously. The information presented in this chapter will also benefit online investigators when accessing and searching within the dark areas of the Internet.

This chapter was dedicated to the deepest layers of the Internet. In the next chapter we will return to the surface to teach you how to use advanced techniques using typical search engines such as Google and Bing to search for OSINT resources online.

Notes

i.   Internet World Stats, "World Internet Users and 2017 Population Stats," November 5, 2017, `www.internetworldstats.com/stats.htm`.

ii.   Netcraft, "October 2017 Web Server Survey," November 1, 2017, `https://news.netcraft.com/archives/category/web-server-survey/`.

iii. Aclweb, "Classifying Illegal Activities on Tor Network Based on Web Textual Contents," November 2, 2017, `https://www.aclweb.org/anthology/E/E17/E17-1004.pdf`.

iv.   Techworm, "Tor and VPN users labeled as criminals will be hacked and spied by FBI under new law," November 5, 2017, `https://www.techworm.net/2016/05/tor-vpn-users-labeled-criminals-hacked-spied-fbi-new-law.html`.

CHAPTER 4

Search Engine Techniques

The number of Internet users is increasing steadily, as is the number of active websites. According to Netcraft's January 2017 Web Server Survey, there are 1,800,047,111 billion websites.[i] The number of pages on these websites changes continually according to many factors. Google Inside Search estimates that there are more than 130 trillion web pages discovered by Google; about 50 billion of them have been included in Google's searchable index as of October 2017.[ii] Do not forget that Google—and similar search engines—cannot index the entire Web, as pages that belong to the deep/dark web cannot be discovered by typical search engines.

As you can see, the number of web pages that exist is huge, and finding your way in this mass media would be very difficult without search engines. A search engine works by sending a *crawler*—automated software—to continually scan active websites to add the discovered content to its index, which is stored in massive databases. The user then queries the search engine index, which returns the results—that may contain a mix of web pages, images, videos, and other file types—as a list of matching sites ranked by relevance.

Without a search engine, a user would need to access and check every website manually when seeking specific information. This would be a daunting task and consume a considerable amount of time for each search. Search engines also help users view only relevant results. For instance, search engine software scans each indexed page and selects a list of keywords from it to categorize it. When a user, for example, searches for *cheap flight to Hawaii*, all pages that offer flights to Hawaii will appear in the search result list. However, the top rank will be for the pages/websites strictly related to user search criteria. Please note that the algorithm for ranking websites in search results is secret for each search engine provider, and the rank for each website—even for the same query—can change hourly. However, the highest rank will be for the websites that satisfy the ranking algorithm criteria in terms of popularity and relevancy of the user's search query.

N. A. Hassan and R. Hijazi, *Open Source Intelligence Methods and Tools*,
https://doi.org/10.1007/978-1-4842-3213-2_4

Typical search engines like Bing and Google offer their services free of charge. They also offer advanced search features that can be used by users to conduct advanced searches. For example, Google offers a powerful Advanced Search (`https://www.google.com/advanced_search`) that gives more specific search results (see Figure 4-1).

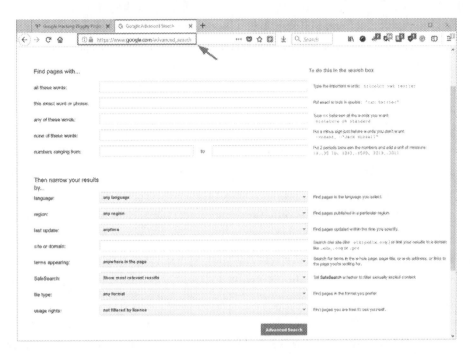

Figure 4-1. *Google Advanced Search functionality returns more specific search results*

The internal mechanism of search engines is not as simple as their interface. The more sophisticated the search engine, the more complicated the algorithm it uses to find and index contents from the Web. In this chapter, we will cover how to use different types of search engines efficiently to locate information online. We will start by focusing on Google because it's considered the largest one and has plenty of specialized operators to conduct advanced searches (also known as Google *dorks*). We will also cover how to search for specific digital file types such as images and videos in addition to using many free online services to validate your findings. Before we begin, let's cover how to select search keywords to return the most relevant results from search engines.

Keywords Discovery and Research

As an OSINT investigator, you need to master the art of online searching, which requires you to use the correct search keywords. Typical search engines discover and index web pages using a variety of criteria. Apparently the most important one is the set of keywords available within the target page.

Keyword discovery help searchers to expand the breadth of their searches to include different variations of the same keyword and uncover synonyms and semantically related terms and phrases so they can better find content that may be rarely accessed by typical users conducting similar searches.

Keywords discovery is used extensively by online marketers in search engine optimization (SEO) to see which keywords are used by different people—using different search engines—to search for a similar topic. Online investigators can use the same technique to search for variations of a phrase/keyword in addition to acquiring intelligence about current search trends.

The following are the most popular keyword research tools:

- Google Keyword Suggest Tool (`http://tools.seochat.com/tools/suggest-tool`): This gives keyword suggestions for Google, Bing, Amazon, and YouTube.

- Google AdWords (`https://adwords.google.com/home/tools/keyword-planner/`) and Google Trends (`https://www.google.com/trends`): These will show search volume and matrices of Google searches for any geographical region in the entire world.

- One Look (`www.onelook.com/reverse-dictionary.shtml`): Enter a word, phrase, sentence, or pattern to search for related words.

Using Search Engines to Locate Information

In this section, we will show how to utilize search engines to get precise results, beginning with the giant, Google.

Google

The Google search engine is the leader among its peers and has the greatest market share with more than 77 percent of global search traffic using it.

The number of daily searches conducted by web users globally on search engines is huge. Table 4-1 shows the number of daily searches per search engine.[iii]

Table 4-1. *Number of Daily Searches by Major Search Engines*

Search Engine	Searches per Day
Google	4,464,000,000
Bing	873,964,000
Baidu	583,520,803
Yahoo	536,101,505
Other (AOL, Ask, etc.)	128,427,264

Most web users have used a Google web search to find something online. A Google basic search is what you see when visiting the Google home page (www.google.com). You type your search query into the Google search box and hit the Google Search button. Alternatively, you can use your voice to enter the search query by clicking the microphone icon. The Google home page offers other useful services such as searching for images, videos, newsgroups, and maps in addition to the Google Translate service. Let's see how you can use some Google words to refine a basic search for better results.

Warning!   When using the following Google search words (symbols), make sure not to put any space between the symbol and the search term (query).

---

1. To search within social media sites, use the symbol @ followed by a social media name; then enter a colon your search query. For example, enter **@facebook:nihad hassan** to search for the term *nihad hassan* within Facebook).

2. To search for hashtags, put a # sign before your search term. For example, enter **#USAelection**.

3. To search for an exact match, surround your search term/phrase with quotation marks. For example, enter **"data hiding"**.

4. The tilde (~) operator searches for the word that comes after it directly and for its synonyms. For example, entering **Excel ~guide** will return Excel tutorials, tips, helper, video trainings, and anything synonymous with the word *guide*.

5. The OR operator in capital letters only—also written as a vertical bar (|)— is used to find pages that contain the searched terms. For example, entering **Apress OR springer** (or entering **Apress|Springer**) will retrieve pages that contain either the term *Apress* or the term *Springer*.

6. To exclude words from your search, put a minus (-) symbol in front of the word (phrase) that you want to leave out. For example, enter **lacoste -animal**.

7. To search for the unknown words, use the asterisk (*) to substitute it with one or more words. For example, enter **data hiding in ***.

8. Use the double dots (..) without spaces to provide a number range such as date, number, or price range. For example, enter **USA earthquake 1980..2000**.

9. To search for similar web pages, put the word *related:* in the front of the web address that you want to see similar pages of. For example, enter **related:springer.com**.

10. Use the word *info:* to return information that Google has about a certain domain. For example, enter **info:springer.com**.

11. Use the word *define* to find a definition of the supplied keyword. For example, enter **define:information**.

12. Use the word *cache:* to return the Google-cached version of the web page. For example, enter **cache:apress.com**.

13. To search for information about a specific song or movie, enter **Music:** or **Movie:** followed by the song or movie name.

14. To check the current weather in any place around the world, use the *weather* keyword. For example, enter **weather:London**.

15. To show the stock price of any company, use the keyword *stocks:* followed by the company ticker symbol. For example, entering **stocks:MSFT** will show stock information for Microsoft Corporation. You can fetch any company stock ticker symbol by going to `https://www.marketwatch.com/tools/quotes/lookup.asp`.

16. Use the keyword *map:* followed by location name and Google will show you map-based results. For example, enter **map:New York**.

17. Enter **time keyword** to check the current date/time of your current location. To find the time of another location, precede the *time* keyword with the location name (for example, enter **time New York**).

Note! `http://localtimes.info` shows an interactive map of the time around the world right now. `www.thetimenow.com` shows the date, time, and a calendar in addition to weather forecasts and more information about the current location. (The current location is detected using your connection IP address, so make sure to update your location if you are using a VPN service that masks your real IP address.)

---

18. Google also can be used as a converter between currencies and measures. For example, enter **(190 cm in feet)** or **(1000 dollars in yen)**.

19. You can even check flight information using Google. Type your airline company name and the flight number in the Google search box and it will show you flight status information graphically (see Figure 4-2).

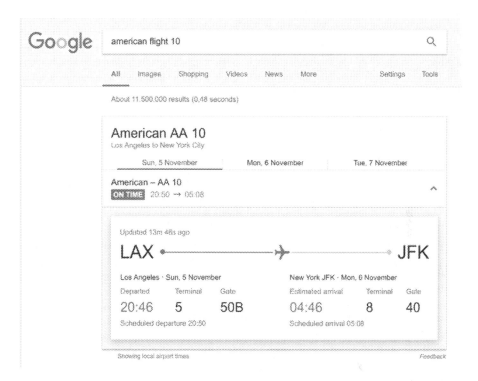

Figure 4-2. *Showing information for the American airline company, flight 10*

Google is also famous for its image search. For instance, to search for a specific image, you can use the Google Advanced Image Search at `https://www.google.com/advanced_image_search`, which allows you to set different image search criteria (such as size, color, type, etc.) to locate your target image.

Basic search is suitable for beginners, and you do not need to worry about the spelling or capitalization of your searched keywords because Google will fix this for you. However, when it comes to fetching relevant information related to a specific topic, you need to use the Google special operators to return information that is difficult to locate through simple search queries.

Google Advanced Operators

The advanced options are also known as *Google hack*ing or *Google dorks*. Google hacking occurs when a user combines search keywords with advanced Google search operators to locate hidden information that is difficult to locate using a basic Google search. For example, Google hacking can be used to find vulnerable web servers or lists of personally identifying information (PII) files for employees/clients in a specific company that could have been left on a company server without protection. Cybercriminals, black hat hackers, and even terrorists use this technique to collect sensitive data online to facilitate launching further attacks against the target.

In the following list, we show examples of advanced Google search operators beginning with the simplest. The general format is as follows: **operator:search_term**. (There is no space between the operator, the colon, and the keyword search).

- The *site* operator asks Google to search within one website or domain. For example, if you enter **hide site:darknessgate.com**, Google will search for the word *hide* within the *darknessgate.com* website only. Using the same operator, you can restrict your search within one domain type. For example, enter **computer forensics site:gov** to search for the term *computer forensics* in all websites with the .gov domain.

- Insert your query search term after the *allintext* operator and Google will restrict its search to all pages that contain the terms specified. For example, enter **allintext:free SMicrosoft service** and Google will only return the pages that have the three terms *free* and *SMS* and *service* within its text.

- Begin your search with the *allintitle* operator and follow it with your search terms. Google will only return the pages that contain your searched query in their titles. For example, enter **allintitle:Nihad hassan** to have Google return all pages that have *nihad hassan* in their title (the page title appears at the top of the browser window), as shown in Figure 4-3.

Figure 4-3. Searching within page titles for a specific term

- If you use the *allintitle* operator in an image search, it will return images in files whose names contain the specified search query.

- Begin your search with the *allinurl* operator followed by your search term and Google will restrict its results to all the pages that contain your searched terms in their URL. For example, enter **allinurl:OSINT intelligence** and Google will return pages with the terms *OSINT intelligence* in their URLs (see Figure 4-4). You cannot include other search operators with the *allinurl* operator.

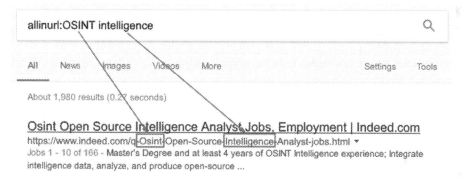

Figure 4-4. *Using the Google allintitle operator*

- When using the *filetype* suffix with your search terms, Google will restrict the results to web pages that end with this extension. For example, enter **osint intelligence filetype:PDF** and Google will return PDF files that match the specified search query.

- To search for more than one file type, add their extensions to the search query as follows: **osint intelligence filetype:pdf OR filetype:doc**. Google supports searching for different file types; the list of indexable file formats is available at (`https://www.google.com/support/enterprise/static/gsa/docs/admin/74/gsa_doc_set/file_formats/file_formats.html`).

All these examples are simple demonstrations of how you can use advanced Google search operators to return accurate relevant results. Online investigators should be creative and work to develop their search skills by utilizing different search operators in one statement to return the best results.

Note!   Google Advanced Search (`https://www.google.com/advanced_search`) allows users to use advanced search operators without typing them manually into the search box, although it still has limitations on conducting more creative searches. However, it's still considered a great tool for casual users to search Google professionally.

Google Hacking Database

The Google Hacking Database (see Figure 4-5) created by Johnny Long contains hundreds of ready-to-use advanced Google search terms that can be used to acquire intelligence online. It can help you to find the following and more:

- Vulnerable web servers

- Files that contain sensitive information such as usernames/passwords in addition to configuration files that contain settings and other important information from Internet devices

- Sensitive directories left without protection

- Error messages generated by servers, databases, and other software that can be exploited to invade information systems

- Information about network devices such as firewalls, IDS logs, and configurations

- Different IoT devices and the control panels of unprotected ones

- Hidden pages such as intranets, VPN services, and others

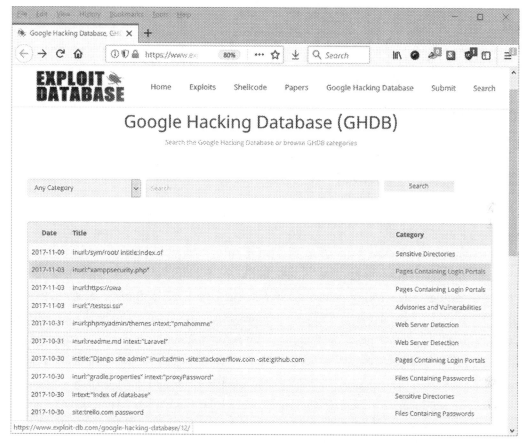

Figure 4-5. *Google Hacking Database (`www.exploit-db.com/google-dorks`)*

Here are some examples search terms that you can use on Google to find sensitive information online:

- *"Index of /backup"*: This will return a list of unprotected servers that contain backup data. Such files can contain sensitive information.

- *"robots.txt" "Disallow:" filetype:txt*: The `robots.txt` file usually resides within the root directory of a web server and instructs search engine crawlers on the parts of your website that you do not them to look at (in other words, that you want ignored from the indexing process). Hackers check `robots.txt` files to see the unindexed files to gain intelligence or to access sensitive locations.

- *budget site:gov filetype:xls*: This query will return all publicly accessible Microsoft Excel spreadsheets with the term *budget* from all websites that have the `.gov` domain name.

Note!   To find updated lists of Google dorks, run the following searches using Google:

allintext:Google Dorks filetype:pdf

allintitle:Google hacking

Search Engines Powered by Google

While Google is great at web searches, it does not have a clean record in terms of respecting a user's privacy. Google and other giant IT providers monitor their users' online activities to some extent to understand their browsing habits and thus target them with customized advertisements. Another disadvantage for using a Google search is the fact that Google records your previous searches and may omit some results from future searches if it finds them irrelevant to your browsing habits. This is dangerous for online investigations because it may limit the result set returned by Google, according to the searcher's previous browsing history.

The Google search algorithm is considered the best one for returning relevant results. However, for privacy-conscious people, there are many search engines that retrieve their search results from Google without invading users' privacy by collecting information about their searches. These are the most popular ones:

- StartPage (`https://www.startpage.com`)

- Lukol (`https://www.lukol.com`)

- Mozbot (`https://www.mozbot.com`)

Bing

Bing is the second most popular search engine after Google; it was developed by Microsoft and is the default search engine in the Internet Explorer and Edge browsers. Bing has many similarities to Google basic search operators. Table 4-2 lists the main search operators that can be used to refine your search on Bing (don't use a space after the colon in the examples).

Table 4-2. *Bing Search Operators*

Operator	Example	Description
" "	**"French food"**	Searches for an exact phrase
NOT or minus sign	**Virus -computer**	Excludes web pages that contain a term or phrase.
OR	**Nokia OR Apple**	Searches for any of these words *Nokia* or *Apple*
define:	**define:computer**	Gets a definition for the specified word
Site:	**Windows site:darknessgate.com**	Limits your search results to one site (searches within one site for a specific word or phrase)
Filetype:	**Bing search operator filetype:pdf**	Searches for results with a specific file type (PDF in this example)
inbody:	**inbody:digital privacy**	Returns web pages that contain the specified term in the body of the page
IP	**ip:193.70.110.132**	Finds all websites hosted by the specified IP address
Language:	**unicef language:ar**	Returns web pages for a specific language; in this example, we searched for the word *UNICEF* in Arabic pages only (Note: To see the list of country, region, and language codes supported by Bing, go to `http://help.bingads.microsoft.com/apex/index/18/en-US/10004`.)
Feed:	**feed:computer security**	Finds RSS feeds on the websites that match your search criteria
Prefer:	**computer hacking prefer:tutorials**	Adds emphasis to a search term or to another search operator to focus the search results on it; in this example, we are searching for the terms *computer hacking* but with an emphasis on tutorials

You can compare the results retrieved by Google and Bing for the same search query by going to `http://bvsg.org/index.html`.

Another useful service that allows you to construct complex search queries for both Google and Bing visually is Advangle (`http://advangle.com`), as shown in Figure 4-6. You can also save your queries in an Advangle account (registration is free) to return to them later.

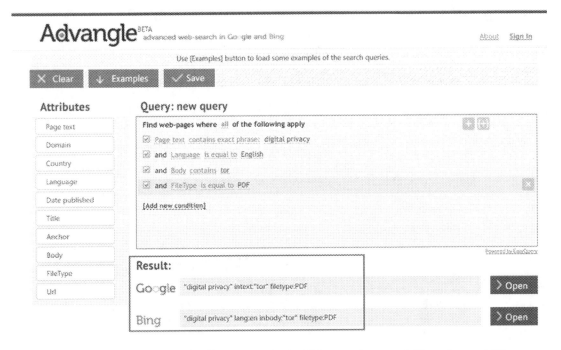

Figure 4-6.   Using the Advangle service to build an advanced Google and Bing query

Privacy-Oriented Search Engines

These are the most popular search engines that don't track user activities:

- *DuckDuckGo* (https://duckduckgo.com/): Online investigators usually use this to search the surface web while using the Tor Browser.

- *Qwant* (https://www.qwant.combased): This is based in France.

- *Oscobo* (https://oscobo.co.uk): This is based in the United Kingdom.

- *Swisscows* (https://swisscows.com): This is a privacy-safe web search based in Switzerland.

- *Privatelee* (https://privatelee.com): Search for web and images privately.

- *Gigablast* (https://www.gigablast.com): This is an open source search engine.

- *Gibiru* (www.gibiru.com): This is an uncensored and anonymous search engine.

Other Search Engines

Many OSINT investigators prefer to use more than one search engine to fetch results. Indeed, you will be surprised at the diversity of results when using different search engines to search for the same query. Table 4-3 lists other popular search engines that can be used to locate information online, by popularity. Bear in mind that you should anonymize your connection before conducting any search, or you can simply use the Tor Browser to conduct your search.

Table 4-3. *Other Search Engines*

Number	Search Engine Name	URL
1	Yahoo! Advanced web search	`https://search.yahoo.com/web/advanced`
2	Yandex	`https://www.yandex.com`
3	AOL	`http://search.aol.com`
4	Dothop	`http://dothop.com/home`
5	Excite	`www.excite.com`
6	Goodsearch	`https://www.goodsearch.com`
7	Factbites	`www.factbites.com`
8	Infospace	`http://infospace.com`
9	Lycos	`www.lycos.com/`
10	Exalead	`www.exalead.com/search/web/`
11	Search	`https://www.search.com/`
12	Search Engine Colossus	`http://searchenginecolossus.com` (contains a directory of search engines from 317 countries and territories worldwide, covering all spoken world languages)
13	Search Engines Directory	`www.searchengineguide.com/searchengines.html`
14	The Ultimate Search Engine Links Page	`www.searchenginelinks.co.uk/`

There are also national search engines that can be used to search for information in specific countries. Table 4-4 lists the main ones by popularity.

Table 4-4. *Popular National Search Engines*

Number	Search Engine Name	URL	Country
1	Yandex	`https://www.yandex.com`	Russia
2	Search	`https://www.search.ch/`	Switzerland
3	Alleba	`www.alleba.com/`	Philippines
4	Baidu	`https://www.baidu.com`	China
5	Eniro	`https://www.eniro.se`	Sweden
6	Daum	`https://www.daum.net (www.naver.com)`	South Korea
7	Goo	`www.goo.ne.jp`	Japan
8	Onet	`https://www.onet.pl`	Poland
9	Parseek	`www.parseek.com`	Iran
10	SAPO	`https://www.sapo.pt`	Portugal
11	AONDE	`www.aonde.com`	Brazil
12	Lableb	`https://www.lableb.com`	Arabic-based search engine

Business Search Sites

Although the term OSINT comes from the military, its value has not been limited to this context only. Nowadays, businesses rely heavily on OSINT to empower their decision-making processes in addition to predicting future events.

Finding information about corporations is essential for any online investigation. For example, business information gathered from OSINT sources can reveal important information such as business profits, current and future projects, business hierarchy, and company dates (such as annual meetings, corporate holidays, or investor meetings). Such information is helpful in many cases (for example, to find out whether a specific company or a person was part of a tax evasion case).

In this section, we will list sites that can be used to retrieve important information about businesses globally.

Find Business Annual Records

An annual report is a document issued by a company to its stockholders once a year. It contains valuable information about a corporation's financial status such as its budget, financial position, profits, loss, management and auditor reports, and cash flow. You can also find a general description about the industry in which the intended company belongs.

The following sites give free access to thousands of annual reports published by different industries:

- `www.annualreports.com` lists thousands of annual records from 5,333 companies worldwide.

- `https://www.reportlinker.com` contains more than 60 million searchable tables, figures, and datasets.

- `https://www.gov.uk/government/publications/overseas-registries/overseas-registries` lists all the company registries located around the world offered by the U.K. government.

- `https://www.sec.gov/edgar/searchedgar/companysearch.html` is the U.S. Securities and Exchange Commission (see Figure 4-7).

Figure 4-7. *Searching for company filings on* `www.sec.gov`

- `www.sedar.com` gives access to public securities documents and information filed by all Canadian securities administrators.

- `https://www.commercial-register.sg.ch/home/worldwide.html` gives a list of government and commercial registers around the globe.

Annual reports can also be found on a corporation's website; simply go to the About Us page or conduct a search for *annual report* using the corporate site search facility to find such files. They usually come in PDF or HTML format.

Business Information (Profiles)

Corporation profile and directory websites provide valuable information about companies such as their addresses, location, branches, contact details, staff names (and may include their business phone numbers and e-mails), types of service or industry, and a lot more. The following are the most popular business profile sites to retrieve such information:

- *Open Corporates* (`https://opencorporates.com`): This is the largest open database of companies in the world.

- *Crunchbase* (`https://www.crunchbase.com`): Provides information about business companies, from early-stage startups to Fortune 1000.

- *Corporationwiki* (`https://www.corporationwiki.com`): This allows you to search for any company and visualize the connection between people working within it. You can also download an Excel file that contains detailed information (including a link to a page on the site containing the person's known address) about each person who works within the company.

- *Zoom Info* (`https://www.zoominfo.com/company-directory/us`): This site lists companies in the United Sates categorized by industry and offers information—including contact details—for people working in these companies. The service is paid and offers a trial to test the service.

- *Kompass* (`https://www.kompass.com/selectcountry/`): This is a global business-to-business portal with information about companies in more than 60 countries.

- *Infobel* (`www.infobel.com`): You can search for a company or a person anywhere in the world.

- *Orbis directory* (`https://orbisdirectory.bvdinfo.com/version-20171019/OrbisDirectory/Companies`): This gives information about private companies globally for free. The paid service offers more detailed reports.

- *Manta* (`https://www.manta.com/business`): This is a business directory for U.S. businesses.

- *Canadian Company Capabilities* (`http://strategis.ic.gc.ca/eic/site/ccc-rec.nsf/eng/Home`): This is a website maintained by the Canadian government; it has a database of 60,000 Canadian businesses categorized according to each one industry. Each business profile contains information on contacts, products, services, trade experience, and technology.

- *Canadian Importers Database* (`https://strategis.ic.gc.ca/eic/site/cid-dic.nsf/eng/home`): This provides lists of companies importing goods into Canada, by product, by city, and by country of origin.

- *LittleSis* (`https://littlesis.org`): This is a powerful profiling website that lists a wealth of information about 185,000 people and 67,000 organizations in varying stages of completion. This site targets powerful individuals and organizations in the public and private sectors such as politicians, businesspeople, lobbyists, business corporations, and nonprofit organizations such as foundations, social clubs, arts groups, and political organizations.

- *Companies House* (`https://beta.companieshouse.gov.uk`): This is a U.K. businesses register (also contains information about individuals in different industries within the United Kingdom).

- *CDREX* (`http://cdrex.com`): This provides information—including GPS location—for U.K. business (about 7 million companies categorized according to location or industry).

- *EUROPAGES* (`https://www.europages.co.uk`): This is an European business-to-business portal that holds 3 million registered businesses in 26 languages.

- *Vault* (`www.vault.com`): This has information about U.S. companies (more than 5,000 companies in 120 industries). Employee reviews and rankings are also available for each listed company. Paid subscribers have access to detailed information.

- *Owler* (`https://www.owler.com`): This is a wealth of information on more than 15 million businesses around the world.

- *The United Kingdom Limited Liability Company list* (`https://www.companiesintheuk.co.uk`): Provides free information and official documents about any Limited Liability company in the UK.

- *Kvk* (`www.kvk.nl`): This is the Dutch Chamber of Commerce, which is a German company registry.

- *International White and Yellow Pages* (`www.wayp.com`): This contains names, addresses, phone numbers, and fax numbers.

Finally, it is worth mentioning Google Finance (`https://finance.google.com/finance`). This gives detailed up-to-date information on world markets and company news.

Metadata Search Engines

When you conduct a search using a typical search engine like Google, your query will get processed by the search engine, which looks up your search query in its index database and retrieves relevant results accordingly. Metasearch engines are different; these engines do not have their own indexes. Instead, they send your search query to other search engines (such as Google, Bing, and Yahoo) in addition to other third-party data sources. Then they retrieve the results, rank them, and present the final output to you through their web interface.

Metasearch engines make agreements with the "true" search engine providers (like Google and Bing) to allow them to search and retrieve content from their indexes. Some meta search engines do use their own ranking schema to present the compiled results to end users. However, they cannot interfere with—or decide—the rank and relevancy of contents delivered to them by their data sources. Thus, you should usually stick to the top results from each partner search engine.

A major advantage of metasearch engines is their ability to compile results from many sources for each user search inquiry. Searching multiple sources instantly will reduce the time required for conducting the search and will return more comprehensive results without forgetting the enhanced privacy compared with other typical search engines (like Google and Bing). In the following list, we discuss the most popular metasearch engines currently available:

- www.etools.ch/search.do compiles its results from major international search engines, preserving user privacy by not collecting or sharing personal information about its users. This search engine is fast and shows a summary for each search query— on the right side—detailing the source of its results (see Figure 4-8).

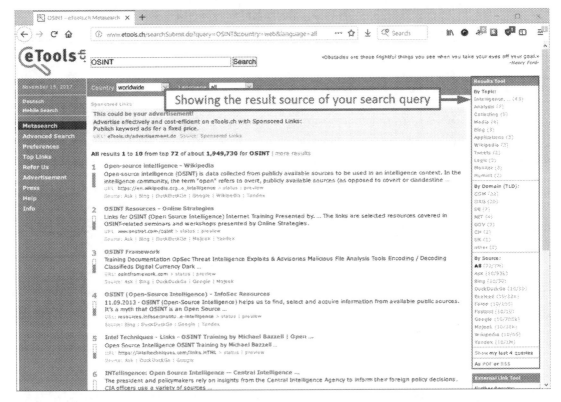

Figure 4-8. *Showing the source result of your search query when using etools.ch*

- All the Internet (https://www.alltheInternet.com) queries major search engines including shopping sites like Amazon and eBay.

- Fagan Finder (www.faganfinder.com/engines) queries the major search engines as well as answer engines and question-and-answer sites and blogs.

- `www.izito.com` aggregates data from multiple sources (Yahoo, Bing, Wikipedia, YouTube, and others) to generate optimal results that include images, videos, news, and articles.

- Metacrawler (`www.metacrawler.com`) aggregates results from Google and Yahoo.

- My All Search (`https://www.myallsearch.com`) aggregates results through Bing, DuckDuckGo, AOL Search, Ask, Oscobo, Mojeek, ZapMeta, and MetaCrawler.

- Carrot2 (`http://search.carrot2.org/`) aggregates results from the Google API, Bing API, eTools Meta Search, Lucene, SOLR, and more. It organizes results into thematic categories (circles and foam trees) helping users to narrow down their search visually by dividing it into many topics (see Figure 4-9).

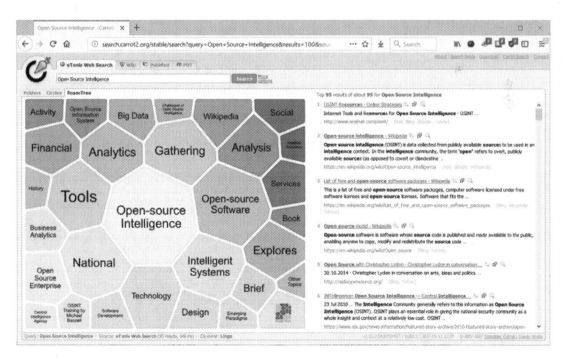

Figure 4-9. *Carrot2 dividing search results into thematic categories*

- elocalfinder (`www.elocalfinder.com/HSearch.aspx`) fetches results from Google, Yahoo, Ask, and Bing and displays them in a table for comparison along with the overall ranking.

- Opentext (`http://fqs.opentext.com/web.htm`) is a metasearch engine based on Google, Yahoo!, Ask, Bing, Wikipedia, and Open Directory. It also offers a search utility to search within social sites like Facebook, Twitter, YouTube, and LinkedIn in addition to news search engines (aggregating results from the Guardian, Reuters, the Washington Post, BBC News, and the Los Angeles Times) and health search engines.

Code Search

As an online investigator, you may encounter cases when you need to search for a snippet of code (for example, to reconstruct embedded software). The following are the major source code search engines:

- Searchcode (`https://searchcode.com`) searches Google code, GitHub, Bitbucket, CodePlex, Sourceforge, Fedora Project, and GitLab.

- Nerdaydata (`https://nerdydata.com/search`) requires a monthly subscription to unlock all features.

- Krugle (`www.krugle.org`) is another one.

- Codase (`www.codase.com`) searches 250 million lines of code.

- The O'Reilly source code search (`http://labs.oreilly.com`) gives access to all code snippets in O'Reilly books.

- Symbolhound (`http://symbolhound.com`) searches code search engines and doesn't ignore special characters.

- Merobase (`http://merobase.com`) is a code search engine for Java software components.

- GitHub Dorks (`https://github.com/techgaun/github-dorks`) searches a Python tool to search sensitive data, such as private keys, credentials, and authentication tokens on different repositories.

FTP Search Engines

File Transfer Protocol (FTP) is an old protocol invented in the early days of the Internet and still used by millions of websites. As its name implies, it is used to transfer files between computers across networks like the Internet. Web hosting companies usually give its customers an FTP account to transfer files to their hosting space. Many companies, universities, institutions, and collaboration projects put large archive files and other downloadable software on FTP servers to facilitate sharing among its employees. FTP accounts can be accessed using a special client such as FileZilla (`https://filezilla-project.org`) that supports uploading, downloading, and renaming files. Companies usually protect their FTP servers with a password. However, you can find plenty of them left unsecured online (without a password), and such public FTP servers can be accessed through web browsers directly to view/download their contents.

According to the IEEE Computer Society,[iv] there are more than 13 million FTP servers in the world, 1.1 million of which allow "anonymous" (public) access. A wealth of useful information can be found on public FTP servers, ranging from music and video files to licensed software, tax documents, and cryptographic secrets in addition to personal files and directories.

When searching for contents on FTP servers using specialized FTP search engines, you are only searching for filenames and directories, as indexing all the content on all FTP servers is difficult and cannot be achieved easily. Let's first begin testing some techniques with Google to find content on FTP servers; see Table 4-5.

Table 4-5. *Advanced Google Search Queries to Find FTP Servers*

Google FTP Search Query	Meaning
inurl:"ftp://www." "Index of /"	This search query can be used to find FTP servers online.
inurl:ftp -inurl:(http|https) "SEARCH QUERY"	Use this to search for all FTP servers that have the specified search query.

The following are some sites to search FTP servers:

- Global file search (`http://globalfilesearch.com`)

- Filemare (`https://filemare.com/en-nl`)

- Archie (`http://archie.icm.edu.pl/archie_eng.html`)

- File watcher (`www.filewatcher.com`)

Automated Search Tools

Automated tools allow an online searcher to automate the search process using major search engines such as Google, Bing, and Shodan. Automated tools are fast and allow you to test large numbers of search queries continually, thus returning more comprehensive results because the search tool can construct complex search queries better than a human. The following sections highlight the most famous automated search tools.

SearchDiggity

This is the most well-known search engine hacking tool; it is a Windows GUI application that connects you to famous search engines' hacking databases such as the Google Hacking Database. It works by automating the search process on different search engine platforms such as Google, Bing, Shodan, CodeSearch, and others, and it presents the results within the program's main interface. See `https://www.bishopfox.com/resources/tools/google-hacking-diggity/attack-tools`.

SearchDome

This is an online service that allows you to automate your search on eBay.com using a wide array of search criteria (see Figure 4-10). See `https://www.searchdome.com/ebay`.

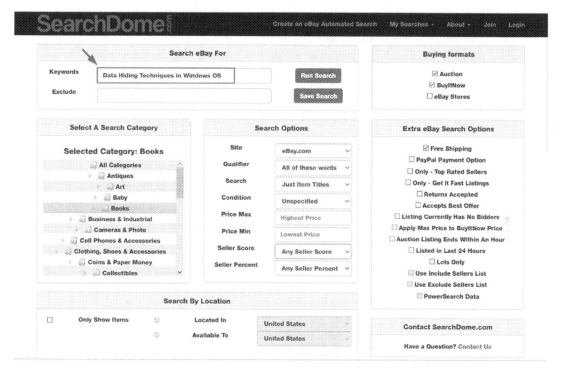

Figure 4-10. Use SearchDome to conduct advanced searches within eBay.com

Jeviz

This is an Amazon advanced search engine currently focused on the United States; it allows a user to search within an Amazon website and find deep links that are difficult to locate using the typical Amazon search engine. See https://www.jeviz.com.

Internet Of Things (IoT) Device Search Engines

There are many dedicated search engines for Internet-connected devices (known as IoT devices). The following are some popular websites that help you discover such devices online:

- *Shodan* (https://www.shodan.io): Shodan is the world's first search engine for Internet-connected devices.

- *123Cam* (http://123cam.com List): This is a free webcam from different countries around the world.

- *AirportWebcams* (`http://airportwebcams.net`): This is the largest database of airport webcams (more than 1,800 webcams) from different countries around the world.

- *Insecam* (`www.insecam.org`): This is a directory of online surveillance security cameras.

- *Lookr* (`https://www.lookr.com`): This lists live webcams from different places around the world.

- *Open Street Cam* (`https://www.openstreetcam.org/map`): This lists street webcams from around the world.

- *Pictimo* (`https://www.pictimo.com`): This searches for live streaming webcams from around the world.

- *Reolink* (`https://reolink.com/unsecured-ip-camera-list`): This is a list of unsecured IP cameras.

- *Webcam-Network Project* (`www.the-webcam-network.com`): This is a webcam directory.

- *Thingful* (`https://www.thingful.net`): This is a search engine for the Internet of Things.

Web Directories

We defined *web directory* briefly in the previous chapter. A web directory—also known as a *subject directory*—is a website that lists and organizes many sites into categories. We can consider it like a phone book. Each letter in this phone book refers to a topic or subject (shopping, news, information technology, blog), and each topic has many websites belonging to it (for example, information security contains `www.DarknessGate.com`).

The directory has a hierarchical structure; it emphasizes linking to a site home page instead of linking to individual pages, thus focusing on the general topic/subject the website belongs to. Directories are usually managed by human reviewers; hence, unlike search engines that use spiders to index web contents automatically, web directories depend on human efforts to add/update their contents. To add a website to a web directory, a webmaster needs to submit a site address and supply some keywords and define its niche. A moderator—from the web directory—then checks the submission for fitness.

A user can use a web directory internal search engine to find a specific website within the directory or can simply browse all websites under a specific topic (see Figure 4-11).

Web directories come in varying sizes. Yahoo and DMOZ are both discontinued now, but you can view a static version of DMOZ at `http://dmoztools.net`. There are huge directories covering all types of Internet sites. Other types are specialized web directories that cover specific subjects and branch to relevant websites within them.

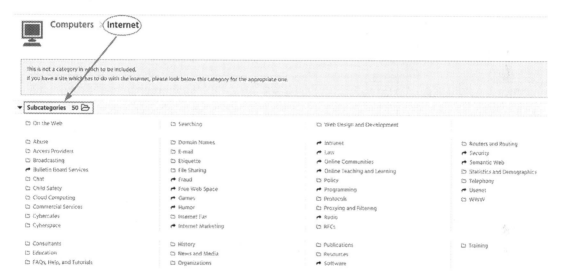

Figure 4-11. *Sample web directory (`http://dmoztools.net`) showing main category and other subcategories*

A web directory can be either free or paid. Free submission sites charge no money for include your site in the directory, while the paid ones require a website owner to pay a little amount of money to include their site in the directory. Some web directories ask for a reciprocal link. Hence, you need to put a link to the directory on your homepage to include yours—freely—in their listing.

While websites use keywords to search and locate information online, web directories organize all the websites according to each site subject, thus enabling you to find groups of relevant sites according to subject, language, and region. Then you can use search engine techniques—for example, a Google custom search—to search within each category for specific information.

Here are the most popular web directories:

- The WWW Virtual Library (`http://vlib.org`)

- DirPopulus (`http://dirpopulus.org`)

- Best of the Web (`https://botw.org`)

- GoWorkable (`www.goworkable.com`)

- 01webdirectory (`www.01webdirectory.com`)

Translation Services

During your web search, you may encounter useful information in other languages. Such information could be valuable and cannot be omitted during your search. There are many free online translation services to translate documents, text, and even whole websites. Check out the following list:

- Google Translate (`https://translate.google.com`) is the most important one; it can translate text and entire web pages into other languages (see Figure 4-12).

Figure 4-12. *Using the Google Translate service to translate a web page from English to Arabic*

- Google Input Tools (`https://www.google.com/inputtools/try`) allows a user to enter text in any supported language using their English (Latin) keyboard, and the text will get converted into its native script. You can download an offline version for Windows and Android or simply use it online (see Figure 4-13).

- The Yamli Intelligent Arabic Keyboard (`https://www.yamli.com/clavier-arabe`) allows you to type in Arabic using Latin characters in a phonetic way, and the site will transform it into Arabic words.

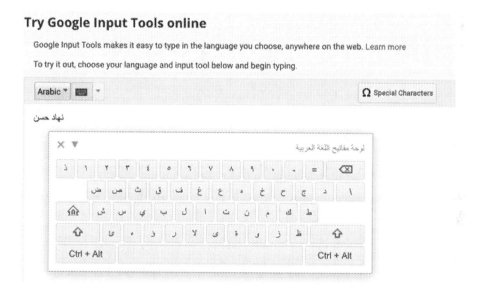

Figure 4-13. *Using Google input to convert written text to any languages supported by Google*

- Apertium (`https://www.apertium.org`) is an open source machine translation platform.

- Babylon (`http://translation.babylon-software.com`) This is a computer dictionary and translation program, developed by Babylon Software Ltd. It offers translation in more than 800 language pairs.

- Bing Translator (`https://www.bing.com/translator`) is another translation service.

- Dictionary (`http://translate.reference.com`) is another translation service.

- Wiktionary (`https://www.wiktionary.org`) is another translation service.

- Free Translator (`www.free-translator.com`) is another translation service.

- No Slang (`https://www.noslang.com`) translates text slang, Internet slang, and acronyms.

- Lexilogos (`https://www.lexilogos.com/keyboard/index.htm`) supports a multilanguage keyboard.

Website History and Website Capture

Sometimes you want to go back in time to investigate something in the past. Website capture is useful for online investigations because you can ensure that a snapshot of a given website will always remain online even if the original page disappears. Please note that saved pages are usually stored without their associated scripts, so some functionality, themes, and menus may not work correctly.

There are many online sites that offer such services; the following are the most popular ones:

- Internet Archive (the Wayback Machine; `https://archive.org/web/web.php`) is the most popular archive site; it has more than 308 billion web pages saved over time, and anyone can capture a web page as it appears now to use it in the future as a clue or a reference (the captured website should allow crawlers). See Figure 4-14.

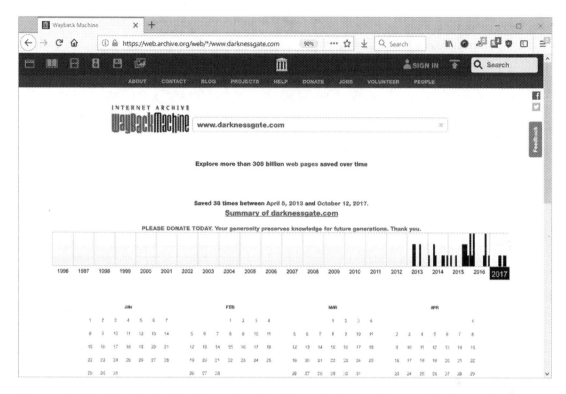

Figure 4-14. *Wayback Machine showing historical data for www.DarknessGate.com*

- Archive (`https://archive.fo/`) is also available.

- Cached pages (`www.cachedpages.com/`) shows previous websites
  captured on three different archive websites (Google cache, Coral,
  and Archive.org).

- `www.screenshots.com` shows screenshot history for any website.

- Way Backpack (`https://github.com/jsvine/waybackpack`) is a tool
  that allows you to download the entire Wayback Machine archive for
  a given web page.

- Library of Congress (`https://loc.gov/websites`) is another one.

- UK Web Archive (`www.webarchive.org.uk/ukwa`) is another one.

- Stanford Web Archive Portal (`https://swap.stanford.edu`) is
  another one.

- Oldweb.today (`http://oldweb.today`) retrieves archived web pages from the different public Internet archives. You can also display archived websites using different web browsers.

- UK Government Web Archive (`www.nationalarchives.gov.uk/webarchive/`) holds U.K. government web archives published on the Web since 1996 to the present. The archived contents include videos, tweets, and web pages.

Website Monitoring Services

Sometimes you might need to know about changes to a specific website when they happen. Tracking down changes to one website can be achieved by visiting it regularly. However, what can you do if you need to track page changes to many sites at once?

There are many online services that allow you to track an unlimited number of pages. This works by sending you an alert e-mail once a change is detected in the specific page (chosen by you). Some paid services allow you to receive SMS alerts also. The following are the major free website-monitoring services currently available:

- Google Alerts (`https://www.google.com/alerts`; see Figure 4-15) is a web content change detection (based on your search phrase or keywords) and notification service offered by Google. To set an alert, you need to go to the Google Alerts page (you need to sign into your Google account first) and enter the search phrase or word (it should be specific, not general, to avoid getting too many results). Google will notify you by e-mail when the specified search phrase or word appears in the newly indexed search results anywhere online (it will not notify you about current results available on the Web).

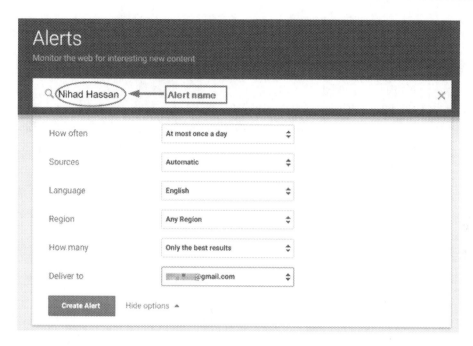

Figure 4-15. *Creating a new Google alert*

- Talk Walker (www.talkwalker.com/alerts) is an alternative to Google Alerts.

- Visual Ping (https://visualping.io) monitors web pages for any detected change; the free account gives you 62 checks per month.

- Follow That Page (https://www.followthatpage.com) gives you two daily checks with the free account.

- Watch That Page (www.watchthatpage.com) gives you 70 weekly checks on all your pages.

- Update Scanner (https://addons.mozilla.org/en-US/firefox/addon/update-scanner) is a Firefox extension that monitors web pages for updates.

RSS Feed

Another method to monitor website changes is to use an RSS feed. So, what does RSS mean?

Really Simple Syndication or Rich Site Summary is an XML (text) file that allows site owners to inform subscribed readers—and other sites—about new content published on their sites. RSS revolutionizes how Internet users can track updated content online. To check for new site updates, a user needs to have an RSS feed reader. The user subscribes to the site RSS feed, and then any new content on this site will appear in their feed reader automatically. Each feed entry will usually contain the title, summary of the published text, date of publishing, and author name.

Subscribing to a website RSS will make a user aware of any updates on to their monitored sites, thus removing the need to visit intended websites continually to check for newly published contents.

Major web browsers offer a mechanism to subscribe to the site RSS feed. Mozilla Firefox comes equipped with built-in RSS support called Live Bookmarks. To subscribe to any website RSS feed through Firefox, follow these steps:

1. Navigate to the website where you want to subscribe to its RSS feed.

2. From the Bookmarks menu, select Subscribe to This Page (if the browser does not detect an RSS feed on the page, this option will be grayed out). Then select your feed. Figure 4-16 shows two feeds for this site because it is a blog, one for the comments and the second for site contents named Feed.

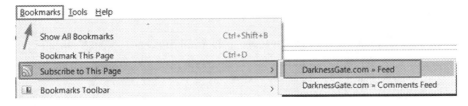

Figure 4-16. *Subscribe to an RSS feed using Firefox*

3. The next page appears. Use the Firefox subscription box at the top to confirm your subscription. Make sure to set the option as in Figure 4-17.

Figure 4-17. *Click the Subscribe Now button to subscribe to the intended RSS feed*

4. After clicking Subscribe Now, a pop-up message will appear allowing you to change the feed name and location. The default settings should be OK. Hit the Subscribe button and you are done!

The built-in RSS feed reader in a browser has limited functionality compared to some dedicated desktop RSS feed reader software. For instance, RSSOwl (`www.rssowl.org/`) comes with powerful features such as searching within feeds, saving a previous feed search, and getting notifications on new content. It is free and comes supported on all major platforms like Windows, Linux, and macOS.

There are also browser extensions—add-ons—for major web browsers in addition to online services that offer feed subscription. However, if you are part of an online investigation, it is preferable to use only the built-in browser feed utility or the RSSOwl software to avoid leaking information about your stored feed. Many browser extensions request access to your browser surfing history, and this may result in a privacy breach if such records fall into the wrong hands.

News Search

A wealth of useful information about anything can be found in news sources. For instance, a corporation can gain deep insight about any competitor like its legal history, partnership agreements, financial status, and any negative mention by searching within news archives. We gave an example for business corporations; however, the same things apply to governments, nonprofit organizations, and high-profile individuals.

Searching in news online is easier than searching in a media broadcast archive. In this section, we will cover how you can customize Google News to know about the latest updates of any search keyword/phrase appearing in global news channels. We will also mention other online news sources and give advice on how to detect fake news.

Customize Google News

Google News offers an up-to-date news service aggregated from various sources around the world. A user can select a topic of interest, and Google will show relevant results about this topic. Online investigators can exploit the Google News service to simplify searching for specific topics or search terms within the news. To do this, follow these steps:

1. Go to https://news.google.com.

2. Go to the left side of the page and click "Manage sections" (see Figure 4-18).

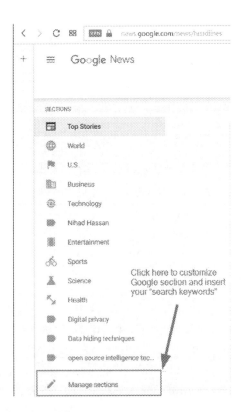

Figure 4-18. *Customizing Google News*

3. The page in Figure 4-19 appears. Enter the topic or keywords in the "Search terms" text box; you can also name the title of the search. Then click the Add Section button.

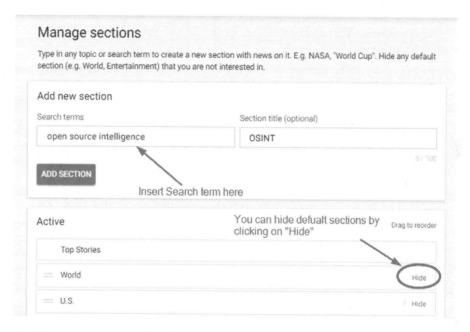

Figure 4-19. *Customizing the Google News sections to include your keywords*

Now, a new section will appear in the left vertical menu of Google News. To search for specific keywords, all you need to do is to click the section name and Google will display the relevant news search results.

Note!   Google keeps an archive of previous news; you can check it at
`https://news.google.com/newspapers`.

News Websites

There are many online news services that offer up-to-date information about all kinds of topics. The following are the most popular ones:

- *1stHeadlines* (`https://www.1stheadlines.com`): This lists breaking news headline.

- *News Now* (`www.newsnow.co.uk`): This lists latest news from around the world.

- *All You Can Read* (`www.allyoucanread.com`): This website lists all major newspapers and news media in each country around the world (usually list the top 30 sites).

- *Daily Earth* (`http://dailyearth.com/index.html`): This is a global newspaper directory.

- *Chroniclingamerica* (`https://chroniclingamerica.loc.gov/search/titles`): Search U.S. Newspaper Directory.

- *Newspaper Map* (`http://newspapermap.com`): This is a global newspaper map.

- *World News* (`https://wn.com`): A collection of world news aggregated from different sources.

- *The Paperboy* (`https://www.thepaperboy.com/index.cfm`): This aggregates news from major news agencies, lists all newspapers from around the world, and shows the front page of major newspapers from around the world.

- *Site Intel Group* (`https://ent.siteintelgroup.com`): This site specializes in news about ISIS and other Jihadist groups.

Fake News Detection

In today's digital age, everything is connected online, and a large number of people receive their news using social media sites, where anyone can post anything using a fake identity. In addition, there are many unreliable news sites that announce news without investigating its source accurately. For instance, any malicious actor can spread misleading news for commercial gain, for propaganda purposes, or to mislead people about something. Such false news can spread instantly because of the simplicity of sharing information across different social media platforms and, consequently, through the entire Internet.

Detecting fake news has become a hot topic today and attracts huge attention. Major social platforms—like Twitter and Facebook—have promised their users they will find a solution to stop or at least decrease the harm of fake news. Researchers continue in this field with emphasis on developing artificial intelligence solutions (such as machine learning and natural language processing) to combat fake news.

As an OSINT investigator, you will certainly encounter fake news during your search for resources. Any suspicious information should not be included in your case files. To help sort true information from false information, you should use the following checklist for investigating suspicious news:

1. Read the entire article or piece of information first. Do not believe anything until you review its source.

2. Read the source of the news/information.

3. If the source comes from a credible or well-known website (for example, a global well-known news agency), do the following:

   a. Go to the source of the news to see whether the same information is presented on its site. For example, if a piece of news is attributed to Reuters (`https://www.reuters.com`), check its website to see whether the same information exists there.

4. If the information comes from an unknown source, you need to conduct an online search to see who else has published the same news.

   a. If a credible and well-known website published the same story from the same source, it is highly likely to be a true story.

   b. Otherwise, you need to check more about the issue or decline to use the information.

Warning!   Do not trust information published on social sites only. Instead, conduct an online search to see whether the same news has been published elsewhere. If you find that this news is false, make sure to report it to the site operators (for example, Facebook allows its users to report posts for review).

You should read news, articles, and other content only on reputable websites. Less-known sites should be investigated thoroughly before considering their news as valid.

There are many sites online that help you to figure out whether something is false news/information. The following are the most important ones:

- Snopes (`https://www.snopes.com`) discovers false news, stories, and urban legends and researches/validates rumors to see whether they are true (see Figure 4-20).

Figure 4-20. *Example of fake news discovered by Snopes*

- Hoaxy (`https://hoaxy.iuni.iu.edu`) checks the spread of false claims (like a hoax, rumor, satire, or news report) across social media sites. The site derives its results from reputable fact-checking organizations to return the most accurate results.

- FactCheck (`www.factcheck.org/fake-news`) is partnered with Facebook to help identify and label fake news reported by its users. It also monitors different media for the false information covering a wide range of topics like health, science, and hoaxes spread through spam e-mails.

- `https://reporterslab.org/fact-checking` gives a map of global fact-checking sites (see Figure 4-21).

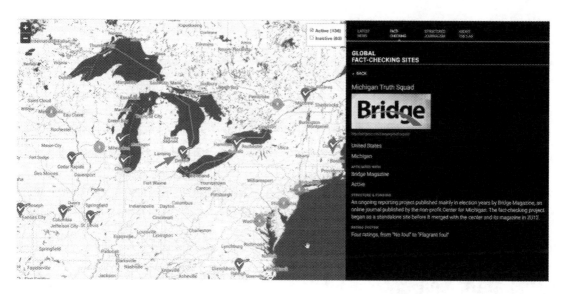

Figure 4-21. *reporterslab.org/fact-checking showing a global of fact-checking sites around the world*

- `www.truthorfiction.com` discovers fake news in different topics such as politics, nature, health, space, crime, police and terrorism, and so on.

- Hoax-Slayer (`www.hoax-slayer.com`) focuses on e-mail scams and social media hoaxes.

- Verification Handbook (`http://verificationhandbook.com`) is a definitive guide to verifying digital content for emergency coverage available in different languages.

- Verification Junkie (`http://verificationjunkie.com`) is a directory of tools for verifying, fact checking, and assessing the validity of eyewitness reports and user self-published content online.

- `https://citizenevidence.org` has tools and lessons to teach people how to authenticate user-generated online contents. It is managed by Amnesty International.

- InVID Verification Plugin (`www.invid-project.eu/tools-and-services/invid-verification-plugin`) supports both Mozilla Firefox and Chrome. This is a tool created by the InVID European project to help journalists verify content on social networks.

Searching for Digital Files

In a previous section, we talked briefly about how to use Google and Bing advanced search operators to search for different types of digital files (documents, images, and videos). In this section, we will continue our discussion and show how to utilize different techniques and specialized search engines to search for files in a variety of formats.

Digital files constitute an important percentage of web contents located on the surface web. Now, with the availability of free cloud file-hosting services (Dropbox, Google Drive) and video-sharing sites (YouTube), individuals and corporations are used to using such services for online sharing. Digital files found online can contain a wealth of information, not only in their contents but also in their metadata (hidden attributes).

Document Search

This section is dedicated to online document search, but before we start, let's first talk about the most common document file formats available online.

DOC and DOCX

DOC and DOCX are the standard file formats for Microsoft Word documents. Microsoft Word is part of the Microsoft Office suite created by Microsoft. The .doc extension is for older versions of Microsoft Word, such as 2003 and older. New editions of Microsoft Word (beginning with 2007) have the .docx extension.

HTML and HTM

Hypertext Markup Language is the standard web page file format to represent content on the Web. Both extensions (.html and .htm) can be used interchangeably. To edit these files, you can use any text editor. However, to decode and display HTML file contents, you need to open the HTML file using a web browser.

ODT

This is a text document file format (formatted using the OASIS OpenDocument XML-based standard) like the Microsoft Word file format; it is used in the open source word processing program named Writer, which comes as part of the Apache OpenOffice suite. ODT can be opened and edited using any OpenOffice-compatible program, including

NeoOffice (Mac), AbiWord (Mac and Windows), and KWord (Unix). You can also open ODT files using Microsoft Word and save them as DOCX files.

XLS and XLSX

XLS and XLSX are file formats for Microsoft Excel used to create spreadsheets. Older editions have the `.xsl` extension, while modern Microsoft Excel files (beginning with 2007) have the `.xslx` extension. Excel is part of the Microsoft Office suite created by Microsoft.

ODS

ODS stands for OpenDocument Spreadsheet; this format was created by the Calc program that is included in the Apache OpenOffice suite. ODS files can be opened and edited using any OpenOffice-compatible program, including NeoOffice (Mac) and LibreOffice (Mac and Windows). They can also be opened in Microsoft Excel and saved as XLS or XLSX files.

PPT and PPTX

PPT and PPTX are file format for Microsoft PowerPoint that are used for creating multimedia presentations. Just like with the Excel and Word programs, `.ppt` is used for older editions, while `.pptx` is used in modern Microsoft PowerPoint editions.

ODP

ODP stands for OpenDocument Presentation. It is used in the Apache OpenOffice Impress program, which comes as part of the OpenOffice suite. Microsoft PowerPoint can be used to open or save a presentation in the ODP format.

TXT

TXT is a basic plain-text file format that can be opened using any text editor on all operating systems.

PDF

PDF stands for Portable Document Format, the most widely used document file format online, originally created by Adobe Systems. Acrobat Reader, which is available as a free download from the Adobe website (`https://get.adobe.com/reader`), allows you to view and print PDF files. The PDF file format has become the most widely used file format by governments, corporations, and educational institutions around the world.

Note!   Apache OpenOffice can be found at `https://www.openoffice.org`, and LibreOffice can be found at `https://www.libreoffice.org`.

Let's begin our search for documents by using some Google operators to find files on different cloud storage providers.

To search a Google doc site, use the following query in the Google basic search engine: **site:docs.google.com SEARCHTERM**. This will search for the specified search term on the Google document website (`docs.google.com`). In the same way, you can search for documents hosted on Google Drive—with public access—using the following search query: **site:drive.google.com SEARCHTERM**.

To search for files hosted on Dropbox, type the following in Google: **site:dl.dropbox.com SEARCHTERM**.

To search for files on Amazon AWS, type the following in Google: **site:s3.amazonaws.com SEARCHTERM**.

To search for files on Microsoft OneDrive, type the following in Google: **site:onedrive.live.com SEARCHTERM**.

File Search Engines

Some specialized search engines can query many file hosting sites.

Fagan Finder

Fagan Finder (`www.faganfinder.com/filetype`) is an old search engine but still works just fine to locate different file types online. Just enter your search term, select the file type you want to search for, and finally select the search engine to conduct your search (see Figure 4-22).

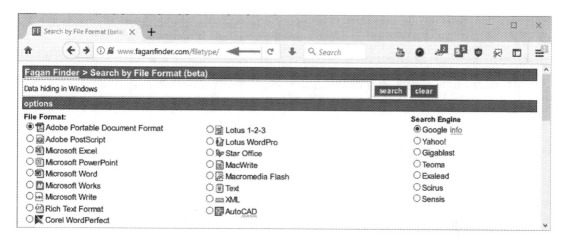

Figure 4-22. *Use the Fagan Finder file search engine to locate a variety of file types on different search engines*

General-Search

General-Search (www.general-search.com) allows you to search for different file types using 11 file-hosting websites. You can select the file type and set a filter to its size (see Figure 4-23).

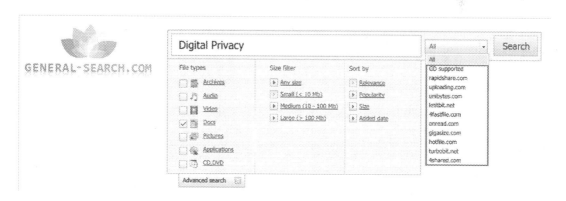

Figure 4-23. *Search for files using 11 file-hosting websites*

ShareDir

ShareDir (https://sharedir.com) lets you specify a file type and search more than 60 file-hosting sites simultaneously. The unique service offered by this site is that it allows you to download 500MB daily—without waiting—from premium file-hosting websites. All you need is to register for a free account to use this feature.

> **Note!**   You can search any file-hosting website using the Google *site* search operator. For example, to search for files on Mediafire.com, type the following operator into the Google search engine: **site:mediafire.com SEARCHTERM**.

Custom Search Engine

We already covered different types of search engines. However, we deferred our discussion of custom search engines until now, so we could cover how to use this technique to narrow down your search for specific file types within a limited set of sites.

The term *custom search* can be misleading at first sight; some users may think that they can create a new custom search engine according to their preferences. However, this is not true. A custom search allows you to use an existing search engine service to preselect the websites you need to limit your search to, the types of results returned (for example, only PDF files), and how the results will be prioritized.

A major provider of custom search is Google, so we will cover how to create one in the following steps:

1. Go to `www.google.com/coop/cse`.

2. You must have a Google account to use this service, so sign in if you have not done this already.

3. Click the "New search engine" button on the left side.

4. On the following page, enter the sites that you want to include in your search in the "Sites to search" section. You can include whole site URLs or individual page URLs. Select the language used to display the GUI of your custom search engine; finally, give your search a name.

5. Click the Create button to create your custom search engine (see Figure 4-24).

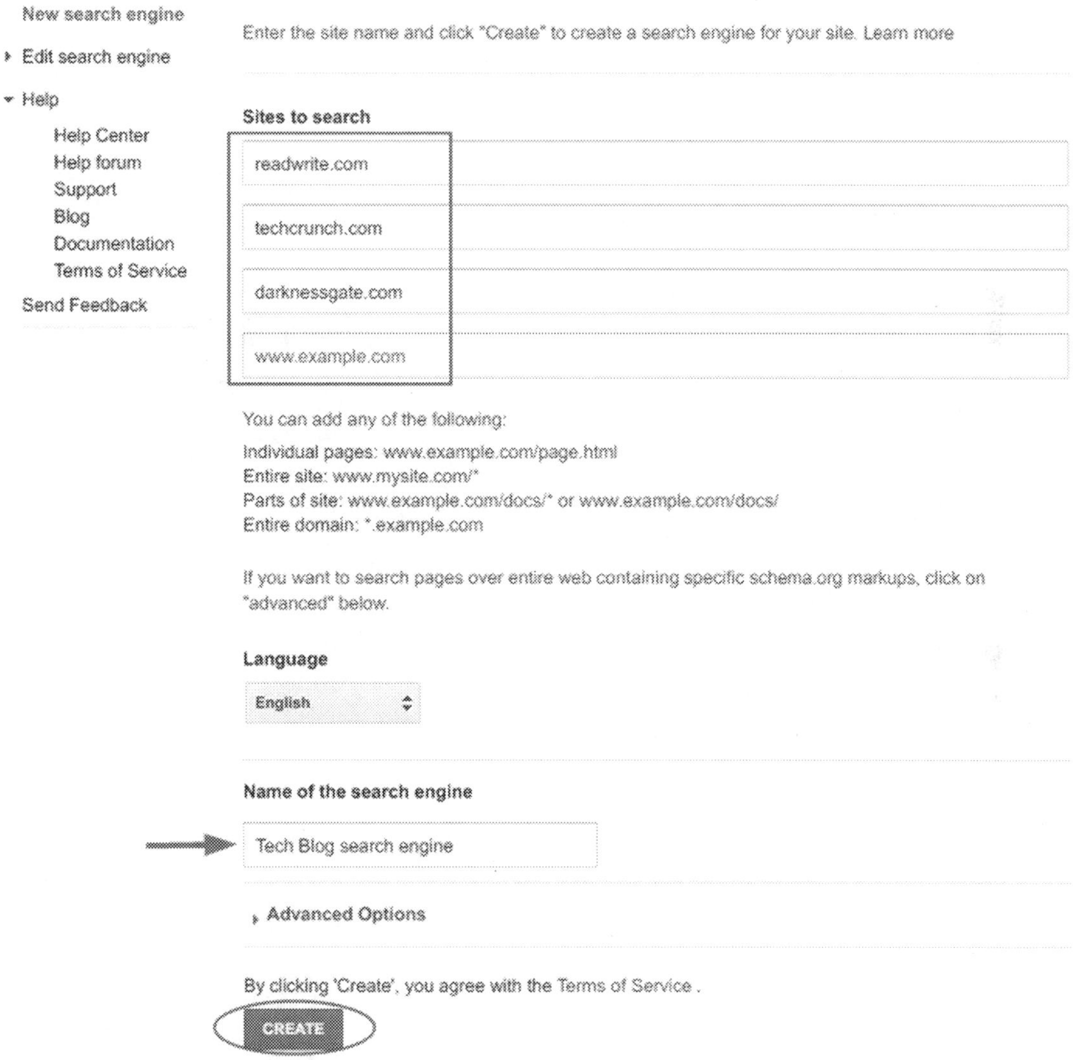

New search engine

▶ Edit search engine

▾ Help
    Help Center
    Help forum
    Support
    Blog
    Documentation
    Terms of Service
Send Feedback

Enter the site name and click "Create" to create a search engine for your site. Learn more

Sites to search

readwrite.com

techcrunch.com

darknessgate.com

www.example.com

You can add any of the following:

Individual pages: www.example.com/page.html
Entire site: www.mysite.com/*
Parts of site: www.example.com/docs/* or www.example.com/docs/
Entire domain: *.example.com

If you want to search pages over entire web containing specific schema.org markups, click on "advanced" below.

Language

English   ⇕

Name of the search engine

Tech Blog search engine

▸ Advanced Options

By clicking 'Create', you agree with the Terms of Service .

CREATE

Figure 4-24. *Create a custom search engine using a Google custom search*

6. After successfully creating your custom search engine, Google
    will display a page showing the public URL of your custom search
    engine. It will also show the HTML code snippet in case you want
    to put it on your website and a link to a custom search engine
    control panel to update its settings (see Figure 4-25).

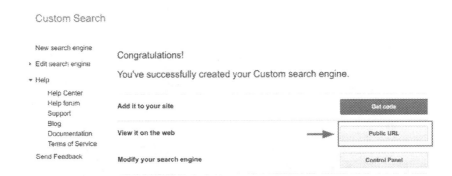

Figure 4-25. *Google custom search engine created successfully*

To access the public URL of your custom search engine, go to `https://cse.google.`
`com/cse/all`, click the custom search engine name you want to access, go to Setup, and
select Public URL (see Figure 4-26).

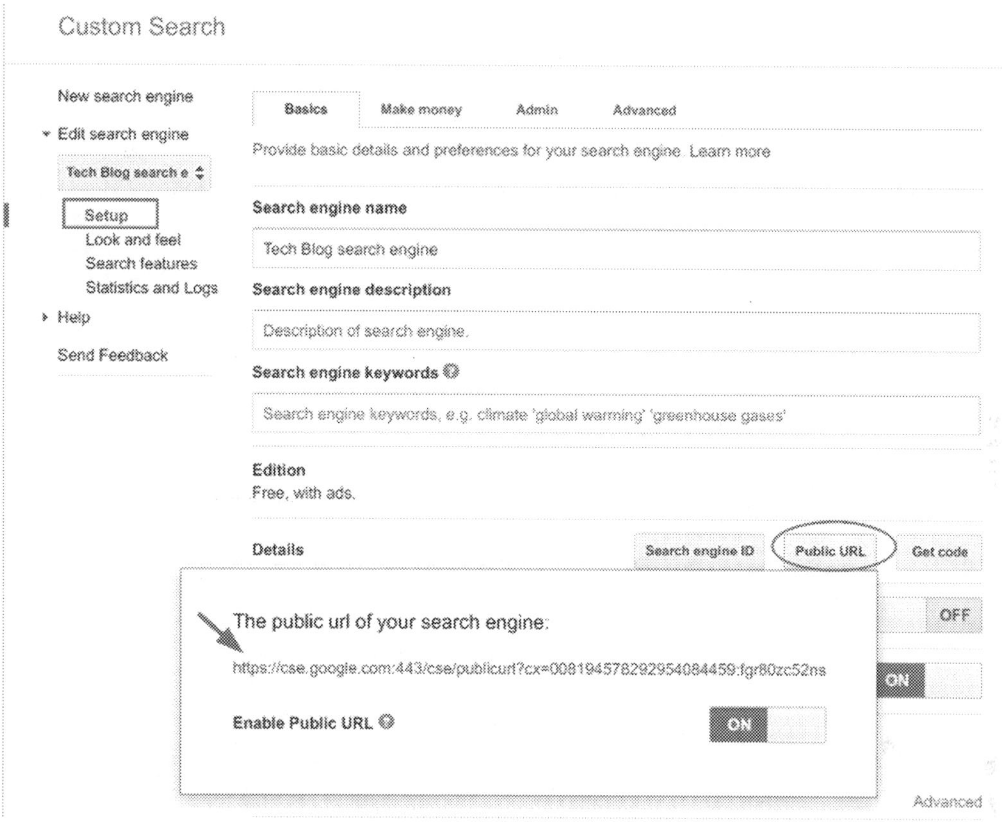

Figure 4-26. *Viewing the public URL of your Google custom search engine*

Google will display a search box to you. Enter your search query, and Google will display relevant results from only the websites that have been entered upon creating your custom search engine.

Many Internet users have already created their own Google custom search engines to locate files and FTP directories online. One of these is located at `https://cse.google.com/cse/home?cx=014863114814409449623%3Ajc-vjhl_c5g`. To use this custom search, enter your search term (file or directory name); you can also specify the file type you want to restrict search results to by clicking the relevant name below the search box (see Figure 4-27).

Figure 4-27. *A Google custom search engine used to search for a variety of file types*

Other useful Google custom search engines for locating OSINT resources online are as follows:

- 300+ Social Networking Sites (`https://cse.google.com/cse/public url?key=AIzaSyB2lwQuNzUsRTH-49FA7od4dB_Xvu5DCvg&cx=0017944 96531944888666:iyxger-cwug&q=%22%22`)

- 250+ Video Sharing Sites (`https://cse.google.com/cse/publicurl ?key=AIzaSyB2lwQuNzUsRTH-49FA7od4dB_Xvu5DCvg&cx=0017944965 31944888666:ctbnemd5u7s&q=%22%22`)

- File Sharing Sites Search (`https://cse.google.com/cse/publicurl? key=AIzaSyB2lwQuNzUsRTH-49FA7od4dB_Xvu5DCvg&cx=00179449653 1944888666:hn5bcrszfhe&q=%22%22`)

- Torrent Search (`https://cse.google.com/cse/publicurl?key=AIza SyB2lwQuNzUsRTH-49FA7od4dB_Xvu5DCvg&cx=0017944965319448886 66:ixpabzzplzy&q=%22%22`)

Note!   You can construct an advanced Google operator to search for PDF files hosted on public servers using the following Google dork: **intitle:index.of +?last modified? +?parent directory? +pdf "Search Term"**.

Gray Literature

As we already said in Chapter 1, gray literature is any material produced by the world's commercial publishing systems. It has mainly two types.

- Gray literature

- Gray information

Gray literature includes books, journals, magazines, and anything that can be obtained publicly through traditional bookstore channels or academic publications. A user usually pays subscription fees to gain access to such resources or buys them directly from bookstores (such as buying books from Amazon.com). Springer (https://rd.springer.com), which provides access to millions of scientific documents such as journals, books, series, protocols, and reference works, is a clear example of a gray literature channel.

Gray information, on the other hand, cannot be obtained easily using traditional bookstore routes. However, it has some specialized channels where you can obtain some of it; you need to pay for specialized subscription agencies to acquire the rest. Gray information includes the following—and more:

- Academic papers

- Preprints

- Proceedings

- Conference and discussion papers

- Research reports

- Marketing reports

- Technical specifications and standards

- Dissertations

- Theses

- Trade publications

- Memoranda

- Government reports and documents not published commercially

- Translations

- Newsletters

- Market surveys

- Draft versions of books and articles

In this section, we will focus on academic and scholarly resources because we already covered the business search engines where you can get gray information about businesses. In the following list, you'll find the most important gray literature websites that can be used to retrieve academic and scholarly resources for free covering all topics:

- Academia (`https://www.academia.edu`) is a platform for academics to share research papers—more than 19 million papers currently uploaded—covering all academic subjects.

- Academic Index (`www.academicindex.net`) is a scholarly academic search engine that lists only selected sets of quality websites chosen by academics, librarians, educators, and library consortia.

- Academic Torrents (`http://academictorrents.com`) is a community-maintained distributed repository for datasets and scientific knowledge. It hosts academic research, courses, datasets, papers, and collections using the Torrent technology where each user of the system can store a research paper and offer it for download using only a home computer. All you need is a Torrent client, and you are ready to download and share (seed) contents.

- American Doctoral Dissertations (`www.opendissertations.com`) provides free access to more than 172,000 theses and dissertations accepted by American universities since 1902 to the present.

- ArchiveGrid (`https://beta.worldcat.org/archivegrid`) holds more than five million archival materials aggregated from archives, libraries, museums, and historical societies. Primary topics include historical documents, and personal and family papers and histories.

- Google Scholar (`https://scholar.google.com/schhp?hl=en`) is a Google search engine to find scholarly research. Results are ranked based on the number of citations (calculated based on the number of people who cite the research) and the publication's credibility. You can also create alerts (like Google alert already covered) so you will get informed when a new scholarly research paper is published that matches your search criteria.

- The Bielefeld Academic Search Engine (`https://www.base-search.net/Search/Advanced`) contains more than 100 million documents.

- Archive Portal Europe (`www.archivesportaleurope.net`) provides access to information on archival material from different European countries covering numerous topics (such as agriculture, health, justice, politics, and science).

- Social Science Research Network (`https://www.ssrn.com/en`) provides more than a half-million research papers covering 30 topics.

- The National Library of Australia (`http://trove.nla.gov.au`) has more than 500 million Australian and online resources covering books, journals, annual reports, images, historic newspapers, maps, music, archives, and more.

- ScienceDirect (`www.sciencedirect.com`) contains more than 250,000 open access (free to read and download) articles in scientific, technical, and medical research.

- PQDT Open (`https://pqdtopen.proquest.com/search.html`) provides open access to dissertations and theses free of charge.

- The National Archive of the United Kingdom (`http://discovery.nationalarchives.gov.uk`) holds more than 32 million descriptions of records held by The National Archives and more than 2,500 archives across the UK, many of them are available for download.

- Oxford Academic (`https://academic.oup.com/journals`) contains journals in law, business, science, social science, art, and medicine.

- Page Press (`www.pagepress.org`) contains open access scholarly journals.

- CERN Document Server (`https://cdsweb.cern.ch`) provides free access to thousands of articles, books, reprints, presentation and talks, multimedia, and outreach covering mostly the physical science.

- High Wire (`http://highwire.stanford.edu/lists/freeart.dtl`) has free online full-text articles.

- Gray Guide (`http://greyguide.isti.cnr.it`) has resources in gray literature.

- Beyond Citation (`www.beyondcitation.org`) gives information about different academic databases and other digital research collections.

- Crossref (`https://search.crossref.org`) searches the metadata (title, author, DOI, ORCID ID, ISSN) of more than 92 million journal articles, books, standards, and datasets.

- Databases (`https://databases.today`) is a directory of publicly available databases to download free resources for security researchers and journalists.

Data Leak Information

Data leaks—sometimes called *data breach*es—are the intentional or unintentional release of confidential information to the public. Leaks mainly occur because of black hat hacker attacks against computerized systems or by disgruntled employees who may uncover secret information about their organizations.

Data leaks can include credit card information, PII, health information of patients, financial information, e-mail/social site usernames and passwords, trade secrets, corporations plans and future works, intellectual property information, and military information belonging to governments.

There is a debate on the legal status of data leak information. For instance, some argue that leaked information has become part of OSINT sources and thus you can handle it as you do with any publicly available information. The opposite opinion suggests that leaked information has been obtained illegally by breaching system or legal rules and thus should not be used as OSINT sources.

OSINT investigations cannot omit the existence of such leaked data while investigating some cases (especially when dealing with leaked intelligence information). However, it is preferred to handle it carefully on a case-by-case basis. For instance, if personal information or a private corporation has secrets leaked online, it is preferable not to publicize the information again and to renounce it in your search. Instead, you can use the useful elements in your investigation while respecting the affected actor's private information that has been already leaked once.

Leaked information such as personal, financial, and corporate information can be found on the darknet (already covered in Chapter 3), but we are not going to cover it because this is made up of illegal sites promoting illegal actions.

Leaked official documents are distributed online using specific websites that focus on different areas, mostly the military, intelligence, and surveillance arenas. The following are the two most popular official data leak repositories online:

- WikiLeaks (`https://wikileaks.org`)

- Cryptome (`https://cryptome.org`)

- Offshore Leaks (`https://offshoreleaks.icij.org`)

Document Metadata

We already talked about digital file metadata and demonstrated how to view/edit it using different tools in Chapter 2, but bear in mind that any digital files acquired online can contain useful metadata that must be investigated.

Image

Digital images, logos, and icons can be of great value in OSINT investigations. Major search engines like Google, Yahoo, and Bing provide basic image search engine functionality. However, there are other more specialized image search engines that can be used to get more precise results.

Basic Image Search

The following sites offer image search services:

- Google Image Search (`https://images.google.com`)

- Bing image search (`www.bing.com/images`)

- Yahoo Images (`http://images.yahoo.com`)

- Yandex (`https://yandex.com/images`)

- Baidu (`http://image.baidu.com`)

- Imgur (`https://imgur.com`)

- Photobucket (`http://photobucket.com`)

- Picsearch (`www.picsearch.com` contains)

- `https://ccsearch.creativecommons.org`)

- SmugMug (`https://www.smugmug.com`)

Google offers Advanced Image Search, where you can set many criteria of your search query such as image color, image type (photo, face, clip art, line drawing, animated), region or country, site or domain name, image format type, and usage rights. Google Advanced Image Search can be found at (`https://images.google.com/advanced_image_search`).

Images shared across social media sites can be found in the following locations:

- *Lakako* (`https://www.lakako.com`): This searches Instagram, Twitter, and Google+ for photos and people.

- *Flickr* (`https://www.flickr.com`)

  - *Flicker map* (`https://www.flickr.com/map`): View uploaded images on a map according to the uploader country of origin.

  - *My Pics map* (`www.mypicsmap.com`): View Flickr photos on a Google map. You need to supply the Flicker username of the image uploader or view photos from a specific photo set.

  - *idGettr* (`https://www.webpagefx.com/tools/idgettr`): Find the Flicker ID number (also works for groups).

  - *Flickr Hive Mind* (`http://flickrhivemind.net`): This is a data-mining tool for the Flickr database of photography.

- *Instagram* (`https://www.instagram.com`)

  - *Websta* (`https://websta.me/search`) is an advanced search for the Instagram website.

  - *Stalkture* (`http://stalkture.com`) is an Instagram online web viewer.

  - *Mininsta* (`http://mininsta.net`) is an advanced Instagram search engine.

- *Pinterest* (`https://www.pinterest.com`)

There are specialized sites that hold images that have appeared in the press and news media. To search for this type of images, try these sites:

- Gettyimages (`www.gettyimages.com`)

- International Logo List (`http://logos.iti.gr/table/`)

- Instant Logo Search (`http://instantlogosearch.com`)

- Reuters Pictures (`http://pictures.reuters.com`)

- News Press (`https://www.news-press.com/media/latest/news`)

- Associated Press Images Portal (`www.apimages.com`)

- PA Images (`https://www.paimages.co.uk`)

- European Pressphoto Agency (`www.epa.eu`)

- Canadian Press Images Archive (`www.cpimages.com/fotoweb/index.fwx`)

HOW TO DOWNLOAD FLASH VIDEOS, ICONS, AND OTHER IMAGES USING FIREFOX

Some websites—like `www.DarknessGate.com`—protect multimedia content by disabling selection and right-click. Many websites are still using Flash videos (SWF files) to display animation. To download SWF files and other multimedia files—when the right-click on a site is disabled—using only Firefox browser, follow these steps:

A. Go to the Firefox menu and select Tools and then Page Info.

B. Go to the Media tab and locate your SWF file or the images you want to download. Select the file and then click the Save As button (see Figure 4-28).

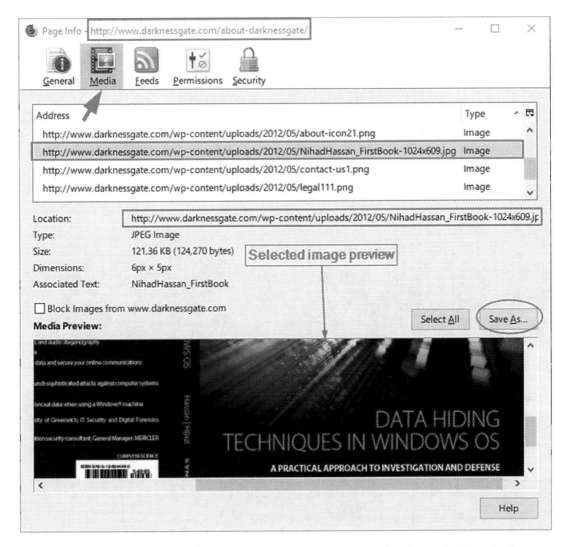

Figure 4-28. *Saving an image from a protected website (right-click disabled) using the Firefox browser. In the same way, you can download SWF (Flash) files embedded within pages. However, you need first to finish playing the movie before downloading it.*

Please note that we are not promoting breaching copyright laws regarding downloading multimedia content from the Internet. However, you may need such techniques in some context.

Always read a website's "terms of use" and regulations and obey the copyright laws announced for each site before collecting any material online.

Reverse Image Search

A reverse image search uses a sample image instead of a search query. It works by uploading an image—or inserting its URL—into a reverse image search engine, which will in turn search its index to find where else this image appears online and display all the other locations. In this way, you can know the original source of photographs, memes, and profile pictures. The following are the most popular reverse image search engine sites:

- *Google reverse search* (`https://www.google.com/imghp`): Google has a dedicated search engine for image reverse searches; you can either paste the image URL in the search box or upload it to Google (see Figure 4-29).

Figure 4-29. *Google reverse image search using an image URL*

- *Karmadecay* (`http://karmadecay.com`): This is a reverse image search on Reddit.com (in beta).

- *TinyEye* (`www.tineye.com`): You can search by image or URL; more than 24 billion images have already been indexed.

- *Reverse Image Search* (`www.reverse-image-search.com`): Conduct a reverse image search with Google, Bing, and Yandex.

- *Imagebrief* (`www.imagebrief.com`): Search for images and use reverse image searches as well.

- *Cam Finds App* (`http://camfindapp.com`): This is an app available for both Android and Apple devices. It uses visual search technology to recognize uploaded pictures and gives instant results about them such as related images, local shopping results, and a vast selection of web results.

- *Image Identification Project* (`https://www.imageidentify.com`): This uses visual search technology to recognize uploaded images.

Image Manipulation Check

OSINT multimedia searches intersect many areas of the digital forensics field. As an online investigator, you should not trust all the multimedia files you acquire. If you are in doubt about any multimedia file (image or video), you should check carefully to assure that it has not been tampered with, meaning manipulated on purpose to hide or alter some facts. Image analysis begins with identifying the source device (camera or mobile phone) used to take the photo. This information is part of image metadata.

As we already mentioned in Chapter 2, all digital file types can include metadata (which is a data about data). Metadata can include a wealth of useful information for your investigation. In Chapter 2 we mentioned some tools to view/edit metadata in images, video, PDFs, and Microsoft Office documents. We will continue here and mention additional tools that are specifically useful for digital images:

- *Forensically* (`https://29a.ch/photo-forensics/#forensic-magnifier`): This site offers free tools for image forensics analysis; it includes clone detection, error-level analysis, metadata extraction, and more.

- *Fotoforensics* (`http://fotoforensics.com`): This offers the forensics analysis of JPEG and PNG files to check for any manipulation using error-level analysis (ELA) techniques.

- *Ghiro* (`www.getghiro.org`): This is an open source tool that can analyze images in bulk and extract metadata information, use GPS metadata to search for nearby images, and perform ELA to detect whether an image has been manipulated. You can download this program as a virtual appliance that is ready to use (it comes installed within Linux Ubuntu).

- *ExifTool* (`https://sno.phy.queensu.ca/~phil/exiftool`): You can read, write, and edit meta-information in a wide variety of files. It supports different metadata formats such as EXIF, GPS, IPTC, XMP, JFIF, GeoTIFF, ICC Profile, Photoshop IRB, FlashPix, AFCP, and ID3.

- *Exif Search* (`https://www.exif-search.com`): This is a commercial search of images by using their metadata.

- *JPEGsnoop* (`www.impulseadventure.com/photo/jpeg-snoop.html`): This analyzes the source of the image to test its authenticity.

- GeoSetter (`www.geosetter.de/en`): You can manipulate/view geodata—and other metadata information—of other images.

- *Lets Enhance* (`https://letsenhance.io`): You can enhance a photo size without losing its quality. The free account allows for 14 images. However, you still need to upload a target image to the server, and this will impose privacy concerns on the uploaded files.

OCR Tools

During your search, you may encounter text written inside images. This text should be extracted first so that it can be edited, formatted, indexed, searched, or translated. The following are popular tools and web services for extracting text from images, known as optical character recognition (OCR):

- FreeOCR (`www.paperfile.net/index.html`)

- Free Online OCR (`www.i2ocr.com`)

- NewOCR (`www.newocr.com`)

Google Drive and Google Docs have integrated OCR support enabled by default. To use this service, you need to upload the image into your Google Drive account (you must have a Google account first) at `https://www.google.com/drive`. Then right-click the uploaded image, select Open With, and choose Google Docs (see Figure 4-30).

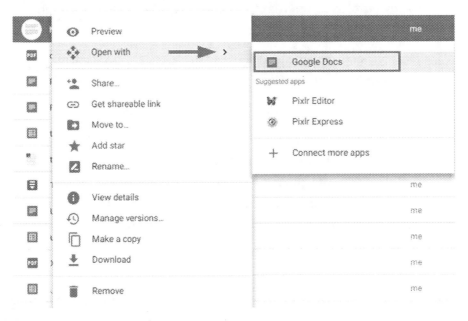

Figure 4-30. *Opening an image file using Google Doc*

You will notice that Google has presented your uploaded image on the top of the document and created an editable OCR text below it (see Figure 4-31).

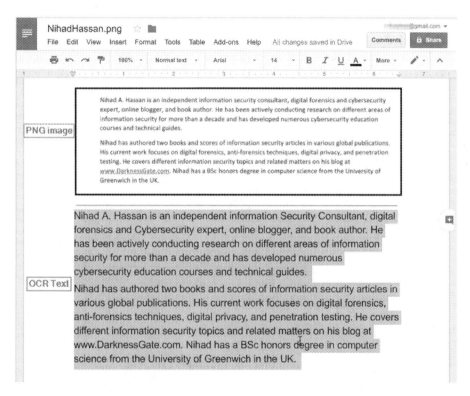

Figure 4-31. *Google Doc changed the text within the uploaded image into editable text*

Video

The technological revolution has affected the way people communicate. For instance, Internet speed is increasing steadily and has become more affordable in most countries around the world. Computing devices such as tables and smartphones are getting cheaper, and almost anyone can acquire one. Many of these devices come equipped with powerful cameras. In fact, people have become used to recording their daily moments using videos; video-sharing websites allow anyone to upload a video file with just a simple click using each site's app.

Video contents can be of great value in any online investigation. In this section, we will list the most important video-sharing sites where you can find different kinds of videos. Then we will cover some techniques and tools to investigate the video content.

Basic Video Search

Here are the most popular sites:

- YouTube (`https://www.youtube.com`)

- Google videos (`https://www.google.com/videohp`)

- Yahoo video search (`https://video.search.yahoo.com`)

- Bing videos (`https://www.bing.com/videos`)

- AOL (`https://www.aol.com/video`)

- StartPage video search (`https://www.startpage.com/eng/video.html`)

- Veoh (`www.veoh.com`)

- Vimeo (`https://vimeo.com`)

- 360daily (`www.360daily.com`)

- Official Facebook video search (`https://www.facebook.com/pg/facebook/videos`)

- Crowd Tangle (Facebook video search) (`www.crowdtangle.com/videosearch`)

- Internet archive open source movies (`https://archive.org/details/opensource_movies`)

- Live Leak (`https://www.liveleak.com`)

- Facebook live video map (`http://facebook.com/livemap`); see Figure 4-32

Figure 4-32. *Facebook live video stream is another source for OSINT investigation*

Here are some other video sites:

- *Meta Tube* (`www.metatube.com`): This is like YouTube.com.

- *Geo Search Tool* (`http://youtube.github.io/geo-search-tool/`
  `search.html`): This searches for all movies according to a specific
  query entered by the user. The result set will be further filtered
  according to the distance from a specific location (city, village,
  intersection) and according to a specific time frame (past hour, past
  two or three hours, etc.).

- *Earth Cam* (`www.earthcam.com`): This is a global network of live
  cameras providing live streaming video from different regions in the
  world.

- *Insecam* (`www.insecam.org`): This is a directory of online surveillance
  security cameras.

> **Note!**   You can use Google to search within any video-sharing site by typing the following search query:
>
> site:*youtube*.com SEARCHTERM
>
> Replace *YouTube* with the video site.

Video Analysis

These are the most popular sites:

- *YouTube DataViewer from Amnesty International* (`https://citizenevidence.amnestyusa.org`): This is an online service that allows you to extract hidden information from videos uploaded to YouTube (see Figure 4-33) like the upload date/time and thumbnails (you can also make a reverse image search on extracted thumbnails using a Google reverse image search).

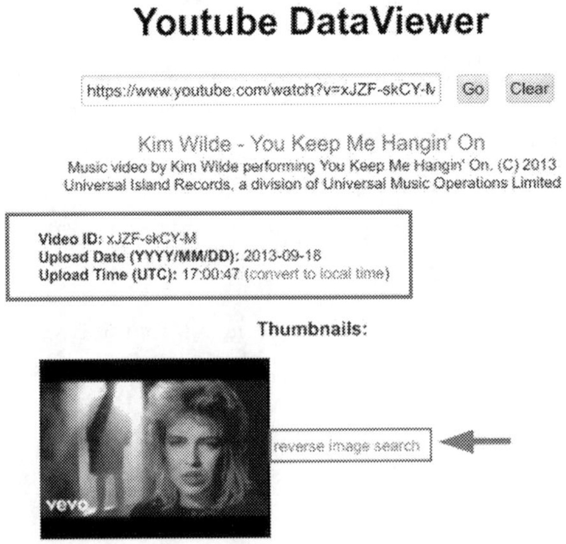

Figure 4-33. *Using YouTube DataViewer to extract metadata about any YouTube video*

- *Ez Gif* (https://ezgif.com/reverse-video): This is a reverse video search and offers many other useful video conversion tools.

- *Print YouTube Video* (https://www.labnol.org/internet/print-youtube-video/28217/): To print a YouTube video storyboard, go to the link provided and add Print YouTube Video to the browser bookmark toolbar. To print any YouTube movie, just access the YouTube video page and click the bookmark (see Figure 4-34). A new page will appear that contains the generated video storyboard images.

Figure 4-34. Print YouTube Videos (source: https://www.labnol.org/internet/print-youtube-video/28217/)

- *Video to Text Converter* (www.360converter.com/conversion/video2TextConversion): This converts video/audio files into text.

- *Montage* (https://montage.storyful.com): This allows team collaborations for analyzing video content.

File Extension and File Signature List

Knowing file extensions and signatures will help you to identify and investigate digital files during your OSINT gathering. The following are two websites for this issue:

- *File Extensions* (`https://www.file-extensions.org/`): This library contains thousands of file extensions and their descriptions.

- *File Signature Table* (`https://garykessler.net/library/file_sigs.html`): List of file extensions and their associated Hex signature.

Productivity Tools

In Chapter 2, we covered some useful tools for making your online investigations more organized. We deferred mentioning the remaining tools until now as they relate to file-searching techniques.

Screen Capture

Sometimes you need to take a screen capture of the whole screen or part of the screen to capture important information (for example, to capture a pop-up message or a portion of online map) and include it in your investigation report. There are many tools to achieve this; these are two popular solutions:

- *Awesome Screenshot Plus* (`https://addons.mozilla.org/en-US/firefox/addon/screenshot-capture-annotate/`): This is a Firefox add-on; it can be used to capture the whole page or any portion of it; annotate it with rectangles, circles, arrows, lines, and text; blur sensitive information; and much more.

- *Greenshot* (`http://getgreenshot.org`): This is an open source screenshot program for Windows. It allows you to create screenshots of a selected region, window, or full screen. It has a built-in image editor to annotate, highlight, or obfuscate parts of the captured screenshots (see Figure 4-35).

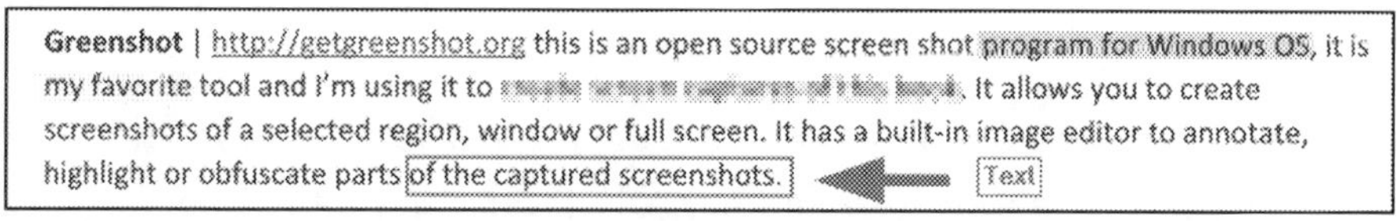

> Greenshot | http://getgreenshot.org this is an open source screen shot program for Windows OS, it is my favorite tool and I'm using it to ▬▬▬ ▬▬▬ ▬▬▬▬ ▬▬ ▬▬. It allows you to create screenshots of a selected region, window or full screen. It has a built-in image editor to annotate, highlight or obfuscate parts of the captured screenshots. ⬅ Text

Figure 4-35. *Greenshot can perform different annotation actions on captured images and is easy to use*

- *Screenshot Machine* (`https://screenshotmachine.com`): This site allows you to take an online screen capture of any specified URL. The captured image can be downloaded to your device.

- *PDF My URL* (`http://pdfmyurl.com`): This is an online service to create PDF documents from any URL in your browser.

Download Online Video

Online investigations require you to search and investigate video files to extract useful hidden information. Sometimes you may need to save (download) a video from the Internet—for example, from a YouTube website—to include it in your investigation or to analyze it further. There are many ways to download videos from the Internet; the easiest method is to use browser add-ons.

Easy YouTube Video Downloader Express

This is a Firefox add-on to download videos from YouTube. It allows the direct download of high-quality video/audio from YouTube (1080p full-HD and 256Kbps MP3) with a single click. You can find it at `https://addons.mozilla.org/en-US/firefox/addon/easy-youtube-video-download`.

YooDownload

If you prefer to use a web service to download videos from different social sites online, YooDownload will help to achieve this easily. Go to `https://yoodownload.com/index.php` and insert the video URL from the social platform (YouTube, Facebook, Instagram, Twitter, Vid, and SoundCloud music); you can also select the video quality before download. The website also offers a browser extension for the Chrome browser.

Dredown

At `https://www.dredown.com`, you can download videos from all major video-sharing sites such as YouTube, Facebook, Instagram, Keek, Twitter, Twitch, Vimeo, Vevo, Tumblr, and more.

You can find other websites for downloading video contents online at `http://deturl.com`.

Video/Audio Converter

You may encounter cases—during your search for videos—where you cannot open a specific video/audio file because of its file format type. To counter such issues, you can use software to convert a video file from its current file format to another one so it can work on supported devices.

- HandBrake (`https://handbrake.fr`): This is an open source program for processing multimedia files and any DVD or Blu-ray disc into a readable format on supported devices; it also supports encoding different audio file types.

- Convert2mp3 (`www.convert2mp3.net`): This is an online service that converts videos with different file formats into MP3 and other audio file formats.

Warning!   There are many web extensions already available to download/convert media files from the Internet. However, we prefer not to use such add-ons as they can gain access to our browser web history, and this may result in a privacy invasion, especially when working on sensitive cases that require secrecy.

Using online services should be more secure when you use these two precaution measures:

A. Do not supply information when using this service (e.g., e-mail, phone number, etc.)

B. Access such services over a VPN connectio n (or using the Tor Browser).

File Search Tools

After collecting a large number of files as part of your online investigation, you may have difficulty finding one specific piece of information when you need it. All operating systems have a built-in search function to locate files and folders on the computer drive. However, they lack an advanced search feature like those offered by some dedicated tools. They are also known to be time-consuming especially when using the Windows search feature on computers with old hardware. (Windows performs background search indexing and consumes a considerable amount of system RAM because it performs thousands of write operations on the hard drive, resulting in slowing down the computer; this problem appears clearly on Windows Vista.)

Being able to search through the files you have collected is an integral part of your OSINT analyzing skills. Your ability to find files fast through automated search will save considerable time than when conducting such searches manually.

To speed up file searches on your computer, you need to have an index of your stored files. The idea is like how people query search engines. When someone queries Google for a search term, Google will search for this term in its index database. When a match is found, the URLs associated with the index search results get retrieved and displayed on the user's browser. Searching for files on computers is similar. You need to have an index of all file names and their locations on your computer hard drives. The list (index) will get stored in a database. Whenever you search for something, you will query the database instead of asking Windows to search manually across all files and folders on the drive. This will effectively give you the fastest results, especially if you have millions of files on your computer hard drive.

Windows can create such an index to locate files faster. However, there are better programs that can do the job better and have more advanced search features. These are some of them:

- *Locate32* (`http://locate32.cogit.net`): Upon the first run, you need to go to the File menu and select Update Databases. This will create the database file that contains the names of all files/folders along with their locations on all hard drives (see Figure 4-36).

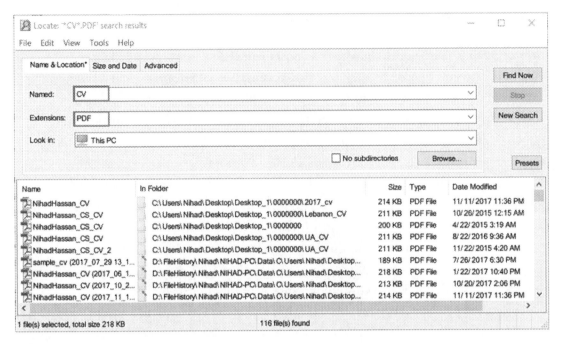

Figure 4-36. *Locate32 sample search result*

- *Everything* (www.voidtools.com): This is a small program that consumes very little system resources; it creates an index database automatically upon start and can index files very fast (it needs one minute to index 1,000,000 files) and can search within file contents. You can search using different methods such as Boolean, regex, wildcards, file types, and macros.

- *FileSeek* (free edition) (https://www.fileseek.ca): This uses multithreading technology to speed up searches and can synchronize search results across different computers in addition to searching within the file's contents using regular expressions.

- *Open Semantic Search* (https://www.opensemanticsearch.org): This open source search engine comes with integrated research tools for easier searching, monitoring, analytics, discovery, and text mining of heterogenous and large document sets and news. It can be installed on your own server or enterprise server and comes with plenty of excellent search features. It is suitable for teams conducting OSINT research on a large volume of datasets.

Summary

In this chapter, we thoroughly covered how to use basic and advanced search engine techniques to locate information online. Although most of your work in this chapter was focused on retrieving data from the surface web, we showed techniques for extracting data from the deep web and provided direct links to a variety of deep web repositories to retrieve information from it.

Major search engines allow its users to search for multimedia content such as videos and images. However, there are specialized search engines for FTP servers and multimedia contents that can return even more results. Bear in mind that images and videos retrieved from the Web can contain useful information associated with them—known as *metadata*—that should be retrieved first. These files must also be investigated using specialized tools to make sure that they have not been manipulated in any way before considering them valid.

In the next chapter, we will continue our discussion of online search techniques, but there we will focus on using different techniques and services to find information about specific people using social media sites and other specialized people-searching engines.

Notes

i.   Netcraft, "January 2017 Web Server Survey" December 05, 2017
     https://news.netcraft.com/archives/2017/01/12/january-
     2017-web-server-survey.html

ii. WWW Size, "The size of the World Wide Web (The Internet)"
     December 05, 2017 www.worldwidewebsize.com

iii. Smart insights "Search Engine Statistics 2017" December 05, 2017
     https://www.smartinsights.com/search-engine-marketing/
     search-engine-statistics

iv. IEEE, "FTP: The Forgotten Cloud" December 05, 2017
     https://www.computer.org/csdl/proceedings/
     dsn/2016/8891/00/8891a503.pdf

CHAPTER 5

Social Media Intelligence

In today's digital age, it is rare to meet a person who is connected to the Internet who doesn't have an account on one or more social media sites. People use social sites to socialize, play games, shop, communicate online, and seek information about anything you can imagine. Facebook, Twitter, YouTube, LinkedIn, and Google have become integral parts of our lives, and hundreds of millions of people spend considerable amounts of time on these platforms daily.

Check out these statistics about the global usage of social media sites:

- As of October 2017, the total worldwide population was 7.6 billion.[i] Of those, 3.5 billion people have an Internet connection, and 3.03 billion of those connected users have an active presence on one or more social media platform.[ii]

- Each Internet user has an average of seven social media accounts.[iii]

- Facebook has 2.07 billion monthly active users as of the third quarter of 2017.[iv]

- As of the third quarter of 2017, Twitter has 330 million monthly active users.

- As of April 2017, LinkedIn has 500 million users in 200 countries.[v]

Social media sites open numerous opportunities for any investigation because of the vast amount of useful information that can be found on them. For example, you can get a great deal of personal information about any person worldwide by just checking this person's Facebook page. Such information often includes the person of interest's connections on Facebook, political views, religion, ethnicity, country of origin, personal images and videos, spouse name (or marital status), home and work addresses, frequently visited locations, social activities (e.g., sports, theater, and restaurant visits),

N. A. Hassan and R. Hijazi, *Open Source Intelligence Methods and Tools*, https://doi.org/10.1007/978-1-4842-3213-2_5

work history, education, important event dates (such as birth date, graduation date, relationship date, or the date when left/start a new job), and social interactions. This can all be found in one Facebook profile, for example. Facebook also helps an outside observer to understand how a particular Facebook user perceives life by just checking the user's current activities and social interactions.

Many estimates show that 90 percent of useful information acquired by intelligence services comes from public sources (OSINT), and the rest comes from traditional covert spying intelligence. Security services gather information in bulk from social sites to gain insight about possible future events worldwide and to profile people on a national scale.

Aside from intelligence gathering, law enforcement uses social media sites as investigative resources to fight crimes. For instance, checking a suspect's Facebook page—or his relatives' and friends' pages—may reveal important information about a criminal case. Sometimes the suspect could be anonymous, but the police could have a picture of him taken by surveillance cameras. In such cases, police use social media sites to engage the public in identifying suspects. Social sites can also be used to track and locate suspects in addition to understanding their behaviors. However, bear in mind that using the information gathered from social media sites in a legal case is generally allowed under these two conditions:

- When acquiring permission from a court to gather information about a specific user, a court order is sent to the intended social media site to hand the information to authorities officially.

- If the information is available publicly (e.g., public posts, images, or videos), then law enforcement can acquire it without a permit, which is the essence of the OSINT concept.

Intelligence gathered from social media can also be useful in the corporate world. For instance, employers can conduct a background check about prospective candidates before offering them a vacancy. The same applies to insurance companies and banks before offering some services (e.g., an insurance contract or a bank loan) to their clients. Global companies—operating in different countries—need to have some form of intelligence about new markets before entering them. Indeed, social media exploitation has become integrated into the majority of businesses to support the decision-making process.

Warning!   Using the information published on social sites to acquire intelligence about a prospect employee should be handled carefully in accordance with the law to avoid triggering a claim of discrimination by the prospective employee.

In this chapter, we will show investigators how to find information on social media sites. There are a plethora of tools and online services to dive beyond basic the search functions available for each social site. We will demonstrate how to use such services/tools to aggregate information about any target online, but before we begin our discussion about how to retrieve information from the most popular social media sites, we'll first explain the term *social media intelligence* and differentiate between the different types of social media sites currently available.

What Is Social Media Intelligence?

Social media intelligence (SOCMINT) refers to the information gathered from social media platforms. The resources available on social media sites can be either open to the public (e.g., public posts on Facebook) or private. Private information cannot be accessed without proper permission (e.g., Facebook private messages or posts shared with friends). There is a debate between privacy advocates and other security experts about whether information available on social media sites is OSINT. Although the majority of social media sites require their users to register before accessing site contents in full, many surveys show that social media users expect to have some form of privacy for their online activities (even when posting content with public access). However, security experts generally consider information shared on social media sites as belonging to the OSINT domain because it is public information shared on public online platforms and thus can be exploited for different purposes.

Note!   Many U.S. states (about 25 states in 2017[vi]) imposed different restrictions regarding employers' access to workers' (applicants or employees) social media accounts. However, this does not mean that your social media interactions will not get observed—secretly—in one way or another.

There are different types of social media sites, but before listing them, let's first see what content people can publish on social media platforms to get to know the types of information that you can expect to gather.

Social Media Content Types

Aside from browsing the content, people interact with social media sites for different purposes. The following are the general interactions used across different social media sites:

- *Post/comment*: People access social sites to post or write paragraphs of text that can be seen by other users. Each social platform has its own name. On Twitter it's called a *tweet*, while on Facebook it's called a *post* or a *comment* when commenting on other user post. This text can be combined with images, videos, and URLs. See Figure 5-1 for a sample LinkedIn post.

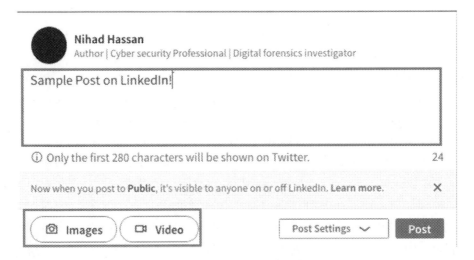

Figure 5-1. Sample post on LinkedIn, which can be associated with either an image or video. The same post can also be shared on Twitter (which requires connecting your Twitter account with your LinkedIn profile).

- *Reply*: This is a text message (can also be an image, video, or URL) that replies to another user's post, update status, or comment.

- *Multimedia content (images and videos)*: Multimedia is popular; a user can upload a video or image as a part of their post. Many social platforms allow their users to upload multiple images/videos to form an album. Live streams also are available on many social platforms such as Facebook and YouTube. This feature allows a user to broadcast live videos and display the recording on their profiles for later viewing.

- *Social interactions*: This is the essence of social media sites, where people get connected online by sending/responding to friend requests sent by their friends, work and study colleagues, roommates, neighbors, family members, and favorite celebrities or actors. The set of online relationships forms what is known as *social networking*.

- *Metadata*: The results from the sum of user interactions with the social platform. Examples include the date and time when a video/image was uploaded, the date and time when a friend request was accepted, geolocation data—if enabled—of the uploaded multimedia file or post, and the type of device used to upload the contents (mobile or a standard computer).

Online investigators want to acquire all these content types—if possible—when conducting their investigations. This ability to do this depends on the privacy control level set by each user when publishing posts/updates online. For example, it is not possible to see other people's updates on Facebook (see Figure 5-2) if they restrict a post's visibility to some friend circles or set it to "Only me."

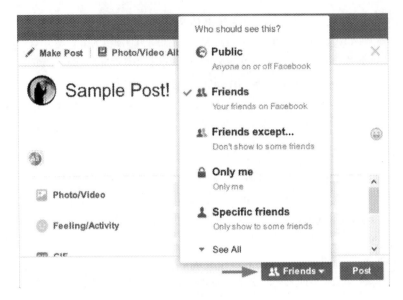

Figure 5-2. *Facebook privacy options to limit a post's visibility*

Bear in mind that information shared on social media sites with family or friend circles cannot be guaranteed to remain private. For example, when you share a personal photo of yourself with a friend and this friend shares this photo in a public status, then others can see your personal photo even though you shared it privately at first.

Classifications of Social Media Platforms

Many people use the terms *social media* and *social networking* interchangeably to refer to Facebook, Twitter, LinkedIn, and related social platforms. This is not absolutely wrong, but it is not accurate because social media is the main umbrella that contains other categories like "social networking" that holds sites like Facebook. Social media contains other types that have similar roles in facilitating interactions between people online.

The following are the main social media types classified according to function:

- *Social networking*: This allows people to connect with other people and businesses (brands) online to share information and ideas. The most obvious examples of this type are Facebook and LinkedIn. (The latter is more focused on the corporate world but shares many similar features with Facebook.)

- *Photo sharing*: Such websites are dedicated to sharing photos between users online. The most popular ones are Instagram (`https://www.instagram.com`) and Flicker (`https://www.flickr.com`).

- *Video sharing*: Such websites are dedicated to sharing videos, including live video broadcasts. The most popular one is `https://www.youtube.com`. Sharing multimedia content is feasible via social networking sites such as Facebook (which offers live video broadcast) and LinkedIn. However, video-sharing sites—like YouTube.com— are dedicated to sharing multimedia content and contain a limited amount of text within them (mainly allowing users to comment on the uploaded videos).

- *Blogs*: This is a type of informational website containing a set of posts—belonging to one topic or subject—organized in descending order according to the publish date. A first blogs were based on static HTML content and created/operated by one author. With the advance of web publishing tools and the emergence of Web 2.0 technology—which simplifies posting content online by nontechnical users—blog usage has been boosted and become available to anyone who wants to have a place online to share his/her ideas. The most popular blogging platforms are WordPress (`https://wordpress.com`) and Blogger (`https://www.blogger.com`), which is powered by Google.

- *Microblog*: This allows users to publish a short text paragraph (which can be associated with an image or video) or a link (URL) to be shared with other audience online. The most popular microblogs are Twitter (`https://twitter.com`) and Tumbler (`https://www.tumblr.com`).

- *Forums (message board)*: This is one of the oldest types of social media. It allows users to share ideas, opinions, expertise, information, and news and discuss it with other users in a form of posted messages and replies. Forums usually come organized into topics. The most popular ones now are Reddit (`https://www.reddit.com`) and Quora | (`https://www.quora.com`).

- *Social gaming*: This refers to playing games online with other players in different locations. Social games allow users to collaborate from different parts around the world to form teams or to challenge other individuals/groups. Facebook has many social games that can be played within a user's web browser; you can check them out at `https://www.facebook.com/games`.

- *Social bookmarking*: These websites offer a similar function to your web browser's typical bookmark. However, they allow you to do this online and share your Internet bookmarks among your friends in addition to adding annotations and tags to your saved bookmarks. Many bookmarking services allow their users to sync the bookmarks with any device or browser, making your bookmarks accessible on multiple devices at the same time. The most popular bookmarking services are Atavi (`https://atavi.com`), Pinterest (`www.pinterest.com`), and Pocket (`https://getpocket.com`).

- *Product/service review*: These websites allow their users to review—give feedback—about any product or service they have used. Other people will find such reviews useful to aid them in their buying decisions. The most popular review sites are Yelp (`https://www.yelp.com`) and Angie's List (`www.angieslistbusinesscenter.com`).

Popular Social Networking Sites

Not all social media sites have the same popularity among users worldwide. Figure 5-3 shows statistics published by Statista.com in September 2017 listing the most popular social media sites ranked by number of active users (in millions). The nature of social media sites is changing rapidly, so such statistics are expected to change frequently during the course of the year. However, the major players are expected to continue dominating the social media market for the near future.

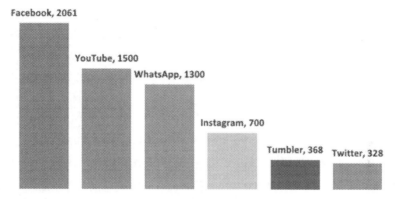

Figure 5-3. *Popular social media sites (source: https://www.statista.com/ statistics/272014/global-social-networks-ranked-by-number-of-users/)*

Investigating Social Media Sites

In this section, we discuss the most popular social media sites and demonstrate how to conduct a smarter search on each one to extract useful and hidden information that cannot be fetched using each site's standard search function. The focus will be on social networking sites because searching within multimedia content was covered in the previous chapter. These sites contain a wealth of personal information and social interactions that can be useful for online investigations.

Facebook

Facebook (www.facebook.com) is the most popular social networking site with the largest active user base on Earth. Facebook has currently more than 2 billion active users worldwide. Facebook is an American company; founded by Mark Zuckerberg in 2004, it was originally developed for Harvard University students to share social information. However, it expanded its membership later to accept students from different U.S. universities. In 2006, Facebook allowed anyone—older than 13 years old with a valid email address—to become a registered member and use its service.

Facebook is so popular that anyone who have an Internet connection worldwide is expected to have a Facebook account! Facebook facilitates sharing different types of online content (images, videos, text messages, live broadcast, check-ins) between people, which is what makes it popular among varied user groups around the globe.

A lot of information can be found in each Facebook user account. For instance, to create a Facebook account, you need to supply your email (or phone number) as a username, a password, your date of birth, and your gender. After creating and activating your Facebook account, you can add more information about yourself such as work and education information, places you have lived in, contact information (email, phone number, address, a public key for receiving encrypted messages), religious and political views, languages, other social accounts (Twitter and LinkedIn), your personal blog or website, family and relationships, and other information about you in addition to live events.

Facebook allows its registered users to do different social interactions such as the following:

- Share updates, photos, videos, and geolocation data (e.g., your current location using the check-in feature) with friends

- See friends' updates/posts, respond with comments, and like or share their updates

- Invite your friends to join groups and attend events

- Chat using Facebook Messenger and send direct private messages to another Facebook member

- Play online games within your web browser (multiplayers games are supported)

- Follow company/brand news

- Make connections with your favorite actors, celebrities, and other public entities

- Use Facebook account credentials to sign into different services across the Web

- Make live video broadcasts using Facebook Live (`https://live.fb.com`)

- Get Facebook support, which implements a variety of privacy settings on all content published by its users to restrict content visibility according to each user need

As noted, the sum of personal information and social interactions available publicly on Facebook provides a wealth of information for any OSINT gathering. As we already said, gathering personal information from Facebook about any target is dependent on the privacy controls set for their updates and social interactions. However, many studies show that the majority of Facebook users do not give much thought to privacy issues when using this platform.

The data volume stored within the Facebook database is huge. Facebook stores about 300 petabytes of data (in March 2017).[vii] This is equal to 300,000,000 gigabytes. Every minute on Facebook, 510,000 comments are posted, 293,000 statuses are updated, and 136,000 photos are uploaded.[viii] To locate information within this jungle, Facebook has developed its own search mechanism to simplify searching for different content types generated by its users' interactions, and this what we will cover in the next section.

Facebook Graph Search

Facebook offers an advanced semantic search engine to locate anything within its database by using natural English language phrases and keywords. This semantic search engine is called Graph Search and was first introduced in early 2013; it allows Facebook users to type in their queries in the Facebook search box to return accurate results based on their questions/phrases or combined keywords. The returned results are quite informative and different from the traditional search approach, which works by returning lists of links based on searched keywords only. For example, you can type **Pages liked by my friends** and Facebook will return a list of pages liked by all your friends list, or you can simply type **Pages liked by ***********, replacing the asterisks with the target's Facebook username, to return a list of pages liked by the specified user.

Note!   You must have a Facebook account to conduct the searches used in this chapter. It is advisable to use a dummy email account when creating this account to avoid revealing your true identity when conducting advanced searches on Facebook (specifically applicable to law enforcement).

Warning!   Facebook policy prohibits opening accounts with false identities. Take this into consideration when using visible Facebook data for a lawsuit.

Now, to use the Facebook Graph Search, you need first to sign into your Facebook account and then change your account language settings to use the English language (US). After doing this, your account is ready to use Facebook Graph Search. To change your Facebook account language, follow these steps:

1. Log in to your Facebook account and click the down arrow shown at the top-right corner of your screen.

2. Click Settings to access the account settings where you can change all your Facebook account settings (see Figure 5-4).

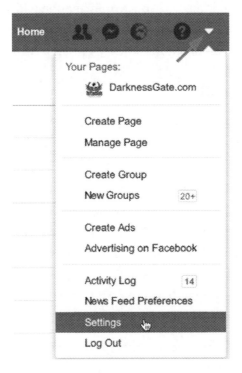

Figure 5-4. *Accessing Facebook account settings*

3. Click Languages on the left side of the page, and make sure that the option "What language do you want to use Facebook in?" is set to English (US), as shown in Figure 5-5.

Figure 5-5. *Setting the Facebook account language to English (US) to use the Facebook semantic search engine known as Graph Search*

After updating your Facebook account to use the English (US) language and thus activating Graph Search, you can type in Facebook search bar anything you want to search for. For instance, you can search for people, your target's friends, places (towns, countries, historical places), things, photos, pages, groups, apps, events, and restaurants, in addition to entertainment such as music, movies or games. Once your search criteria is entered into the search bar, Facebook will show a list of suggestions; you can either select something from the list or opt for your entered one (see Figure 5-6).

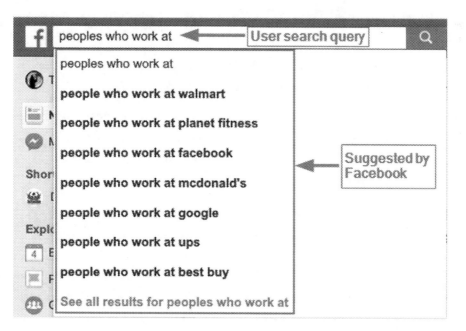

Figure 5-6. *Facebook showing suggested searches based on your entered search query*

215

Knowing how to use Facebook Graph Search is important for online investigators to exploit Facebook's repository of data. Each Facebook account—or page—is linked to its user social interactions (like, tag, share, friends list, work, university/school and education information, movie, song, events, geolocation data, and locations). The investigator has to type the right search query to fetch such results. In a nutshell, Graph Search helps you to map each Facebook account to its associated activities on Facebook.

Now we'll give some examples of Facebook Graph Search queries to activate your imagination on how to build different search queries to extract accurate results from Facebook.

To search for people on Facebook, use these queries:

- *Peoples named [FirstName LastName] who live in [City, State].* Here's an example: **people named Nihad Hassan who live in Buffalo, New York**.

- *People who live in [city, state] and are [single/married] and like [something].* Here's an example: **people who work in Seattle, Washington and are single and like Lebanese restaurants**.

- *People who are [Profession Name] and live in [City, State]. Here's an example:* **People who are Programmer and live in London, UK**.

- *People who like [Page Name] and live in [Place].* Here's an example: **people who like apress and live in New York, USA**.

- *People who work at [Company].* Here's an example: **people who work at Apress**. This query can be refined to search for people working at the Apress company as authors: **people who work at Apress as author** (see Figure 5-7).

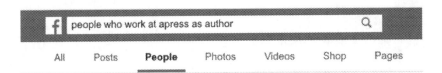

Figure 5-7. *Finding people who work at a specific company with a specific role*

- *People who live in [Country] and like [Page Name].* Here's an example: **people who live in USA and like Al-Qaeda**.

To search for specific pages on Facebook, try the following queries:

- *Pages named [Name].* Here's an example: **pages named Al-Qaeda**.

- *Pages liked by [Name].* Here's an example: **Pages liked by Mark Zuckerberg**.

- *Pages liked by [Profession].* Here's an example: **pages liked by teachers**.

To search for professions, businesses, or services, try the following search queries:

- *Dentist in [City].* Here's an example: **Dentist in Manhattan, New York**.

- *[Profession Name] named [Name].* Here's an example: **Teachers named John Walker**.

To search for posts, use these:

- *Posts liked by people who like [Page].* Here's an example: **Posts liked by people who like Apress**.

- *Posts liked by people who live in [city, state] and work at [company].* Here's an example: **Posts liked by people who live in Dallas, Texas and work at Google**.

- *Posts by [FirstName LastName] from year.* Here's an example: **Posts by Nihad Hassan from the year 2011**.

Tip!   Monitoring a target's "post time" on Facebook may reveal what time the person wakes up each day.

Note!   Using Facebook Graph Search may return a large number of results. To refine your search results, you can use the Graph Search filters on the left side of the page (see Figure 5-8).

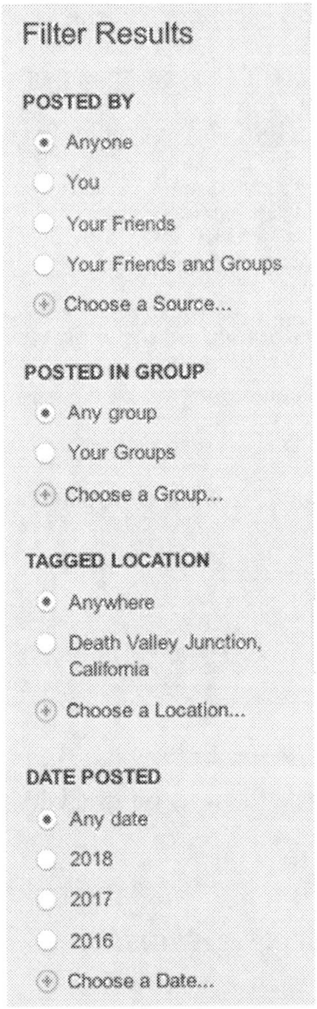

Figure 5-8. *The Facebook Graph Search filters help you to refine your search results*

To use the advanced Facebook Graph Search, you need to know the target's Facebook profile ID (pages and groups also have their own IDs). To get the target's Facebook profile ID manually, do the following:

1. Go to the target's Facebook page, right-click the page and select View Page Source (see Figure 5-9).

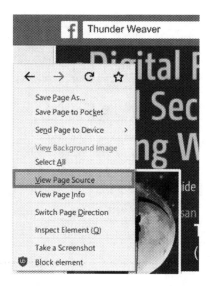

Figure 5-9. *Viewing a target's Facebook page HTML code to find their profile ID*

2. Press Ctrl+F (in IE, Firefox, Chrome, or Opera) to search within
    the HTML source code. Enter **profile_id** as the search criteria.
    The number beside it is the target Facebook unique profile ID
    (see Figure 5-10).

Figure 5-10. *Finding the unique Facebook profile ID*

After knowing how to find target Facebook profile ID (the same applies to Facebook
pages and groups), let's use it to find a list of publicly viewable photos of a target. This
time, you will insert your search query in a browser's address bar instead of using the
Facebook search bar.

A Graph Search web address always starts with this: https://www.facebook.com/
search/.

To search for photos liked by a target Facebook user, type the query shown in
Figure 5-11 in a browser's address bar (the highlighted number points to the target's
Facebook profile ID).

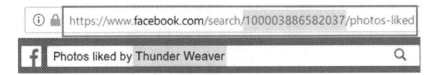

Figure 5-11. *Searching for photos liked by a target Facebook user*

In the same way, you can modify the query to return photos commented on or tagged by the target user.

Note!   Replace the number 100003886582037 with your target Facebook profile ID in all the following queries.

Use `https://www.facebook.com/search/100003886582037/photos-commented` to find photos commented on by the target.

Use `https://www.facebook.com/search/100003886582037/photos-tagged` to find all photos tagged with a target profile.

The *photos-of* query returns all photos uploaded by the target's profile in addition to all photos where the target was tagged or mentioned; consider this query as a container for showing all publicly available photos of a target profile: `https://www.facebook.com/search/100003886582037/photos-of`.

Note!   Facebook Photo queries also work for Videos. Replace `photos` with `videos` in your search query.

To see a list of places visited by your target profile, use this: `https://www.facebook.com/search/100003886582037/places-visited`.

To see a list of places liked by target profile, use this: `https://www.facebook.com/search/100003886582037/places-liked`.

To see a list of places checked in at, use this: `https://www.facebook.com/search/100003886582037/places-checked-in`.

To see the target's friend list (if it is set to public), use the following: `https://www.facebook.com/search/100003886582037/friends`. This will also reveal when each Facebook friendship began (see Figure 5-12).

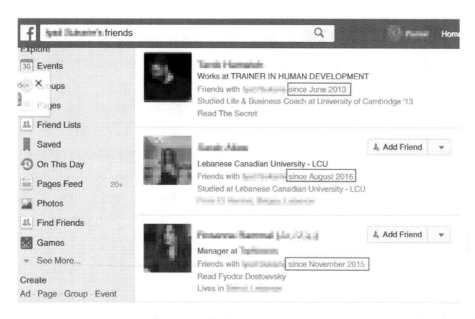

Figure 5-12. *Investigating the target's Facebook friend list will reveal when the target friendship relationship began*

To see a list of events attended by target profile, use this: `https://www.facebook.com/search/100003886582037/events-joined`.

If your target Facebook account has not restricted their friend list from public view, you can also conduct the following queries on your target Facebook friends:

- To see a list of photos uploaded by target friends, type the following query: `https://www.facebook.com/search/100003886582037/friends/photos-uploaded`.

- To see a list of photos liked by target friends, use this: `https://www.facebook.com/search/100003886582037/friends/photos-liked`.

- To see a list of photos commented on by target friends, use this: `https://www.facebook.com/search/100003886582037/friends/photos-commented`.

- To see the places visited by target friends, use this `https://www.facebook.com/search/100003886582037/friends/places-visited`.

- To see the friends of target friends, use this: `https://www.facebook.com/search/100003886582037/friends/friends`.

Note!   Before using Facebook Graph Search, always begin your search on Facebook using your target's full name (if you have it). Although Facebook prohibits registering with false names, there is a great number of Facebook accounts with false names, so you cannot always depend on searching by name. As a second option, try to search using the target's Facebook email address and phone number (if you have them). Please note that searching using email and phone numbers will return no results if the target's privacy control is set to prevent them from appearing on Facebook search. If nothing gives you the required results, try to access the target target's known associate profiles; you may find something that can help you to find your target's real profile.

Other Useful Facebook Graph Search Commands

To search for all people who like a specific page on Facebook, type the query shown in Figure 5-13 in your browser address bar, replacing the highlighted number with your target page profile ID.

Figure 5-13.   *Finding all people who like a specific page on Facebook*

Tracking Photos Downloaded from Facebook to Its Source Profile

When a user uploads a photo to Facebook, its name will get changed upon saving it in the Facebook database. The new name will usually consist of three long numbers, and the file will be in the JPG format. The second number is relevant to the Facebook profile that upload this image to Facebook originally. To know the source Facebook account behind this image, copy the second number and paste it after Facebook web address www.facebook.com/. This should take you to the source Facebook profile (see Figure 5-14). For this tip to work, the image of interest should be posted publicly or your Facebook account must be a friend of the target profile if the image was originally shared with the friend circle.

Figure 5-14.   *Tracking a picture downloaded from the Internet to its source Facebook account uploader*

Note!   Many Facebook users use the same profile photo across different social platforms. To conduct a reverse image search to see where a particular Facebook profile photo appears online, use a service like Google Images (`https://images.google.com`) or Tineye (`www.tineye.com`).

Using Google to Search Facebook Content

Google can be used effectively to search within Facebook public pages using the *site:facebook.com* search operator, which limits a Google search to a specified website only. Other Google advanced search operators—already covered in Chapter 4—can be used to locate accurate information within Facebook. See Figure 5-15 for an example.

Figure 5-15. *Using a Google advanced search operator to locate information within Facebook*

Search for Hashtags on Facebook

To search for posts, photos, or pages that have hashtags, type the Facebook address into the web browser address bar followed by the specified hashtag, as in `https://www.facebook.com/hashtag`.

For example, entering **https://www.facebook.com/hashtag/Terrorism** will display related contents on Facebook that carry the *#Terrorism* hashtag.

Tip!   You can search multiple social media sites (Facebook, Twitter, Pinterest, Instagram) for a specific hashtag by going to `https://www.hashatit.com`.

Using Automated Services to Facilitate Facebook Graph Search

Searching using Facebook Graph Search is easy; you need to use your imagination and create queries that best suit your needs. There are online services that facilitate using Graph Search; all you need to do is to enter target Facebook username or profile ID, and the online service will conduct the advanced search queries—already discussed—for you (of course, only public viewable information will appear). The following are the most popular Facebook Graph Search generators.

Facebook Scanner

This website (`https://stalkscan.com`) allows you to investigate the public information of any Facebook user. To use this service, enter the Facebook URL of the target profile, and the site will populate the page with all the public social interactions produced by the profile of interest (see Figure 5-16).

Figure 5-16. *This site can reveal public information from any Facebook profile*

Graph

This site (`http://graph.tips`) offers a simple graphical user interface to use the Facebook Graph Search to locate public information about any Facebook user. You need to supply the target's Facebook username (which can be extracted from visiting the target's Facebook profile page, as shown in Figure 5-17), and the website will do the remaining work for you.

Figure 5-17. *The Facebook username (highlighted) is different from the name chosen by the user when creating an account (which appears in the Facebook search bar when visiting the target's profile page)*

peoplefindThor

This site (`https://peoplefindthor.dk`) is a Facebook Graph Search generator with the most commonly used filters (see Figure 5-18).

Figure 5-18. *peoplefindThor Facebook search filter*

Socmint

This site (`http://socmint.tools`) facilitates fetching information using Facebook Graph Search.

Facebook Graph Search is continually evolving as are its commands. Success in exploiting this search engine requires trial and error to find the query that returns the best results. You can achieve this by trying different variations of the same query (changing the query wording) to get the desired result. Bear in mind that Graph Search can be somehow dependent on your friend and mutual friend lists; the spread and diversity of your Facebook network can affect the overall Graph Search's generated results.

Online Facebook Search Tools/Services

There are many online services that simplify the process of acquiring/analyzing information from Facebook accounts. The following are the most useful ones:

- *Lookup ID* (`https://lookup-id.com`): This site helps you to find Facebook personal IDs. These IDs are necessary to conduct advanced searches using Facebook Graph Search.

- *FindMyFbid* (`https://findmyfbid.com`): Find your Facebook personal numeric ID.

- *Facebook Page Barometer* (`http://barometer.agorapulse.com`): This site gives statistics and insight about specific Facebook profiles or pages.

- *Facebook Search Tool* (`http://netbootcamp.org/facebook.html`): Conduct advanced searches on Facebook.

- *LikeAlyzer* (`https://likealyzer.com`): Analyze and monitor Facebook pages.

- *Facebook Live video search* (`https://www.facelive.org`): Showing live Facebook video braodcast.

- *Wallflux* (`https://www.wallflux.com`): This site provides RSS feeds and updates for recent posts in Facebook groups and pages.

- *Facebook People/Pages/Places name directory* (`https://www.facebook.com/directory/people`): This site lists people who have public search listings available on Facebook.

- *Information for Law Enforcement Authorities* (`https://www.facebook.com/safety/groups/law/guidelines`): Offers information and legal guidelines for law enforcement/authorities when seeking information from Facebook and Instagram.

- *Who Posted What?* (`https://whopostedwhat.com/staging`): This is a Facebook keyword search generator. It searches Facebook posts and limits the results to a specific date.

- *Signal* (`https://www.facebook.com/facebookmedia/get-started/signal`): This service is used by journalists to collect relevant trends, photos, videos, and posts from Facebook and Instagram to include them in their media broadcasts. The service is available for free for journalists.

Collecting Local Copy of Target Facebook Data

If you are collecting evidence from Facebook for a lawsuit, make sure to save a copy of your findings (evidence) somewhere on your computer. Facebook is managed by its users, and any public post/photo can be suddenly deleted or become private by its owner. To save a copy of the posts or public profiles, save the page using your browser by selecting File and then Save Page As. Or you can simply print the specified page on paper. You can also take a screen capture of the page and save it as an image on your local computer.

OSINT analysts may need an offline version of the target's Facebook data to make an advanced offline analysis or to create reports about a specific user profile or page. The Facebook native user interface does not provide any means of saving or printing a profile data for offline use, and saving a public profile page as an HTML page may not be a convenient solution, especially when you want to save a long page. `http://le-tools.com` has developed a tool named ExtractFace to automate the extraction of data from Facebook profiles. To use this tool, follow these steps:

1. Download the tool from `https://sourceforge.net/projects/extractface/?source=typ_redirect`. Currently, the following prerequisites should be implemented before using this tool:

   - You need to access your Facebook account using the Firefox ESR edition, which can be downloaded from `https://www.mozilla.org/en-US/firefox/organizations/all/`.

   - You need the MozRepl add-on, which can be found at `https://addons.mozilla.org/en-US/firefox/addon/mozrepl/`. After installing this add-on, you need to start it or set the "Activate on startup" option to start it automatically when Firefox launches (see Figure 5-19).

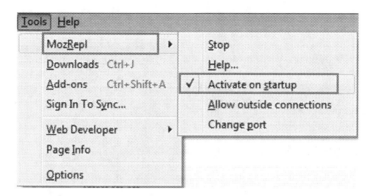

Figure 5-19. *Starting the MozRepl add-on or setting it to start automatically upon launching Firefox*

- And of course you need to have a valid Facebook account, and you must sign into it when using this tool.

Warning!   Deactivate your firewall or allow connections to port 4242 before using this tool.

---

2. To begin harvesting the target's Facebook data, go to the target's profile and right-click the ExtractFace icon—which is located in the Windows taskbar—to launch its options menu (see Figure 5-20).

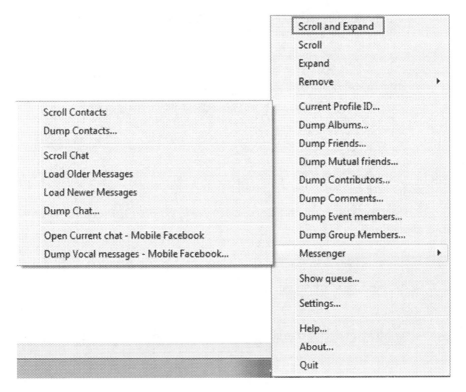

Figure 5-20. *Viewing ExtractFace options*

3.   The first option in the menu is Scroll and Expand. It is advisable to
     use this option first before collecting the target's friends, timeline,
     and comments (posts, photos, and video comments) as it will
     automate the process of scrolling through the entire page until the
     end before harvesting its data. This is necessary to avoid acquiring
     partial results from this tool when visiting lengthy pages or when
     you have slow Internet connection.

For example, to harvest a target's Facebook friend list, go first to the target's
Facebook friend page, click the Scroll and Expand option to begin scrolling across the
entire page, and click Dump Friends. A pop-up menu will appear asking you to select
where you want to store your dump files. Select the location, and finally click the "Dump
now" button (see Figure 5-21).

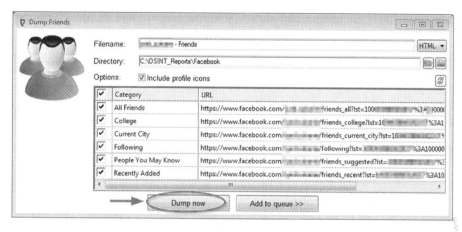

Figure 5-21. *Dumping a target's Facebook friends list using the ExtractFace tool*

Most ExtractFace tool functions work with all people, pages, and group profiles.

Tip!   Facebook does not notify the user when someone visits their Facebook profile or views their photo or video.

If you come across a locked-down Facebook profile (we mean here an account that has tightened privacy controls by hiding its friend list), you can reverse engineer the list of friends from the likes and tags associated with this account.

Twitter

Twitter is the most popular microblogging social media platform with an average 330 million active users monthly (as of the third quarter of 2017).[ix] It launched in 2006 with a main focus on sending SMS mobile communications messages online. Twitter allowed its users to post tweets with 140 characters. In 2017, Twitter expanded its characters count to allow 280 characters. Tweets can contain photos, short videos, and URLs in addition to text.

Twitter is mainly used to connect people with the same interests based on the content posted. To build online communities, Twitter use hashtags (prefixed with pound symbol, #) to group similar topics or subjects. People—even when they do not know each other—can engage in conversation based on a hashtag.

To register on Twitter, you need to have a phone number or email address to activate your account. In addition to a password, Twitter does not enforce using real names when registering for an account. Twitter uses the name *handle* to mean a Twitter username. A Twitter handle begins with the @ sign followed by alphanumeric characters without spaces (e.g., @darknessgate). A Twitter handle can be used to mention someone in public tweets or to send someone a private message. When using Twitter, you can follow other Twitter public profiles, and their updates will appear in your timeline.

Twitter allows you to conduct live video broadcasts using the Twitter Periscope service; you need to use the Twitter official app for this to work using your Android or Apple device.

Although the nature of Twitter does not provide the wealth of personal information provided by Facebook or LinkedIn (covered next), it's still considered a powerful social media platform that can reveal useful OSINT information about some targets when investigated properly. For instance, geolocation data, personal interests, political and religious views, trips, and friends can be revealed by checking someone's Twitter account.

Twitter Search

Twitter has a simple search functionality located in the upper-right side of the screen—when using the Twitter web interface—after logging into your Twitter account. A Twitter simple search allows you to perform a basic search within the Twitter database. However, do not underestimate this little box, as you can add advanced search operators—similar to Google advanced search operators—to your search query to force it to dive deep and return accurate results, as you are going to see next.

The best place to begin your Twitter search is to go to the Twitter search home at https://twitter.com/search-home (see Figure 5-22). From here, you can either conduct simple searches (e.g., search for Twitter profiles or tweets) or click "advanced search" to go to the Twitter advanced search page where you can set different filters on your search.

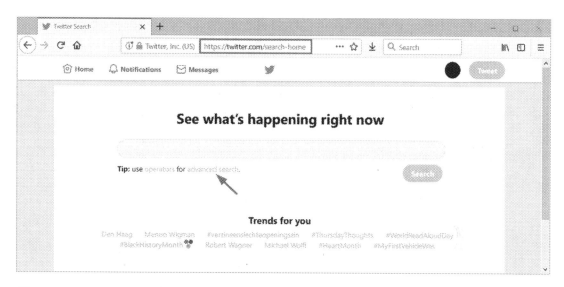

Figure 5-22. *Twitter home search page*

Twitter Advanced Search Operators

The Twitter database is getting larger daily. About 8,000 tweets are posted each second.[x] This is equal to 480,000 tweets each minute. To find your way within this huge volume of data, it is necessary to use advanced search operators to refine your searches. The following search operators can be incorporated into a Twitter simple search to find related tweets more precisely:

- Use the "" operator to search for an exact phrase or word. Here's an example: **"OSINT intelligence"**.

- To search for more than one search term, use the *OR* operator. Here's an example: **OSINT OR intelligence** (this will search for tweets containing either the word *OSINT* or the word *Intelligence* or both).

- The negation operator (-) is used to exclude specific keywords or phrases from search results. Here's an example: **virus -computer**. (This will search for tweets with the word *Virus* but not related to computer viruses.) The negation query can be expanded to exclude more words/phrases using the *OR* operator like this: **Eiffel tower-(trip OR new year OR vacation)**. This will search for *Eiffel tower* and exclude tweets about *trip* and *new year* and *vacation*.

- To search for tweets containing a specific hashtag, use the (#) pound sign. Here's an example: **#OSINT** (this will search for all tweets containing the *OSINT* hashtag).

- To search for tweets sent from a specific Twitter account, use the operator *from*. Here's an example: **from:darknessgate** (this will retrieve all tweets sent from the *darknessgate* account. You can filter the results based on people, photos, news, etc. (see Figure 5-23).

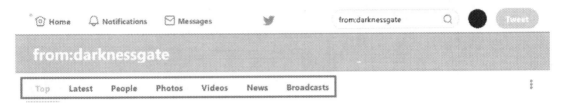

Figure 5-23. *You can use Twitter default filters to narrow your search results within a specific result set after using the From operator*

- The *to* operator followed by the Twitter handle will show all tweets sent to a specific person. Here's an example: **to:darknessgate** (this will retrieve all tweets sent to the *darknessgate* account). You can filter the results based on people, photos, news, etc., as we did with the *from* operator.

- To find all tweets that reference a specific Twitter account, use the @ operator. Here's an example: **@darknessgate** (this will retrieve all tweets that reference the *darknessgate* account).

- To search for tweets sent from a specific location, use the *near* operator followed by the location name. Here's an example: **"happy birthday" near New York** (this will search for tweets containing the exact phrase *happy birthday* and sent from near *New York*).

- To search for tweets sent from within a specific distance from a specific location, use the *within* operator. Here's an example: **near:LA within:15mi** (this will return tweets sent within 15 miles from Los Angeles).

- To search for tweets sent since a specific date, use the *since* operator followed by the date. Here's an example: **OSINT since:2014-11-30** (this will return all tweets containing *OSINT* and sent since November 11, 2014).

- To search for tweets sent up to a specific date, use the *until* operator. Here's an example: **OSINT until:2015-11-30** (this will return all tweets containing *OSINT* and sent until date November 30, 2015).

- To find all tweets that ask a question, use the *?* operator. Here's an example: **OSINT ?** (this will return all tweets containing *OSINT* and asking a question).

The *Filter* operator is powerful to filter results based on different criteria. The following are examples of the most popular filters:

- To search within a Twitter conversation, use the *filter* operator with the *replies* keyword. Here's an example: **OSINT Filter:replies** (this will return all tweets that contain the keyword *OSINT* and are replies to other tweets).

- Use the *images* keyword to return tweets that contain an image within it. Here's an example: **OSINT Filter:images** (this will return all tweets that contain the keyword *OSINT* and have an image embedded within them).

- To return tweets with video embedded with them, use the *videos* keyword (similar to the *images* filter). Here's an example: **OSINT Filter:videos**.

- To return tweets containing an uploaded video, Amplify video, or Periscope video, use the *native_video* operator. Here's an example: **OSINT filter:native_video** (this will return all tweets containing the search keyword *OSINT* that have an uploaded video, Amplify video, or Periscope video).

- To return tweets with either image or video, use the *media* operator. Here's an example: **OSINT Filter:media**.

- To return tweets with a news URL linked to them, use the *news* keyword. Here's an example: **OSINT Filter:news** (this will return tweets containing *OSINT* within them that are mentioned by a news source).

- To return tweets that contain a link (URL) within them, use the *links* keyword. Here's an example: **OSINT Filter:links**.

- To return text-only tweets, use the *text* keyword. Here's an example: **OSINT Filter:text**.

- To return tweets from verified users only (verified accounts have a blue check mark near their names), use the *Verified* operator. Here's an example: **OSINT Filter:verified**.

Tip!   You can use the negation operator (-) with the *Filter* operator to reverse the examples already mentioned. For example, typing **OSINT -Filter:images** will return all tweets containing the *OSINT* search keyword but not containing images embedded within them.

- To search for video uploaded using the Twitter Periscope service, use the *Periscope* filter. Here's an example: **OSINT filter:periscope** (this will search for all tweets containing the *OSINT* keyword with a Periscope video URL).

To search for tweets according to the number of likes, replies, and retweets, use the following operators:

- Use the *min_retweets:* operator followed by a number. Here's an example: **OSINT min_retweets:50** (this will return all tweets containing the *OSINT* search keyword that have been retweeted at least 50 times).

- Use the *min_replies:* operator followed a number to return all tweets with NUMBER or more replies. Here's an example: **OSINT min_replies:11** (this will return all tweets containing the *OSINT* search keyword that have 11 or more replies).

- Use *min_faves*: followed by a number to return all tweets with NUMBER or more likes. Here's an example: **OSINT min_faves:11** (this will return all tweets that have at least 11 or more likes and that contain the *OSINT* search keyword).

- To exclude retweets, use the *-RT* operator. Here's an example: **OSINT—RT** (this will search for all tweets containing the *OSINT* search keyword but exclude all retweets).

- To search for tweets from a specific source, use the *source* operator followed by the source name. Here's an example: **OSINT source:tweetdeck** (this will return all tweets containing *OSINT* and sent from *tweetdeck* (common sources are *tweetdeck, twitter_for_iphone, twitter_for_android*, and *twitter_web_client*).

- To limit Twitter returned results to a specific language, use the *lang* operator. Here's an example: **OSINT lang:en** (this will return all tweets containing *OSINT* in the English language only). To see a list of Twitter-supported language codes, go to `https://dev.twitter.com/web/overview/languages`.

Note!   Twitter allows you to save up to 25 saved searches per account. To save your current search result, click "More search actions" at the top of your results page and then click "Save this search."

Please note that you can combine more than one Twitter advanced search operator to conduct a more precise search. For example, type **"OSINT intelligence" from:darknessgate -Filter:replies lang:en** to get only the tweets containing the exact phrase *OSINT intelligence* from the user *darknessgate* that are not replies to other users and in the English language only.

Twitter Advanced Search Page

The Twitter advanced search page (`https://twitter.com/search-advanced`) allows you to set different filters (language, location, keywords, date/time range) to return the best results. You can search for people, hashtags, and photos in any topic (see Figure 5-24).

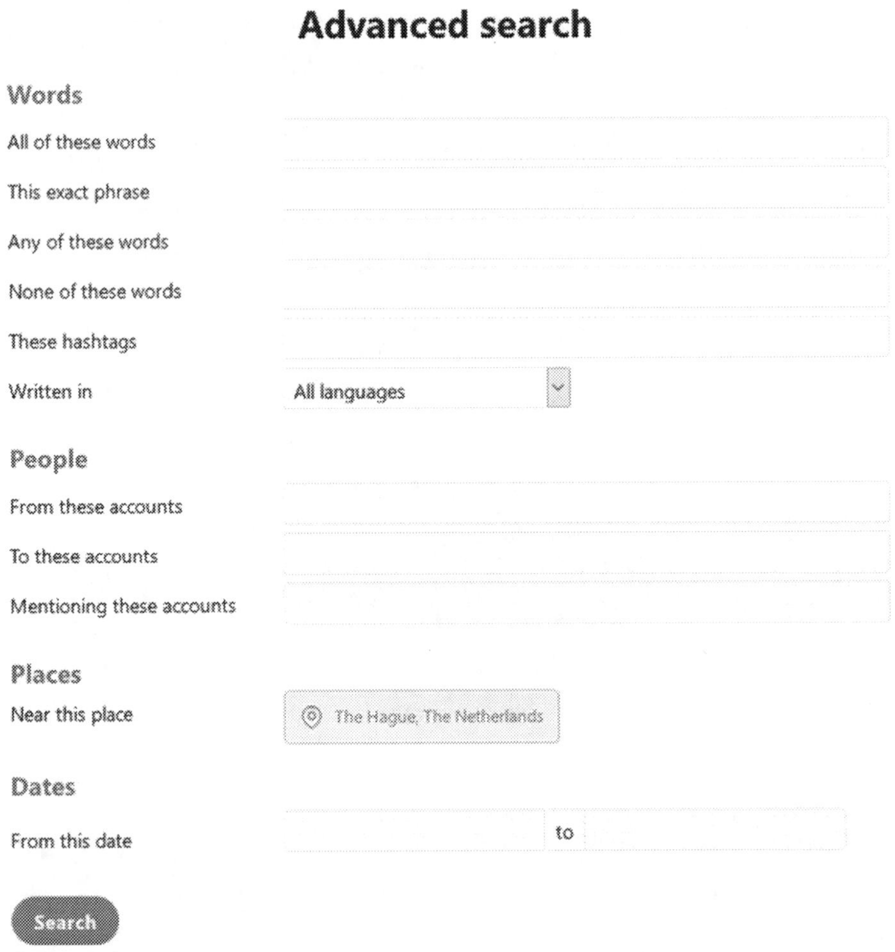

Advanced search

Words

All of these words

This exact phrase

Any of these words

None of these words

These hashtags

Written in   All languages

People

From these accounts

To these accounts

Mentioning these accounts

Places

Near this place   ⊙ The Hague, The Netherlands

Dates

From this date   to

Search

Figure 5-24. *Twitter advanced search page*

Online Twitter Search Tools/Services

The following are online services to help you find information on Twitter:

- *TweetDeck* (`https://tweetdeck.twitter.com`): This is a social
  media dashboard application for managing Twitter accounts in a
  web browser such as Chrome or Firefox. It is popular among desktop
  users and gives you flexibility to manage more than one Twitter
  account using a simple, sleek interface. It also allows you to share an
  account with your team without sharing your password, as you can
  set different access permission on your owned accounts. TweetDeck

shows all Twitter-related activities (activities, messages, notifications, and searches) on one screen. You can add more column types to your screen (e.g., notification, search like, list, collection, activity, messages, mentions, followers, schedule, trending); scroll the page from left to right to see all columns. TweetDeck can be used effectively to search within Twitter and save current searches to see any updated contents reflected automatically. You can also refine your search query using advanced Twitter search operators through an easy-to-use graphical user interface.

- *All My Tweets* (`https://www.allmytweets.net`): View all public tweets posted by any Twitter account on one page.

- *Trendsmap* (`https://www.trendsmap.com`): This shows you the most popular trends, hashtags, and keywords on Twitter from anywhere around the world.

- *Foller* (`http://foller.me`): Analysis Twitter public account data (e.g. profile public information, number of tweets and followers, topics, hashtags, mention).

- *First Tweet* (`http://ctrlq.org/first/`): Find the first tweet of any search keyword or link.

- *Social Bearing* (`https://socialbearing.com/search/followers`): Analyze Twitter followers of any particular account (a maximum of 10,000 followers can be loaded).

- *Twitter Email Test* (`https://pdevesian.eu/tet`): This tests whether an email address is used for a Twitter account. It is useful to know whether a particular user has a Twitter account—maybe under a false name.

- *Twicsy* (`http://twicsy.com/`): Search more than 7,374,661,011 Twitter photos.

- *Follower Wonk* (`https://moz.com/followerwonk/analyze`): Analyze a Twitter user's followers.

- *Sleeping Time* (`http://sleepingtime.org/`): Predict the sleeping schedule of anyone on Twitter.

- *Simple Twitter Profile Analyzer* (https://github.com/x0rz/tweets_analyzer): This is a Python script.

- *Tag Board* (https://tagboard.com): Search for hashtags on Twitter, Facebook, and Google+.

- *TINFOLEAK* (https://tinfoleak.com): Get detailed information about any Twitter account and see what each account leaks. You need to supply your email address to receive the detailed report.

- *TET* (https://pdevesian.eu/tet): Check whether the entered email address is used for a Twitter account.

- *Spoonbill* (https://spoonbill.io): Monitor profile changes from the people you follow on Twitter.

- *Export Tweet* (https://www.exporttweet.com): This is an advanced Twitter analytical service; you can download the generated report for offline usage. To unlock the full features, you need to pay.

Warning!   Many social media analysis services may require you to give them wide access to your Twitter account to function. If you are using a dummy account, you can do this safely; otherwise, make sure not to give permission to services that require access to your account (see Figure 5-25).

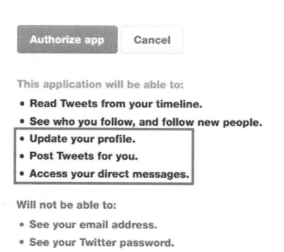

Figure 5-25. *Sample warning issued by Twitter about a third party that requires wide access permission to your account*

Google+

This is a social networking site owned by Google. It is theoretically considered the second largest social media site—after Facebook—in terms of number of registered users. (Google has more than 1.2 billion active monthly users of its free Gmail email service.)However, we cannot conclude that the same number of users is really using the social platform Google+.

The most popular service offered by Google is Gmail, which gives free email service to any Google registered user around the globe, with excellent features in terms of reliability, availability, and storage space. To use any of Google products (e.g., YouTube, Google Drive, Gmail, Google Maps, Google Docs), you need to have a Google account. After signing up for a Google account, you can activate a Google+ account with one click. The nature of this means that the actual number of Google+ users may be much less than the announced statistics. In fact, a study conducted in 2015[xi] shows that the number of active users on Google+ is less than 1 percent of the total Google users. A recent statistic conducted in September 4, 2017,[xii] showed that the total number of unique Google+ monthly visits is 34 million, which is far less than its direct rival Facebook.

Google+ offers similar social interactions to Facebook; people can post status updates, and these updates can be text only or contain—in addition to text—a photo, poll, link (URL), or location. The privacy level of each post can be adjusted according to a user's needs. The Google+ approach to privacy controls is through *circles*. Contrary to Facebook, anyone can add someone to their circle (which is conceptually a list of people) without the need for the other person to add the requester back. This approach is similar to Twitter; people can follow each other to see their updates, but a follow relationship can occur in one direction only (e.g., Nihad can follow Susan, but Susan does not have to follow Nihad).

The Google+ default circle names are Friends, Family, and Acquaintances. The user can create as many circles as needed and can add other people to them. When posting updates to Google+, a user selects which circles they want to share these updates with (see Figure 5-26). Please note that circles are private, so other people will not know in which circle you have put them.

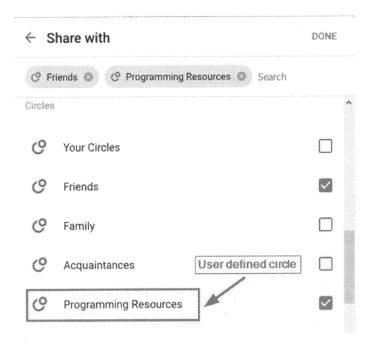

Figure 5-26. *Google+ privacy controls*

We will not delve deeply into Google+ as the actual number of active users is significantly small. In the next section, we will show some techniques to search for people within this platform.

Searching Google+

Similar to other social networks, Google+ allows its users to have a profile that shows some personal information about them. They can adjust the privacy settings of each section of the profile. Some Google+ profile information will also appear across all Google services. The shared data with other Google services includes the following: contact information, education, places (similar to the Facebook check-in feature), links (e.g., personal blog or LinkedIn profile), personal information (gender, birthday), skills, and personal photos.

To begin your search, start with the search bar located at the top of the page and type the person you want to search for. Google+ will give suggestions while you type. The returned results—on the next page—will be grouped into four categories: Communities, People and Pages, Collections, and Posts (see Figure 5-27).

Figure 5-27. *Searching within Google+ using its built-in search functionality*

Google+ Advanced Search Operator

Like Twitter, Facebook, and LinkedIn, Google+ has specialized search operators to help you find precise results easily. The following are the most popular ones.

Note!   Before using the Google+ advanced search operators, you need to know how to find a Google+ profile ID of any user (the username).

1. Log in to your Google+ profile.

2. Click the Profile tab on the left side of the screen.

3. Look at the URL in the address bar. The set of characters after `http://plus.google.com/` is your Google ID (see Figure 5-28).

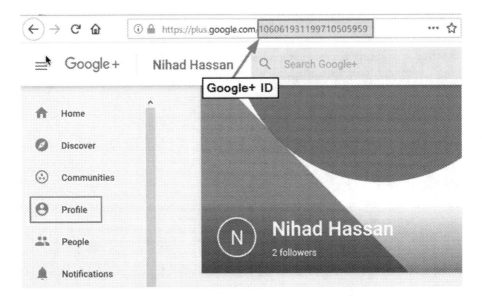

Figure 5-28. *Extracting the Google+ ID from a URL*

4. To see other users' Google IDs, go to each user profile and check the URL in the address bar for the target Google profile ID.

Please note that many Google+ profiles are still using numbers. However, active users have the option to use a customized URL that reflects their real names. Fetching Google+ IDs composed of letters is similar to ones with numbers; you need to copy the letters from the URL (beginning at the +sign).

- To search for hashtags—similar to Twitter—use the pound (#) symbol. Here's an example: **#OSINT**.

- Use the *form* operator to search for posts posted by a specific user. Here's an example: **from: 106061931199710505959** (replace the number with your target Google ID, which can also be composed of letters for some accounts).

- To search for posts by specific type of content, uses the *has* search operator. Here's an example: **OSINT has:photo** (this will return all posts containing *OSINT* that have an image embedded within them). The *photo* part can be replaced with any of the following types: *attachment, poll, video, doc, slides, spreadsheet.*

- To search for posts before or after a specific date, use the *before* or *after* operator. The date format should be as follows: YYYY-MM-DD. Here's an example: **OSINT before:2017-01-16 | OSINT after:2018-01-01**.

- To find posts commented on by a specific user, use the *commenter* operator followed by the target Google ID. Here's an example: **commenter:106061931199710505959**.

- To find all posts that mention a specific user, use the *mention* operator. Here's an example: **mention: 106061931199710505959**.

- To search for posts in a specific community or collection, use the *in* operator. Before giving examples on how to search within communities/collections, follow these steps to find the community or the collection ID on Google+.

  1. Log in to your Google+ profile.

  2. Go to the target community/collection, check the browser address bar, and copy the string of numbers and letters at the end of the URL (see Figure 5-29).

Figure 5-29. *Community ID (highlighted in colors) extracted from Google+ community URL*

- To search within Google+ communities, use *[Search Keyword] in:community* (replace the word *community* with the target's community ID). Here's an example: **pentesting in:112627574116901792152** (this will search for the keyword *pentesting* in the target's community, which has the Google+ ID 112627574116901792152).

- To search within Google+ collections, use *[Search keyword] in:collection* (replace the word *collection* with the target's collection ID). Here's an example: **hacking in:gAAAZ** (this will search for *hacking* within a collection named *gAAAZ*).

- Google+ allows you to use the three logical operators (AND, OR, NOT), but you must write them in capital letters. Here's an example for using each one:

  - Use the NOT operator for negation. Here's an example: **from:106061931199710505959 NOT has:photo** (this will search for all posts sent by the user whose Google ID 106061931199710505959 and not containing a photo). Please note that the NOT operator can be replaced with the minus sign (-) (**from:106061931199710505959—has:photo**).

  - The AND operator is used to search for multiple search keywords. Google+ will automatically add it when separating your search keywords with a space, so there is no need to add it manually. Here's an example: **from:106061931199710505959 AND from:101607398135470979957** (this will search for posts from two Google+ accounts).

  - The OR operator is used to search posts for one or more search keywords. Here's an example: **OSINT has:doc OR has:photo OR has:spreadsheet** (this will search for the keyword *OSINT* in posts that contain *doc* or *photo* or *spreadsheet* within it).

Using Google to Search Within Google+

The Google search engine can be used effectively to search within Google+. As you have done many times before, use the *site* operator to limit your search to Google+ only (site:plus.google.com). Here are some examples:

- **"PERSON NAME" site:plus.google.com** (replace PERSON NAME with target name)

- **"Work at COMPANY NAME" site:plus.google.com** (replace COMPANY NAME with target company)

Searching Google+ Using a Google Custom Search Engine

Here are the most popular Google custom search engines to search within Google Plus profiles:

- Google+ Collections & Communities (http://goo.gl/A8MB7z)

- Google Plus Stalker (https://cse.google.com/cse/publicurl?cx=0 01394533911082033616%3Asvzu2yy2jqg)

- Google+ Photos Custom Search Engine (https://cse.google.com/ cse/publicurl?cx=006205189065513216365:uo99tr1fxjq)

- Google-Plus Profiles (https://cse.google.com/cse/publicurl?cx= 009462381166450434430:cc5gkv2g7nk)

- Retrieve Google+ profiles that have an email address and phone number shared publicly (https://cse.google.com/cse/publicurl? cx=009462381166450434430:cotywcrgpru)

Other Useful Services for Google+

Here are some more sites to check out:

- *Google+ to RSS* (https://gplusrss.com): Create an RSS feed of any Google+ profile or page. The free version allows for two feeds.

- *Google+ User Feed* (http://plusfeed.frosas.net): With this site, you can monitor the feeds of Google+ users. It's useful to monitor your target's posts without visiting their Google+ page.

LinkedIn

LinkedIn is a social networking service dedicated to professional interactions in the business world. Individuals maintain a profile—similar to a résumé—where they present their skills, employment history, and work/project achievements, while corporations maintain a page to promote their business activities and announce vacancies.

LinkedIn started in 2003, so it is considered among the older social media sites. LinkedIn offers its service in 200 countries, and its interface supports 20 languages. The majority of LinkedIn users are in the United States; the second largest segment comes from India followed by Brazil. In December 2016, Microsoft acquired LinkedIn. Currently, LinkedIn has more than 546 million active users worldwide.[xiii]

To have a LinkedIn profile, you must supply your first and last names, email, and a password. LinkedIn has a policy to enforce using real names only; actually it does not make sense to have a false profile here as the essence of LinkedIn is to make connections in the business world, and you need to offer real information to make useful business connections. For privacy-minded people, LinkedIn offers different access permissions that allow each user to tailor their profile's viewable data.

The majority of LinkedIn contents cannot be seen without first logging into your LinkedIn account. If you try to see a LinkedIn profile while you are not logged in, you will encounter a page asking you to register or sign into your account (see Figure 5-30). Some LinkedIn users set high privacy control settings on their accounts to prevent other LinkedIn members from viewing parts of their profile—including the profile picture—unless they become connected on LinkedIn.

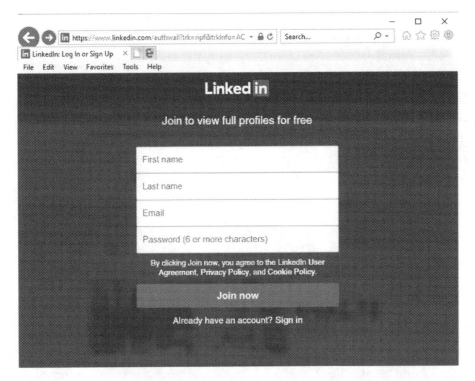

Figure 5-30. *A profile view when the requester is not logged into LinkedIn*

Individual profiles on LinkedIn (see Figure 5-31) hold their name, profession, education, job history (current and previous employment), featured skills and endorsements, recommendations, accomplishments, languages spoken, honors and awards, projects, and interests. People can connect with other professionals on LinkedIn; they can also follow other people or corporate pages, and their updates will appear in the user timeline feed.

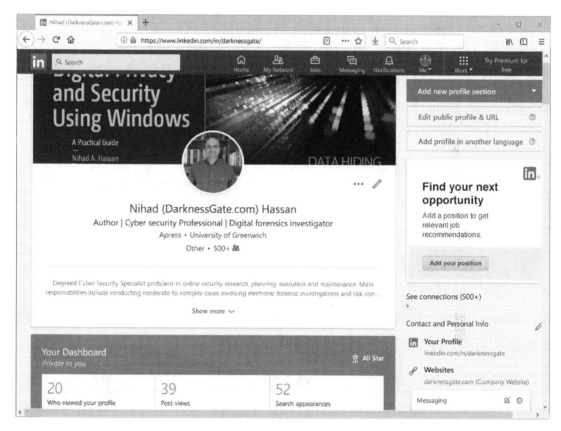

Figure 5-31. *Sample LinkedIn individual profile showing author profile on LinkedIn*

LinkedIn Search

While you are not logged into LinkedIn, you can perform a simple search for people using their first and last names. The search form is located at the bottom of the home page (see Figure 5-32).

Figure 5-32. *Using simple LinkedIn search form located on home page next to "Find a colleague" section to search for people while you are not logged into LinkedIn*

The result of a LinkedIn search—while you are not logged—is a list of matched names with a summary for each one. If you want to access more information about any profile, you need to log in to LinkedIn.

For logged-in users, LinkedIn provides a search bar on top of the page to search for people, jobs, posts, companies, groups, and schools. Using this search bar, you can begin your simple search, and after fetching the results, you can refine your results set using LinkedIn advanced filters.

For example, to search for the keyword *Apress*, type the search keyword **Apress** in the search bar and hit the Enter button. (Note that while typing your search keywords, LinkedIn will give search suggestions that appear in the drop-down list as you type.) Look at the top of the results page and click All Filters (see Figure 5-33) to filter the results according to your needs (see Figure 5-34). Please note that some LinkedIn pages may display LinkedIn search filters on the right side of the page.

Figure 5-33. *Accessing LinkedIn advanced search filters to narrow down your results*

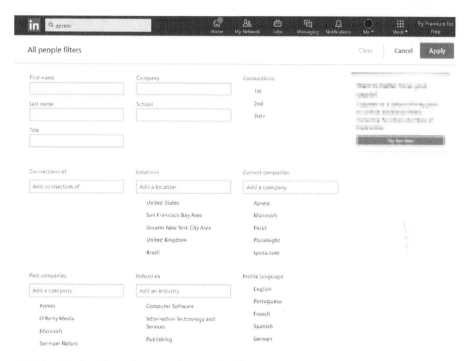

Figure 5-34. *LinkedIn advanced search filters*

Warning!   Whenever you visit someone's profile on LinkedIn, your visit gets recorded, and the visited profile will know about it. You can surf LinkedIn anonymously—after changing your privacy setting (profile viewing options), but you will in turn lose the ability to know who viewed your profile. Please note that users with premium LinkedIn accounts will know who viewed their profile even when the visitor uses LinkedIn in private mode.

LinkedIn advanced search allows you to search according to the target's first and last names, company, school, and title. You can also specify the geographical location of the target to limit your search to one area only. The search can be refined to add other LinkedIn members who might have a connection with this target. In addition, you can filter according to profile language and target current/previous work.

Advanced LinkedIn Search Operators

Similar to Twitter, LinkedIn allows you to use advanced search operators to refine your search. The following are the most popular ones:

- To search for an exact phrase, enclose it in quotation marks. The same technique can be used to search for profiles that have multiple words. Here's an example: **"OSINT intelligence"** (this will search for the exact phrase enclosed within the quotes).

- Use the NOT operator to exclude a particular term. Here's an example: **developer NOT designer**.

- Use the OR operator to include one or more terms together. Here's an example: **developer OR designer** (searches for either a developer or a designer or both).

- Use the AND operator to include two or more terms together. Here's an example: **developer AND designer** (searches for both designer and developer). There's no need to use the AND operator in your search because LinkedIn will add it automatically when you search for more than one term together; just enter a space between your search terms.

- Use parentheses to combine search terms. Here's an example: **penetration tester NOT (developer OR designer)**. This will search for a penetration tester and ignore both developer and designer from search results.

- You can leverage Google to search within LinkedIn using the Google *site* operator. Here's an example: **"Nihad Hassan" site:linkedin.com**.

Searching LinkedIn Using a Google Custom Search

Google custom search engines can become handy to retrieve some results that cannot be fetched easily using typical search engines. The following are a selected set of Google custom searches that prove useful in retrieving data from LinkedIn:

- *Recently Updated Profiles* (https://cse.google.com/cse/public url?cx=009462381166450434430:luit7gbqx2a): This will retrieve recently updated profiles from LinkedIn.

- *LinkedIn Contact Extractor* (`https://cse.google.com/cse/publi curl?cx=001394533911082033616:tm5y1wqwmme`): This will extract LinkedIn profiles that have their contacts publicly accessible. The extracted information includes the Contact, Email, Email2, and Email3 fields.

- *LinkedIn Résumés* (`https://cse.google.com/cse/publicurl?cx=0 10561883190743916877:qa_v6ioerxo#gsc.tab=0`): This will search for updated LinkedIn profiles that have been updated within the past month or two.

- *LinkedIn People Finder (International)* (`https://cse.google.com/cse/home?cx=009679435902400177945:psuoqnxowx8`): Filter the results according to the following countries: United States, Canada, United Kingdom, Ireland, India, New Zealand, China, and Australia.

For your OSINT search work, LinkedIn is considered the first place to search for people who work in a particular profession to find their employment history. For instance, you can figure out a user's experience by seeing their endorsement skills and employment history. The people who endorse the target can also become a target for your search to see their relationship with the main target (e.g., their work relationships, date when worked together, and which projects they worked on). Remember to adjust your account privacy settings to prevent others from knowing your identity when conducting searches on LinkedIn.

General Resources for Locating Information on Social Media Sites

There are many online services that can be used—in accordance with the search techniques already discussed—to find useful information about any target who has a presence on one or more of the social media sites.

- *Buzz Sumo* (`http://buzzsumo.com`): Find the most shared topic or subject that is currently trending on major social media platforms.

- *Key Hole* (`http://keyhole.co`): This offers hashtag and keyword tracking across different social media sites; you can track Twitter accounts, mentions, and URLs.

- *MIT PGP Public Key Server* (http://pgp.mit.edu): Search on the PGP Public Key Server, which can reveal the target's email address. You can use it to conduct further investigations if a target uploaded their public key to such servers.

Note!   You can see a list of all PGP public key servers and check their status at https://sks-keyservers.net/status.

Other Social Media Platforms

We mentioned the most popular social media sites in this chapter. However, talking about all social platforms that exist in the world today would require a book on its own. There are hundreds of active social media sites in the world, and some of them are popular within their own societies only (like the Chinese sites). Table 5-1 lists the other—less popular— social media sites that must also be considered when conducting online investigations.

Table 5-1. *Less Popular Social Media Sites*

Name	Category	URL	Comments
		International Sites	
Reddit	Social news	https://www.reddit.com	Social news aggregation, web content rating, and discussion website
Instagram	Photo sharing	https://www.instagram.com/?hl=en	
Tumblr	Microblogging	https://www.tumblr.com	
Tinder	Location-based social search mobile app	https://tinder.com	
Pinterest	Social network	www.pinterest.com	Multimedia-sharing website
Flickr	Photo sharing	https://www.flickr.com	
classmates	Social sharing	www.classmates.com	

(*continued*)

Table 5-1. (*continued*)

Name	Category	URL	Comments
China			
Qzone	Social network	`http://qzone.qq.com`	Largest Chinese social networking site with more 500 million active users
Sina Weibo	Microblogging social platform	`http://weibo.com/`	A mix between Facebook and Twitter
Baidu	Social forum network	`https://tieba.baidu.com/index.html`	
Russia			
Moemesto.ru	Bookmarking service	`http://moemesto.ru`	
Vkontakte	Social network	`https://vk.com`	Popular in Russia, Ukraine, Belarus, and Kazakhstan
Diary.Ru	Bookmarking site	`www.diary.ru`	
Other Countries			
Draugiem	Social network	`www.draugiem.lv`	Latvia
Hatena	Bookmarking site	`http://b.hatena.ne.jp`	Japan
Facenama	Social network	`www.facenama.com`	Iran
Taringa	Social network	`www.taringa.net`	Latin America

Pastebin Sites

Pastebin is a text-sharing service; it allows any Internet user to post a large amount of text data without even registering at the Pastebin site. Although it is intended to share legitimate data, many black hat hackers are using it to distribute stolen data such as compromised social media accounts (username and passwords), private IP addresses and subnets belonging to various corporations around the world, and user credentials taken from different breached online services.

The following are some popular Pastebin sites and services:

- *Pastebin* (`https://pastebin.com/trends`): This is a text-sharing service.

- *PasteLert* (`https://andrewmohawk.com/pasteLert`): This is a Pastebin alerting service dedicated to the Pastebin.com website.

- *Custom PasteBins Search Tool* (`https://inteltechniques.com/osint/menu.pastebins.html`): This custom search page indexes 57 paste sites.

- *Dump Monitor* (`https://twitter.com/dumpmon`): This is a Twitter account that monitors multiple paste sites for password dumps and other sensitive information.

Social Media Psychological Analysis

Social media sites have become integrated into our daily lives. People are using them increasingly to publish all types of digital contents online. Up until now, we have focused on harvesting data from social sites. However, there is a point that we should not omit when conducting analysis of the harvested data: the psychological status of the person posting the contents on their profile can also give important information, even more than the content itself (in some cases). For instance, the true identity of an anonymous Twitter account can be revealed by performing linguistic analysis of the suspect account. In addition, suspects can be tracked online by examining the way they use language when they chat or when they broadcast their thoughts online (for example, the way a target uses capitalization, omits or includes words , and pronounces some words). The advances in artificial intelligence systems will make analyzing social media accounts more effective and will help investigators uncover the true identity of anonymous social media accounts.

Note!   Analyzing online content—especially content found on social media platforms—becomes important to the forensic context of crime investigation, OSINT intelligence, cyber-exploits, trials, and judicial procedures. This science is known as *forensic linguistics.*

Analyzing the target's psychological status of their online content is outside this book's scope. However, there are some online services that can aid you to analyze online contents and predict the psychological status of the target upon posting it.

Tone Analyzer

This online service (`https://tone-analyzer-demo.mybluemix.net`) offers free linguistic analysis to detect human feelings—such as joy, fear, sadness, anger, analytical, confident, and tentative tones—found in text such as tweets, emails, and Facebook messages (see Figure 5-35).

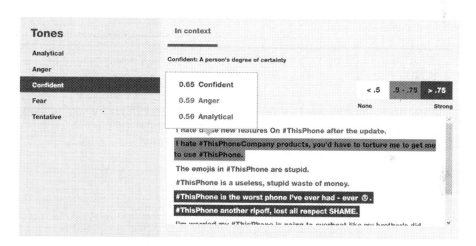

Figure 5-35. *Performing linguistic analysis to understand a text writer's psychological status*

Watson Tone Analyzer

This (`https://www.ibm.com/watson/services/tone-analyzer/`) is a cloud-based server created by IBM. It analyzes emotions and tones in online content (e.g., Facebook posts, reviews, and tweets) to predict the emotional status of the writer. This service can be used in different scenarios—other than intelligence—such as understand customer needs to better serve them.

Facebook and Twitter Prediction

This site (`https://applymagicsauce.com/demo.html`) predicts your psycho-demographic profile. The service can analyze your Facebook and Twitter posts and give insight about your personality, which is useful to see what your current social profile says about you or about any target. You can also insert any text in the website to predict the psycho-demographic profile of its author.

Fake Sport

This site (`https://www.fakespot.com`) analyzes Amazon, Yelp, TripAdvisor, and Apple App store user reviews to check the credibility of them.

Review Meta

With this site (`https://reviewmeta.com`) you can investigate user reviews on Amazon to check which one is likely to be fake or misleading.

TweetGenie

This (`www.tweetgenie.nl/index.php`) is a Dutch project that predicts the target's age and gender from a Twitter username.

Summary

In this chapter, we covered the most popular social media sites worldwide, focusing on the one with the highest number of monthly active visitors. In today's digital age, it is rare to see an Internet user who does not have at least one account on one or more social media site. People use social media services to post all types of contents online such as photos, videos, text messages, and geolocation data. They also mention their education, employment history, and the addresses where they live. Personal information such as social connections, places visited, habits, likes and dislikes, family members, spouse, and more can all be found easily. Although social networking sites allow their users to tighten their privacy controls to prevent others from seeing posted content, few people care about such issues and post many of their activities—especially text posts and check-ins—in public status. This makes a large volume of accessible data readily available to different kinds of online investigations.

This chapter explained how to search popular social media sites to locate information beyond the typical search functionality offered by each service. In the next chapter, we will continue the discussion of how to locate information about people online by focusing on a specific type of search engines known as people search engines. These engine are similar to typical search engines. However, they index content related to individuals only. The next chapter will also cover government records (also known as *public records*). These are confidential records produced by local governments, and they contain valuable information about specific country citizens. By combining the information from people search engines and government records with the information harvested from social media sites, you can—almost—find all the information available about a specific person online.

Notes

i. Worldometers, "Current World Population," February 5, 2018, `www.worldometers.info/world-population/`.

ii. We Are Social Singapore, "Global Digital Statshot Q3 2017," February 14, 2018, `https://www.slideshare.net/wearesocialsg/global-digital-statshot-q3-2017`

iii. Globalwebindex, "Internet users have average of 7 social accounts," February 14, 2018, `https://blog.globalwebindex.net/chart-of-the-day/internet-users-have-average-of-7-social-accounts`

iv. Statista, "Number of monthly active Facebook users worldwide as of 4th quarter 2017 (in millions)," February 14, 2018, `https://www.statista.com/statistics/264810/number-of-monthly-active-facebook-users-worldwide/`

v. LinkedIn, "The Power of LinkedIn's 500 Million Member Community," February 10, 2018, `https://blog.linkedin.com/2017/april/24/the-power-of-linkedins-500-million-community`

 vi. National Conference of State Legislatures, "STATE SOCIAL MEDIA PRIVACY LAWS", February 11, 2018, `www.ncsl.org/research/telecommunications-and-information-technology/state-laws-prohibiting-access-to-social-media-usernames-and-passwords.aspx`

 vii. Smartdatahq, "The Data Volume Stored By Facebook Is... ", February 12, 2018, `https://smartdatahq.com/data-volume-stored-by-facebook/`

 viii. Microfocus, "How Much Data is Created on the Internet Each Day?," February 11, 2018, `https://blog.microfocus.com/how-much-data-is-created-on-the-internet-each-day`

 ix. Statista, "Number of monthly active Twitter users worldwide from 1st quarter 2010 to 4th quarter 2017 (in millions)," February 14, 2018,

 x. Internet Live Stats, "Twitter Usage Statistics," February 12, 2018, `www.internetlivestats.com/twitter-statistics/`

 xi. stonetemple, "Hard Numbers for Public Posting Activity on Google Plus," February 14, 2018, `https://www.stonetemple.com/real-numbers-for-the-activity-on-google-plus/`

 xii. Statistic Brain Research Institute, "Google Plus Demographics & Statistics," February 14, 2018, `https://www.statisticbrain.com/google-plus-demographics-statistics/`

 xiii. LinkedIn, `https://about.linkedin.com`, February 14, 2018, `https://press.linkedin.com/about-linkedin`

CHAPTER 6

People Search Engines and Public Records

In today's digital age, most people have some kind of online presence, either directly or indirectly. Other entities—such as government and local authorities—also store some type of information about their citizens in publicly accessible databases. Searching for someone is not always as easy as typing their name into Google or Facebook; people with a small online presence will not appear easily when searching for them online. In the previous chapter, we demonstrated the importance of social media sites to find people online. In this chapter, we will continue our discussion of how to find people online using specialized websites known as *people search engines* in addition to looking up people in government records (also known as *public records*).

Covering these topics in one chapter is convenient because when you search for people online, a considerable amount of information is derived from public databases.

In this chapter, we will list the main people search engines currently available (focusing on the free services) and talk briefly about the distinct features offered by each one. We will also cover government record sites and categorize them according to the information offered. The information in this chapter combined with the previous chapter will help you find information about most targets online.

What Is a People Search Engine?

People search engines are similar to typical search engines; people search engines index online content but focus on people's personal details and store the results in huge databases to return information upon request. Different parameters are used to search for people on these sites such as target e-mail address, phone number, social username, and full name. Some websites offer additional search parameters such as relative

© Nihad A. Hassan, Rami Hijazi 2018
N. A. Hassan and R. Hijazi, *Open Source Intelligence Methods and Tools*,
https://doi.org/10.1007/978-1-4842-3213-2_6

names, mailing address, date of birth, known aliases, ages, and even photographs using a reverse image search technique. The databases used by people search engines to locate information are diverse. For instance, many people search engines search within the deep web to extract information from source databases that typical search engines cannot reach; these include birth and death databases, public records (such as criminal and tax records), and other overlooked sources (such as information stored in proprietary databases). Please bear in mind that the people search engines will also index results from social media platforms such as Facebook and LinkedIn, making them a convenient solution to return comprehensive result sets.

Online investigators (such as law enforcement and intelligence services) need people search engines to acquire accurate information about their targets; other parties are also interested in using such services. For example, employers can conduct background checks on their perspective employees, and individuals can look up the amount of personal information that is revealed about themselves online.

What Are Public Records?

We already talked about people search engines; these sites derive part of their results from public repositories. So, what do we mean when we say *public records*?

Public records consist of information that has been—mostly—produced by government entities and is meant to be nonconfidential.

Every person on Earth has a set of public records. For example, the most important—mandatory—public records of every human is their birth and death records! Different countries handle public records differently, as public records will contain personally identifiable information (PII) about people, and exposing such details to the public is subject to law.

In the United States, access to national public records is governed by the Freedom of Information Act (FOIA),[i] which clearly states that any person has the right to obtain access to government information in executive branch agency records. Until now, the United States was the only country in the world that gives unrestricted access to public records of its citizens. This means searching for United States citizens and residents returns richer results compared with other countries.

Government records come in different types such as text, photographs, and maps, and they are stored in paper and electronic formats as well such as CD/DVDs, tapes, and computer databases.

Aside from laws regulating access to public records, what you need to know is that many online services offer access to such data for free or in exchange for a small fee.

Example of Public Records

Public records contain different types of information. The following list categorizes the records into groups based on type of information; however, the following list is not inclusive of all types:

- Birth records
- Death records
- Marriage records
- Divorce records
- Address records
- Criminal records
- Court/litigation records
- Voting records
- Driver license records
- Education history
- Property records
- Tax/financial records
- Weapon permits
- Traffic violations
- Bankruptcy records
- Sex offender records
- Professional licenses
- E-mail records
- Telephone records
- Census records

Searching for Personal Details

This is the main section of this chapter. We will start by talking about general people search engines and then narrow our discussion to cover specific services—mostly public records—specializing in searching for particular types of information.

General People Search

The following are the most popular sites used to locate information about people online.

Note!   Before starting your search using these services, make sure—if possible—to prepare as much detail as you can about your target.

- Full name

- E-mail, phone number

- Mailing address

- Friends, exes, family members, social circle names, study mates, business partners, known neighbors, or anyone who may know the target

- Where they live or lived before (country, city, state)

- Education history (school, university)

- Age

TruthFinder

TruthFinder (https://www.truthfinder.com) is one of the most popular people search engines; it is a public search record that gives instant access to a wide set of personal information about anyone living in the United States. TruthFinder has a huge database of social media profiles, address history, contact information, public records (federal, country, and state data sources), and other commercial sources. You can search using the target's first and/or last name in addition to the city/state where the target lives or lived before.

TruthFinder scans the deep web of Internet resources to fetch results from places that conventional search engines cannot operate; it also searches the dark web for exposed personal information, providing a great service for anyone who may suspect that their personal details have been sold on the dark web (it offers a free dark web monitoring service for its registered members). A valid search in TruthFinder will produce a report with detailed information about the target such as birth and death records, property records, criminal records, education history, work history, location history, social media and dating profiles, relatives' names, family members, contact information, and more.

411

On 411 (`https://www.411.co`) you can search for people within the United States. Search parameters include the full name, location, reverse phone lookup, e-mail, and business. The free account returns basic information such as location, contact information, and possible relatives; however, the paid subscription returns in-depth results.

Pipl

Pipl (`https://pipl.com`) is another popular people search engine that covers the entire world. It allows you to search for people using their e-mail address, phone number, or social username. Pipl collaborates with other people search engine services to return comprehensive results. These services can be accessed by clicking the sponsored links that appear on your search result page. The current associates are Peoplelooker.com, Archives.com, and Spokeo.com. These services charge fees for giving deeper details about the person of interest.

Other

These are other important people search engines that you should consider during your search:

- *Spokeo* (`https://www.spokeo.com`): This is a commercial people search engine that gives detailed reports about any target.

- *TruePeopleSearch* (`https://www.truepeoplesearch.com`): You can search by target name, reverse phone, and reverse address. The service is free and shows the contact information (phone and e-mail) in addition to current and previous addresses.

- *US Search* (`https://www.ussearch.com`): This gives basic information about the person of interest such as address, relatives, work, and age. To unlock the full profile, you need to pay for a premium subscription. The service is limited to the United States only.

- *Peek You* (`https://www.peekyou.com`): This aggregates information from social media profiles, news sources, blogs, and other public databases. To unlock the full details, you need to pay.

- *Zaba Search* (`www.zabasearch.com`): You can find people in the United States using a name or phone number. The service is free, and you can register using your Facebook account—for free—to get the benefits of the premium service.

- *White Pages* (`https://www.whitepages.com`): You can search for people within the United States using their name, phone number, business, or address. The White Pages database includes more than 500 million people. The free subscription account gives the following information about the person of interest: landline numbers, current and previous residences, relatives, and associates.

- *Been Verified* (`https://www.beenverified.com`): You can search for people within the United States using their name, phone, e-mail, or mailing address. The basic report gives general information about the subject, while the commercial subscription gives a detailed report about anyone, including criminal records (where available) and property tax records. This service is popular in the United States and used by millions each year.

- *Address Search* (`https://www.addresssearch.com`): You can search for someone's e-mail or mailing address using a name and location. The service is limited to the United States.

- *Lullar* (`http://com.lullar.com`): You can search social media websites using the target's e-mail address or first and last names or username.

- *Yasni* (`www.yasni.com`): You can search for people based on their work history.

- *My Life* (https://www.mylife.com): This shows the reputation score of any target based on the information gathered from government, social, and other sources, plus personal reviews written by others. To unlock the full report, you need to register and pay for the service.

- *Snoop Station* (http://snoopstation.com/index.html): You can search for people using their full name and location. This is a commercial service.

- *Advanced Background Check* (https://www.advancedbackgroundchecks.com): You can give basic details about the target such as mailing address, phone, and e-mail; to unlock the full details, you need to pay.

- *Family Tree Now* (http://familytreenow.com): Discover your family tree by searching with first and last names and city/state. This is a free service.

- *Radaris* (https://radaris.com): This is a public record deep search engine; it returns comprehensive information about a target. It also lists the online mentions about the target such as résumé, business records, publications, videos and images, social networking profile, and web references.

- *Profile Engine* (http://profileengine.com): This is a social network search engine.

- *Info Space* (http://infospace.com): This is a metasearch engine that returns comprehensive results from different public data sources and other people search engine sites.

- *Cubib* (https://cubib.com): You can search millions of online data records for free. Aggregated data is derived from people search, marketing data, property records, vehicle records, court records, patents, business registration, domain name registration, and White House visitation records.

- *Fast People Search* (https://www.fastpeoplesearch.com): This is a reverse name, address, or phone lookup for free.

- *Speedy hunt* (`https://speedyhunt.com`): You can search for people in the United States and return a detailed report—where available—about them, which include arrest and sex offender records. You need to pay to use this service.

- *That's Them* (`https://thatsthem.com/people-search`): You can search for people using their name, address, phone, and e-mail for free.

- *Webmii* (`http://webmii.com`): You can search for people and for their visibility score for free.

- *How Many of Me* (`http://howmanyofme.com/search/`): You write the name, and the site will return the number of people in the United States who have your entered first and last names.

- *Genealogy* (`www.genealogy.com`): You can search family history records using the information originally posted in GenForum.

- *Sorted By Name* (`http://sortedbyname.com`): This is a list of links to genealogy details—based on the first letter of the person's surname—mentioned on other websites.

Online Registries

An online registry is a kind of wish list published online. The most obvious example of such registries is when a couple formulates a list of things they need to purchase for their marriage. They compile a list and publish it online publicly. When one of their friends or relatives buys them an item from the list, the registry provider will remove this item from the list and ship the purchased item to the couple.

For the purpose of OSINT investigation, online registries are useful to uncover personal details/wishes of the people of interest in addition to close friends (as many registries allow friends to post their wishes to the wall of the registry owner), especially after knowing that many people leave their registries available online after the ceremony's end.

There are different types of online registries. The most well-known types are wedding, baby, graduation, birthday, holiday, and gift registries. The following list the most popular online registries:

- *The Knot* (`https://www.theknot.com`): Find a couple's wedding registry and website.

- *Registry Finder* (`https://www.registryfinder.com`): Search for registries.

- *Amazon Registry* (`https://www.amazon.com/wedding/home`): This is the Amazon registry.

- *My Registry* (`https://www.myregistry.com`): This is a global online gift registry service.

- *Checked Twice* (`https://www.checkedtwice.com`): This is a gift registry.

Vital Records

Vital records are government records usually created by local authorities. They include birth and death records, marriage licenses, and divorce decrees. When searching for vital records, the returned result will usually come with the target's personal details. For instance, a birth record will usually come with the parent's full name, the child's name, and the place where the event took place. The death record will come with the location where the person buried, a death certificate, and the name of the person who reported the event to the authorities. Marriage records will hold the couple's parents' names and the place where the marriage was registered. Finally, the divorce record will hold information about the couple's children's names. Other related records such as ancestry records (offered by some databases) and the mailing address of the person of interest can also appear when searching in vital records.

The following are the most popular vital record databases:

Note!   As we already said, most public records online relate to U.S. citizens because of U.S. law. However, we will list other international public records database where available.

- *Sorted by Birth Date* (http://sortedbybirthdate.com): This site uses the Death Master File as of March 2014. The Death Master File is a database made publicly available by the US Social Security Administration since 1980, it contains personal information about people who had Social Security numbers and whose deaths were reported to Social Security Administration from 1962 to present.

- *DeathIndexes* (www.deathindexes.com): This site holds a directory of links to websites with online death indexes categorized by state and country.

- *Family Search* (https://www.familysearch.org/search/collection/1202535): This is a U.S. Social Security death index.

- *Find a Grave* (https://www.findagrave.com): You can find information about people, including their birth, death, and burial information, and it may include pictures, biographies, family information, and more. The site holds more than 170 million memorials in its database.

- *Deaths of U.S. citizens in foreign countries* (https://www.archives.gov/research/vital-records/american-deaths-overseas.html): This is a record of deaths overseas.

- *Obits Archive* (www.obitsarchive.com): You can search more than 53 million U.S. obituaries here.

- *U.S., Department of Veterans Affairs BIRLS Death File, 1850–2010* (https://search.ancestry.com/search/db.aspx?dbid=2441): This database contains birth and death records for more than 14 million veterans and VA beneficiaries who died between the years 1850 and 2010.

- *Melissa* (https://melissadata.com/lookups/deathcheck.asp): This displays a list of people who have died in the last 24 months within the United States.

- *Deceased Online* (https://www.deceasedonline.com): This is the central database for U.K. burials and cremations.

- *National Records of Scotland* (https://www.nrscotland.gov.uk/research/visit-us/scotlandspeople-centre/useful-websites-for-family-history-research/births-deaths-and-marriages): This includes links to births, deaths, and marriage government records in Scotland and selected countries like the United States and Canada.

- *Find My Past* (https://search.findmypast.co.uk/search-united-kingdom-records-in-birth-marriage-death-and-parish-records): You can search for vital records in the United Kingdom, Australia, New Zealand, the United States, Canada, and Ireland.

- *Forebears* (http://forebears.io/germany): International genealogical records are kept here. Select your country and record type to display related results (see Figure 6-1).

Figure 6-1. *International genealogical records offered by* http://forebears.io

Note!   A major portal for locating vital records within the United Sates is Vitalrec (`www.vitalrec.com`). This site tells you how to obtain vital records (birth certificates, death records, and marriage license information) from each state and territory in the United Sates. All you need to do is to select the person of interest's state and then browse the available vital records links for that area. This should be your first place to search for vital records in the United Sates. Please note that Vitalrec.com does not store any information in its database; it just offers links directly to each state's page, and it mentions where and how to get state's vital records. The international section (`www.vitalrec.com/links2.html`) gives details on where to find such information in other countries.

Criminal and Court Search

Criminal and court records include different categories of information such as people with search warrants (arrest warrants and wanted people), jail records, and sex crimes (this category has a dedicated website in the United States that contains full details about each offender). Any person who has been convicted of criminal acts can be found in such public databases. The following are the most important criminal records sites (mostly belonging to U.S. databases):

- *National Sex Offender Public Website (NSOPW)* (`https://www.nsopw.gov/en`): This gives the public access to sex offender data in the United States; returned results include an offender's photograph.

- *Criminal Searches* (`www.criminalsearches.com`): This stores entries for hundreds of millions of adults with a criminal record across the United States.

- *Black Book Online* (`https://www.blackbookonline.info/index.html`): This is a directory of free public record lookup services covering the entire United States. Just select the state to see the available county court records within an area.

- *Ancestor Hunt* (http://ancestorhunt.com/most-wanted-criminals-and-fugitives.htm): These are the most wanted criminals and fugitives in America. Select the state to see the list.

- *The Inmate Locator* (www.theinmatelocator.com): This lists inmate locator services in the United Sates.

- *Federal Bureau of Prisons* (https://www.bop.gov/inmateloc): Here you can locate the whereabouts of any federal inmate incarcerated from 1982 to the present.

- *The Global Terrorism Database* (GTD) (www.start.umd.edu/gtd/): This is an open source database that holds information about terrorist events around the world (bot international and domestic) beginning from 1970 until 2016.

Note!   FBI crime statistics can be useful in some instances when you need to research crime statistics in a specific area and within a specific year. You can find it at https://ucr.fbi.gov.

Tip!   To see a list of badges—mainly security forces badges—from all countries around the world, go to http://allbadges.net/en.

Property Records

Use these sites to get information about properties and their residents:

- *U.S. Realty Record* (https://usrealtyrecords.com): This is a major property information provider in the United States.

- *Zillow* (https://www.zillow.com): This site offers buying, selling, renting, financing, and remodeling properties in the United States.

- *U.S. Title Records* (https://www.ustitlerecords.com/property-records): This lists property records, lien searches, title searches, and deeds. This is a commercial service.

- *GOV.UK* (https://www.gov.uk/search-property-information-land-registry): Here you can find information about a property in England or Wales.

- *Neighbor Report* (https://neighbor.report): This gives data about addresses, residents, and phone numbers in the United States. This service is unique as it allows anyone to post complains or thanks about their neighbors.

Tax and Financial Records

You can find tax and financial information about a person of interest in public record searches.

- *VAT Search* (https://vat-search.eu): This is a site for doing a VAT tax search in all European Union countries.

- *Real Property Tax Database Search* (https://otr.cfo.dc.gov/page/real-property-tax-database-search): This site gives access to property information in the United States.

- *The National Archives (UK)* (www.nationalarchives.gov.uk/help-with-your-research/research-guides/taxation): This is a site for searching British government records on taxation.

Very Important Site!   Go to https://publicrecords.netronline.com for the U.S. Public Records Online Directory, which contains links to official public databases including U.S. citizens' public tax records.

Social Security Number Search

You can perform a reverse Social Security number lookup (for the United States only) by going to `https://www.ssn-check.org/lookup/?state=AK&year=1936`. The database contains Social Security numbers that were issued between 1936 and 2011.

Another site that offers free Social Security number search and lookup tools is SSN-Verify (`https://www.ssn-verify.com/tools`).

Note!   You can find voter registration records in the United States at `https://voterrecords.com`.

Username Check

You can check specific usernames to see where they are being used (e.g., social media sites) or to know whether a particular username really exists.

- *Check User Name* (`http://checkusernames.com`): Check the use of a specific username on 160 social networks. This is useful to discover target social media accounts to see if they are using the same username on multiple platforms.

- *Namechk* (`https://namechk.com`): Check to see whether a specified username is used for major domain names and social media sites.

- *Namecheckr* (`https://www.namecheckr.com`): Check a domain and social username availability across multiple networks.

- *User Search* (`https://www.usersearch.org`): Scan 45 popular social media websites.

E-mail Search and Investigation

Free services can help you to locate people according to their associated e-mail address. E-mail validation services check whether an e-mail address exists and gives other detailed technical information about it.

- *E-mail Dossier* (https://centralops.net/co/emaildossier.aspx): This site gives detailed technical validation reports about e-mails.

- Emailhippo (https://tools.verifyemailaddress.io): Free Email address verification service.

- *Hunter* (https://hunter.io/email-verifier): This website offers free Email address verification service/100 email per month.

- *E-mail Checker* (https://email-checker.net): You can use this site to verify whether an e-mail address is real.

- *Mail Tester* (http://mailtester.com/testmail.php): This site offers e-mail address verification.

- *Byte Plant E-mail Validator* (https://www.email-validator.net): You can validate e-mail addresses in bulk.

- *E-mail Format* (https://email-format.com): Find the e-mail address formats in use at thousands of companies.

- *E-mail Permutator+* (http://metricsparrow.com/toolkit/email-permutator): This is a free e-mail permutator service.

- *Emails4Corporations.com*(https://sites.google.com/site/emails4corporations/home): Provide e-mail address patterns for more than 1,000 companies.

- *Scam Dex* (www.scamdex.com): This is a huge archive of scam e-mails.

- *E-mail Header Analysis* (https://www.iptrackeronline.com/email-header-analysis.php): Get detailed technical information extracted from e-mail headers. This includes the sender IP address, e-mail, and sender ISP in addition to geographical information. To use this service, you need to copy the e-mail header and paste it into the E-mail Header Analysis engine and click "Submit header for analysis." See the following note to learn how to extract the Gmail message header.

Note!   Follow these steps to extract e-mail headers from Gmail:

1. Open the target e-mail.

2. Click the down arrow located next to the Reply button and select "Show original" (see Figure 6-2).

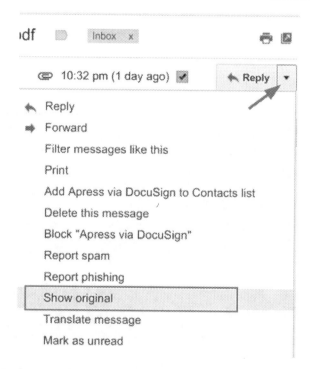

Figure 6-2. *Displaying Gmail e-mail header*

Data Compromised Repository Websites

These sites hold a list of websites that have suffered from a data breach in the past. When a site suffers from a data breach, registered user details—especially usernames and passwords—usually get revealed to the public. Many people have a bad practice of using the same password for more than one account (e.g., using the same password for Facebook and for an e-mail account), so knowing one password may grant access to other social accounts/services belonging to the same user.

The following sites are popular websites that list information from a data breach; you can use them to gain intelligence about any target online:

- Have I been Pwned (`https://haveibeenpwned.com/Passwords`): This site lists half a billion real-world passwords previously exposed in data breaches. You can also download the Pwned Passwords list, which contains additional data about each breached account (such as the number of times that password had been seen in the source data breaches). This site can be searched using a target e-mail address or the password itself to see whether it appears in plain text on any public password dump list (see Figure 6-3). This is a recommended site.

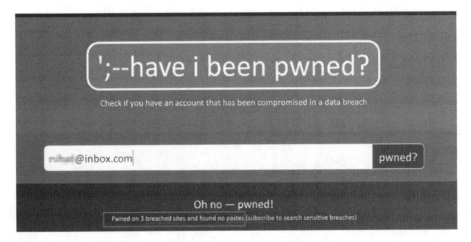

Figure 6-3. *Searching for e-mail that has been pwned previously*

- *Breach Alarm* (`https://breachalarm.com`): Enter your e-mail address to see whether your associated online account passwords have been exposed in a previous data breach. Results will get sent to the specified e-mail address.

- *Global Cyber Vandalism Statistics* (`https://defacer.id`): This site holds information about the most active website hackers, most active hacker groups, recently hacked government and academic websites, recently reported hacked websites, and reported defacements on hold (not verified).

- *Hacked E-mails* (https://hacked-emails.com): Check anonymously whether your e-mail has been compromised in a previous data breach.

Note!   The darknet contains many public databases that list pwned accounts with passwords in clear text. The last known password dump file found on the darknet contained 1.4 billion clear-text credentials in a single file.[ii]

For the individual, it is illegal to access other people's accounts using stolen credentials on pwned databases. For OSINT investigators, the debate continues whether leaked information is a legal source of OSINT or not!

Phone Number Search

A reverse phone lookup service is useful to find out who is behind a specific phone number. Some services also specify the carrier name and type in addition to phone number type. The following are some phone lookup services:

- *Z lookup* (https://www.zlookup.com): This is a site that does international reverse phone lookups including cell phones.

- *Reverse Phone Lookup* (https://www.reversephonelookup.com): This site traces a telephone back to its owner for free.

- *Inter800* (http://inter800.com/index.html): Search for phone numbers within the United States.

- *Twilio* (https://www.twilio.com/lookup): Identify phone number formats, find caller names, find caller types (business or personal), identify phone number carrier, and check phone number type (landline, VoIP, or mobile).

- *Spy Dialer* (https://www.spydialer.com): This is a reverse phone lookup for cell phones and landlines.

- *Who calld* (https://whocalld.com): This is a reverse phone lookup service for international numbers.

- *Info Bel* (`www.infobel.com`): Search for the phone number of a person or company anywhere in the world.

- *Fone Finder* (`www.fonefinder.net`): Search for U.S./Canadian telephone numbers.

- *True Caller* (`https://www.truecaller.com`): This is an international reverse phone number lookup.

- *Free Carrier Lookup* (`http://freecarrierlookup.com`): This is a carrier lookup service.

- *Phone Lookup* (`https://www.phonelookup.com`): This is a reverse phone number lookup service.

Note!   You cannot get reverse phone lookup for mobile phones easily for free; however, there are many paid websites that offer such services.

Employee Profiles and Job Websites

Job sites can reveal a great amount of information about individuals and companies' private details. For example, you can find out the type of hardware and software implemented in the company of interest by looking at the technical vacancies posted by it (e.g., posting a technical vacancy for an IT administrator with experience in Windows Server technology means that the target company is using Windows OS in its infrastructure). A person's expertise, education, and job history can be found easily by looking at their résumé on job websites; an individual's résumés can also reveal important technical information about the companies where they previously worked. The following are the most popular job websites:

- *LinkedIn* (`https://www.linkedin.com`): This was already covered thoroughly in Chapter 5.

- *Recruit in* (`https://recruitin.net`): This is a third-party website that uses Google to search the profiles on LinkedIn. This returns deeper results compared to LinkedIn.

- *Byte* (`https://www.bayt.com`): This is a popular Middle East job website.

- *Market Visual* (www.marketvisual.com): Search professionals by name, company, or title. The site maps business relationships visually between the person of interest and other entities. It displays further data about the target such as the previous and current affiliations and education. The resulted search data can be downloaded in various forms for later analysis.

- *Xing* (https://www.xing.com): This is a business networking site.

- *Indeed* (www.indeed.com): This is a job search website.

- *Eluta* (https://www.eluta.ca): This is the official job search engine of Canada's top 100 employers.

- *CareerBuilder* (https://www.careerbuilder.com): This is a job search website.

- *Euro Jobs* (https://www.eurojobs.com): This is a European job site.

- *Glassdoor* (https://www.glassdoor.com/index.htm): This is an international job site.

- *Monster* (https://www.monster.com): This is an international job website.

- *Head Hunter* (https://www.headhunter.com): This is a management and executive job platform.

- *Jobs* (https://www.jobs.pl): This is a Polish job website.

- *Job site* (https://www.jobsite.co.uk): This is a U.K. job website.

- *Seek* (https://www.seek.com.au): This is an Australian job website.

- *Simply Hired* (https://www.simplyhired.com): Job search within the US.

- *Zip Recruiter* (https://www.ziprecruiter.com): Search over 8 million jobs in the US.

Dating Website Search

Useful information about people and their relationships can be found on dating websites. This information cannot be omitted when conducting OSINT investigations about a person of interest.

- *Ashley Madison* (`https://www.ashleymadison.com`): This is an international dating site.

- *First Met* (`https://www.firstmet.com/index.php`): This is an online dating site with 30 million users.

- *Badoo* (`https://badoo.us`): With more than 380 million users, this network is—currently—considered the largest social discovery network on Earth.

- *Plentyoffish* (`https://www.pof.fr`): This is a dating website for non-English speakers.

- *EHarmony* (`https://www.eharmony.com/verify`): This is an international dating site with a diverse group of individuals of all ages and countries.

- *Zoosk* (`https://www.zoosk.com`): This is an international dating website with more than 40 million users.

- *Black People Met* (`https://www.blackpeoplemeet.com`): This site specializes in locating black singles only.

- *True Dater* (`www.truedater.com`): Find reviews of people on dating websites; search using the dater's username.

- *Our Time* (`https://www.ourtime.co.uk`): This is a dating site for people older than 50.

- *Hater Dater* (`https://www.haterdater.com`): This website helps people who hate the same stuff to gather and communicate online.

- *UK Match* (`https://uk.match.com`): This is a U.K. dating website.

- *Pheramor* (`https://www.pheramor.com`): This is a dating app for those currently working in Houston, Texas.

- *Tinder* (`https://tinder.com`): This is a social search mobile app that allows people to interact online. It is similar to dating websites.

- *Beautiful people* (`https://www.beautifulpeople.com/en-US`): International online dating service. You can register via your Facebook account - if you have one.

- *Meet Up* (https://www.meetup.com): A website that facilitate meeting with people with the same interest/hippies.

- *Okcupid* (https://www.okcupid.com): Free international online dating website that use math algorithms to find the best correct match according to each user profile.

Note!   You can find a comparison of online dating websites at https://www.consumerreports.org/dating-relationships/online-dating-guide-match-me-if-you-can.

Other Public Records

There are other types of online public records that can prove useful in some cases.

- *Search Systems* ((http://publicrecords.searchsystems.net): This is a public records search engine; it includes links to premium databases (and requires payment).

- *Unites States patent records* (https://www.uspto.gov): This lists patent records.

- *Google Advanced Patent Search* (https://www.google.com/advanced_patent_search): Search for patents here.

- *Federal Election Commission* (https://classic.fec.gov/finance/disclosure/norindsea.shtml): This lists individual contributions made by individuals, Native American tribes, partnerships, sole proprietorships, limited liability companies (LLCs), and contributions by candidates to all political committees.

- *Follow That Money* (https://www.followthemoney.org): This lists how money is spent in federal elections.

- *Political Money Line* (www.politicalmoneyline.com): This tracks money spent in politics.

- *EHDP* (https://www.ehdp.com/vitalnet/datasets.htm): This contains lots of health data sets of the United States.

- *Data.GOV.UK* (https://data.gov.uk/data/search): This is a huge collection of U.K. government data.

- *Stats* (www.stats.govt.nz/browse_for_stats.aspx): This is a New Zealand data government data set.

Note!   Local libraries in the United States offer access to proprietary databases like ReferenceUSA (a huge directory service) and America's Newspapers (full-text obituaries) for a small fee. In many instances, such services can be offered remotely in exchange for a valid library subscription card.

Summary

When searching for a person online, make sure to try different websites to do the job because each service aggregates its information from different databases. The indexing mechanisms also differ between sites. It is also advisable to begin your search on social media; if you find useful information about the target, you can conduct a more thorough search using the sites covered in this chapter.

In the next chapter, we will continue our discussion of how to locate people online, but this time using the geographical information that comes with people's Internet usage and social media activities.

Notes

i.   Archives, "Freedom of Information Act (FOIA)", March 11, 2018,
     https://www.archives.gov/foia

ii. Medium, "1.4 Billion Clear Text Credentials Discovered
     in a Single Database", March 11,2018, https://medium.
     com/4iqdelvedeep/1-4-billion-clear-text-credentials-
     discovered-in-a-single-database-3131d0a1ae14

CHAPTER 7

Online Maps

Tracking users' geolocation information has become increasingly popular with the advance of computing devices, mobile communications, and social media platforms because these technologies make posting someone's current location online a matter of clicking one button.

Nowadays, many types of electronic devices come equipped with satellite tracking sensors to determine their location on the map. Almost all handheld devices—such as smartphones and wearable devices—are now location aware. Many apps in major software stores such as Apple and Google Play have the ability to use the geolocation sensor of the smartphone/tablet to offer a customized experience or to offer certain functions to the device's user. In fact, most applications, online services, and social media platforms can track a user's location in one way or another.

In this chapter, we will demonstrate how you can exploit the geolocation information that comes with many users' online activities to determine their current and previous locations. We will also cover many useful online services that can help you to track everything online including vehicles, ships, shipments, airplanes, and people. You'll also learn how to research different online map repositories to gather intelligence.

But before we begin, we will describe in simple terms how navigation systems— which are responsible for determining people's current locations—work.

The Basics of Geolocation Tracking

Most people do not care about the underlying technology responsible for delivering location-based services to them. People enter the address of the location they need to look up on the map, or they use the built-in feature available in smartphones to geotag digital files (such as images and videos) so they record the current location of images/ videos as a meta tag automatically. In other instances, many social media platforms,

© Nihad A. Hassan, Rami Hijazi 2018
N. A. Hassan and R. Hijazi, *Open Source Intelligence Methods and Tools*,
https://doi.org/10.1007/978-1-4842-3213-2_7

especially Facebook and Twitter, allow their users to post their current location online (called a *check-in* on Facebook) with just a single click, and the rest is handled by the electronic device.

To determine someone's current geographical spot, location-aware devices need to communicate with a satellite navigation system that is in turn is responsible for delivering the exact coordinates of the location on Earth.

The Global Positioning System (GPS) is an American satellite navigation system developed and operated by the U.S. government; it is considered the most popular navigation system on Earth and is used by a large number of electronic devices worldwide. Of course, there are other navigation systems such as the Russian system named GLONASS, the BeiDou system owned by China, or the Galileo run by the European Union. These systems are supported by different device manufacturers.

For GPS to know your current location, it needs to determine the exact coordinate where you are currently standing. So, what do we mean by the geographic coordinate?

A *geographic coordinate system* is a system that locates points on Earth using two coordinate values: latitude and longitude. By knowing the two values, you can visualize any point on Earth on a map.

How to Find the GPS Coordinates of Any Location on a Map

To find the GPS coordinates (latitude and longitude) of any geographical spot on Earth using Google Maps, follow these steps:

1. Go to Google Maps at `https://maps.google.com`.

2. Click anywhere on the map where you want to see the GPS coordinates. A small box appears in the bottom of the Google Maps page showing the current location GPS coordinates (see Figure 7-1).

3. To further investigate a selected location, click the coordinate numbers, and Google will take you to a closer view of the target location in addition to giving you its mailing address (if applicable).

Note!   The first GPS number represents the latitude, and the second represents the longitude.

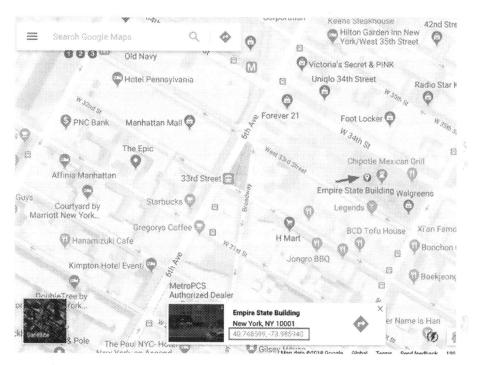

Figure 7-1. *Finding the GPS coordinates of any location on Earth using Google Maps*

Note!   You can also find the latitude and longitude of a point by going to `http://itouchmap.com/latlong.html`. Click the map and drag the marker to the desired location. You can also enter the address (street, city, state, and country) in the search box to look up the GPS coordinates on map.

To convert latitude and longitude to decimal, go to `https://andrew.hedges.name/experiments/convert_lat_long`.

How to Find the Geocode Coordinates from a Mailing Address

If you have an address for a specific location on Earth but you do not know how to find its geocode coordinates on the map, go to the following free services:

- *Batch Geocoding* (`https://www.doogal.co.uk/BatchGeocoding.php`): This service converts multiple address at the same time into their equivalent geocode coordinates (latitude and longitude) using Google Maps.

- *GPS Visualizer's Quick Geocoder* (`www.gpsvisualizer.com/geocode`): This service converts an address into its equivalent geocode coordinates (and works for both Google and Bing).

- *Batch Reverse Geocoding* (`https://www.doogal.co.uk/BatchReverseGeocoding.php`): This service converts geocode coordinate numbers from various coordinate systems to their equivalent approximate mailing address.

General Geospatial Research Tools

There are many online services that can help you when researching online maps for different kinds of information. The following are the most popular services:

- *Digital Globe* (`https://discover.digitalglobe.com`): This is an easy-to-use global map imagery tool with advanced search filters.

- *Bing Maps* (`https://www.bing.com/maps`): This is an alternative to Google Maps.

- *Yandex Maps* (`http://maps.yandex.com`): This is a Russian alternative to Google.

- *Baidu Maps* (`http://map.baidu.com`): This is a Chinese alternative to Google.

- *Daum* (`http://map.daum.net`): This is a Korean map.

- *N2yo* (`www.n2yo.com`): This offers live streaming from different satellites. It also gives information about the tracked satellites and their coverage area.

- *Wigle* (`https://wigle.net`): This shows a Wi-Fi network mapping around the globe. It shows the Wi-Fi network name along with the access point MAC (hardware) address, in addition to the possible locations where free Wi-Fi might be available.

- *BB Bike* (`https://mc.bbbike.org/mc`): Here you can compare two maps. For example, you can compare the same location on maps from Bing and Google Maps to see the differences in the target location.

- *Newspaper Map* (`https://newspapermap.com`): This lists all newspapers around the globe on a map; you can filter them according to location and newspaper language.

- *USGS* (`https://earthexplorer.usgs.gov`): Here you can search a world map using different search criteria such as address, place name, or location coordinates. This map version is newer than Google Maps.

- *Google Street View* (`https://www.google.com/streetview`): Here you can view a specific location (which must exist within the Google Street View database) as if you are there.

- *Google Maps Street View Player* (`www.brianfolts.com/driver`): This shows a street view—where available—between two points on the map.

- *RouteView* (`http://routeview.org/`): This is another Google map street viewer.

- *Street View Movie Maker* (`www.streetviewmovie.com`): Here you can see the Google street view between two locations—where available— and download the movie to your PC for offline viewing.

- *Open Street Cam* (`http://openstreetcam.org/`): Here you can view open street cameras in a specific location—where available.

- *Zoom Earth* (`https://zoom.earth`): Here you can view international cloud imagery—updated each day—from NASA satellites.

- *Hivemapper* (`https://hivemapper.com`): This builds a smart 3D map from airborne video, uncovering changes humans can't see.

- *Liveuamap* (`https://liveuamap.com`): This is an open data media platform that shows the latest news, pictures, and videos from different conflict zones around the globe on a map. This service is important to gain intelligence from various media sources in conflict zones.

- *Terrapattern* (`www.terrapattern.com`): This is a visual search tool for satellite imagery; it allows you to search a wide geographical area for specific visual effects. Currently, the search works in the following cities: New York, San Francisco, Pittsburgh, Berlin, Miami, and Austin.

- *dominoc925* (`https://dominoc925-pages.appspot.com/mapplets/cs_mgrs.html`): Here you can view Military Grid Reference System (MGRS) coordinates.

- *Google Map Alert* (`https://followyourworld.appspot.com`): You can receive an alert when new imagery is available in both Google Maps and Google Earth. You need to supply the latitude and longitude of a target location.

- *Mapillary* (`https://www.mapillary.com`): Here you can view street-level imagery uploaded by people around the world. This service gives a 3D view of many places (its database currently has 259,200,042 images), which is useful to discover/investigate a specific location while you are not there.

- *Address Lookup* (`https://ctrlq.org/maps/address`): Find the address of any place on Google Maps; just move the marker to the specific location on a map, and the relevant address will appear in the pop-up window (see Figure 7-2).

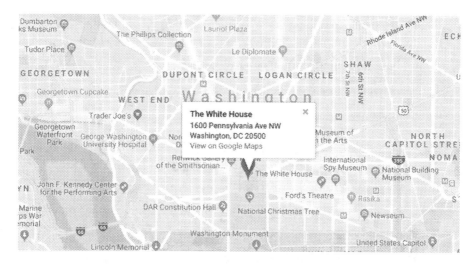

Figure 7-2. *Locating the address of any geographical point on Google Maps*

- *Inspire Geoportal* (http://inspire-geoportal.ec.europa.eu/discovery): This site gives access to European spatial data.

- *Hiking and Biking Map* (http://hikebikemap.org): This is a map for hiking and biking.

- *Viamichelin* (https://www.viamichelin.com): This shows tourist, restaurants, hotels, traffic, and weather on a world map.

- *CORONA Project* (http://corona.cast.uark.edu): This lists more than 800,000 images collected by the CORONA spy satellite launched by the United Sates and was in operation between 1960 and 1972. The pictures are high-resolution and cover different geographic area around the globe, especially in the countries that belonged to the socialist block during the Cold War.

- *Ani Maps* (www.animaps.com): Here you can create maps with interactive animations.

- *Trip Geo* (www.tripgeo.com/Directionsmap.aspx): Here you can create a direction map using Google Street View data.

- *GeoGig* (http://geogig.org): This is an open source tool that imports raw geospatial data (currently from Shapefiles, PostGIS, or SpatiaLite) into a repository to track any changes to the data.

- *GRASS GIS* (`https://grass.osgeo.org`): This is open source Geographic Information System (GIS) software used for managing and analyzing geospatial data, spatial modeling, and visualization.

- *Timescape* (`https://www.timescape.io`): This is a map-based storytelling platform.

- *Polymaps* (`www.polymaps.org`): This is a JavaScript library for making dynamic, interactive maps in modern web browsers; it supports different visual presentations to place on.

- *Mapquest* (`https://www.mapquest.com`): This helps you to find places on a map (such as hotels, restaurants, coffee shops, grocery stores, pharmacies, airports, and more). You can also use this service to find the best route—the shortest one and the estimated time to arrive—when going from one place to another (see Figure 7-3).

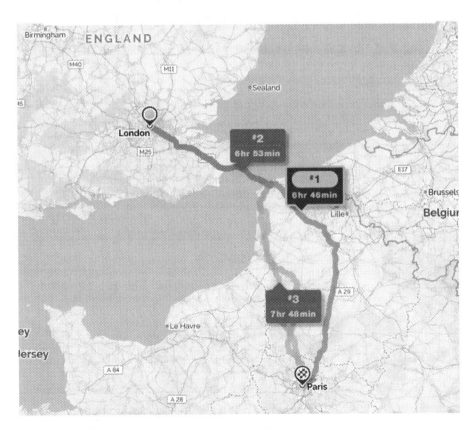

Figure 7-3. *Finding the best routes between two locations*

- *NGA GEOINT* (`https://github.com/ngageoint`): This is the National Geospatial-Intelligence Agency official repository of map-related tools on GitHub.

- *Free Map Tools* (`https://www.freemaptools.com/radius-around-point.htm`): Here you can find the radius around a point on the map.

- *Maphub* (`https://maphub.net`): Here you can create an interactive map by adding points, lines, polygons, or labels in addition to customized backgrounds.

- *Crowdmap* (`https://crowdmap.com`): This is an annotation tool that allows you to visualize information on a map and timeline.

- *Maperitive* (`http://maperitive.net`): This is Windows software for drawing maps based on OpenStreetMap and GPS data.

- *Perry-Castañeda Library Map Collection* (`https://legacy.lib.utexas.edu/maps/index.html`): This lists online maps of current interests around the world in addition to different maps—including historical maps—of different locations around the world.

- *United Nations Geospatial Information Section* (`www.un.org/Depts/Cartographic/english/htmain.htm`): This lists different types of maps such as general maps for countries and the mapping mission of the United Nations.

- *Roundshot* (`www.roundshot.com/default.cfm?DomainID=1&TreeID=172&language=en`): Here you can view live cameras from selected regions around the world. Additional information is available for each selected location that includes physical coverage of camera on map, weather forecasts, and some historical data/pictures.

- *Live Earthquake Map* (`http://quakes.globalincidentmap.com`): This site gives real-time information about earthquakes that have taken place around the world; it also covers important incidents happening around the globe such as Amber alerts, disease outbreak, gang activity, border security issues, nonterror aviation incidents, terrorism event predication, and more.

- *Universal Postal Union* (`www.upu.int/en/the-upu/member-countries.html`): Here you can find postal codes for all countries.

Note!   A database of location names with different spellings in different languages is available at `www.geonames.org`.

To see a list of cities and towns around the world, go to `www.fallingrain.com/world`.

Commercial Satellites

There are many global providers of high-resolution satellite imagery that offer their services to government security agencies and civil companies to help them predict future threats and make decisions accordingly. The following are the most popular providers of high-resolution satellite imagery:

- *European Space Imaging* (`www.euspaceimaging.com`): Provides -commercial- very high resolution imagery of earth using the following satellites: DigitalGlobe: WorldView-1, WorldView-2, WorldView-3, GeoEye-1, QuickBird and IKONOS (archive).

- *Digital Globe* (`https://www.digitalglobe.com/industries/defense-and-intelligence`): This is popular for providing high-resolution satellite images of conflicts around the world.

Date/Time Around the World

There are many free services that offer—in addition to the current date and time in any place around the globe—important statistics about a location, such as the current weather, GPS coordinates, important addresses, nearby airports, and famous places. The following are the popular services:

- *Wolframe Alpha* (`www.wolframalpha.com`): Enter a specific city/town or any location, and the site will retrieve important information about it such as population, current local time, current weather, nearby cities, nearby airports, geographic properties, and more.

- *SunCalc* (`http://suncalc.net`): This shows sun movement during the course of the day for any given location on the map.

- *SunCalc* (`https://www.suncalc.org`): This shows solar data for selected location in addition to other geographical information about this location.

- *Mooncalc* (`https://www.mooncalc.org`): This shows lunar data for a selected location on Earth.

Location-Based Social Media

Major social media platforms allow their users to geotag some of their activities when using them. In this section, we will discuss how you can use the geolocation feature offered by major social media platforms to collect intelligence about a specific target or subject.

YouTube

To search for videos tagged with geocoordinates on YouTube, you can use a dedicated tool called Geo Search Tool (`https://youtube.github.io/geo-search-tool/search.html`). You can search for videos at a given address and in a given timeframe. You can also specify a distance from the location entered; hence, the search can be as broad as 1,000 KM or as narrow at 1 KM. The returned results can be filtered according to each video upload time. Final results appear graphically on a map as a red marker (see Figure 7-4).

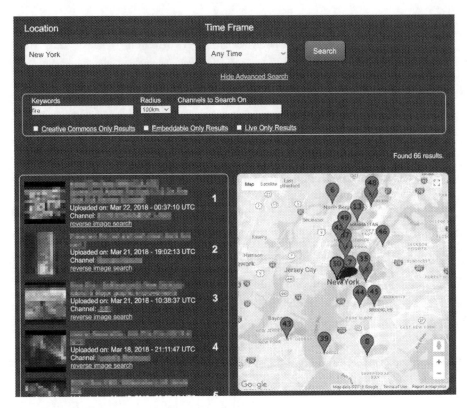

Figure 7-4. *Geolocation YouTube movies search*

Facebook

Facebook is the number-one social networking site. It allows its users to geotag posts, photos, and videos, in addition to posting status updates with their current geolocation. We already covered how to search within Facebook thoroughly. In this section, we will focus on searching for locations within Facebook user-generated content.

Using Facebook Graph in the Location Search

We already covered how to find a specific user's (or page/group's) Facebook profile_id value. The following links will demonstrate how to use a Facebook Graph Search to fetch results based on geotagged content.

Note!   Replace the number 100003886582037 with your target's Facebook profile ID in all the following queries.

- To display the places visited by target profile, type the following in your browser address bar: `https://www.facebook.com/search/100003886582037/places-visited/`.

- To display the recent places that were "checked in" by the target profile, type the following in your browser address bar: `https://www.facebook.com/search/100003886582037/places-checked-in/`.

- To display common places where two targets have "checked in" previously, type the following in your browser address bar: `https://www.facebook.com/search/Facebook_Profile_ID_1/places-checked-in/ Facebook_Profile_ID_2/places-checked-in/ intersect/`.

- To display common events where two targets have attended previously, type the following in your browser address bar: `https://www.facebook.com/search/ Facebook_Profile_ID_1/ events/ Facebook_Profile_ID_2/events/intersect/`.

- To see a list of posts written in a specific location, type the following in the Facebook search bar: **Posts written in Seattle, WA**.

Tip!   Finding the intersections between two Facebook profiles can reveal the relationships between them and open the door for further investigation.

Facebook Live

Go to Facebook Live (`https://www.facebook.com/live`) to see where there are live videos currently broadcasting. Live videos appear on a global map; a user can click any live video—represented as a blue dot—to view/save it.

Twitter

Twitter allows users to post tweets combined with current location data (see Figure 7-5). Such tweets can help investigators to determine the current/previous locations of a target at a specific point in time. In this section, we will cover how to locate tweets based on their geolocation information.

Figure 7-5. Posting a tweet with location information

Search for Tweets in a Specific Geographical Location

The Twitter search functionality allows you to search for tweets posted within a specific location using GPS coordinates. To locate all tweets posted from a specific location on Earth, follow these steps:

1. Open Google Maps, navigate to the target location, and click the exact point on the map to see its GPS coordinates (see Figure 7-6).

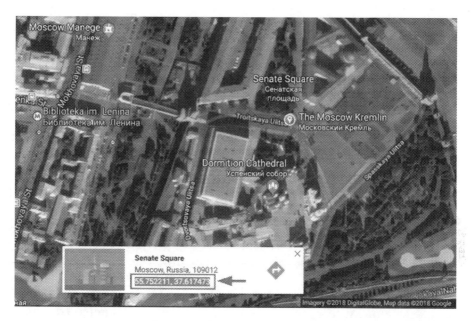

Figure 7-6. *Extracting the GPS coordinates of the target on Google Maps*

2. Go to the Twitter search box and type **near:** followed by the
   target's latitude and longitude enclosed in quotation marks
   (see Figure 7-7).

Figure 7-7. *Searching for all tweets that match the entered GPS coordinates*

3. You can add more advanced Twitter search operators to the
   previous search to further filter its results (see Figure 7-8).

Figure 7-8. *Adding advanced Twitter search filters to refine your search*

As shown in Figure 7-8, note that three filters are applied on the previous location search.

- *Within:3mil*: This limits the results to three miles from the target GPS coordinates.

- *Filter:images*: This returns tweets that contain images within it.

- *Since:2018-03-18*: The tweet's date must be from the date specified and later.

To see the exact time when any tweet was posted, hover your mouse over its timestamp (see Figure 7-9). Please note that the date/time that appears is according to the time zone of your Twitter account settings, not the uploader's date/time.

Figure 7-9. *Finding a tweet's date/time*

Tweet Mapper

Tweet Mapper (`https://keitharm.me/projects/tweet`) is a free service that lists all geotagged tweets (all tweets posted while the location feature is ON). All you need to do is to enter the target's Twitter handle and then press Enter. A map will appear showing red markers (see Figure 7-10) over all the geographical locations where this target posts their geotagged tweets. Click any marker to see related tweets below the map.

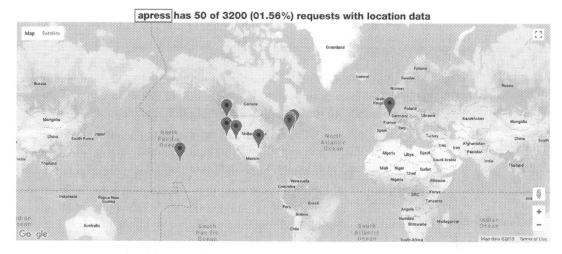

Figure 7-10. *Showing a tweets map for the user Apress*

One Million Tweet Map

View the world's last one million tweets on a map at https://onemilliontweetmap.com.
This is an interesting map to see live tweets from around the globe in real time. Different
filters can be applied to refine the results.

Qtr Tweets

Qtr Tweets (http://qtrtweets.com/twitter) allows you to find all tweets within a
specific distance from the target location on map. You can also search for keywords and
filter the results according to predefined criteria such as tweets with images and tweets
with nonlocation data.

Tweet Map

Tweet Map (https://www.mapd.com/demos/tweetmap) allows you to visualize all tweets
on a global map. Click the points—which represent tweets—to read tweet content. You
can also see top hashtags and tweets and search for them.

Periscope Map

Periscope Map (www.periscopemap.live) shows Twitter Periscope live videos on a
world map.

Other Social Media Platforms

There are hundreds of social media services, and many of them allow users to geotag published contents, but in this chapter we focused on the most popular two: Facebook and Twitter.

To enrich your thinking about the wide possibilities of OSINT gathering offered by geo-enabled social media services, we will briefly cover an additional service that uses users' geolocation data to offer functions. This service is called Strava, and it is used mainly as a social networking app for athletes to measure and share their activities.

Strava Heat Map

A Strava heat map (`https://www.strava.com/heatmap`) is a performance measurement sporting app for athletes; it works by monitoring athletic activities through the GPS sensor existing within their smartphone (supports Apple and Android) or any other supported device like GPS watches and head units and uploading such data to its servers to make it available for sharing. This is a free app, but it reserves some premium features for paying users (e.g., showing advanced statistics about user activities). The most popular usage of this app is tracking users' activities while cycling and running.

A Strava heat map shows "heat" made by aggregated, public activities over the last two years; this map is updated monthly. At the beginning of 2018, Strava revealed several military base locations in Syria and Afghanistan because the military personals inside these—secret—bases were using this app to measure and track their fitness exercises. Base locations appeared clearly as the soldiers were moving around inside the base, drawing a clear border of each base.

What happened with Strava shows clearly that despite all security measures, the lack of user security training can lead to revealing military secrets that are available for intelligence gathering.

Note!   Investigating a Strava heat map can reveal important information about users' sporting activities and the run routes they use.

You can view photos uploaded to Flickr on a map by going to `https://www.flickr.com/map`. Snapchat also has a live map to see snaps of events, breaking news, and more from around the world at `https://map.snapchat.com`.

Conducting Location Searches on Social Media Using Automated Tools

There are many tools that can prove useful when searching for data (both geotagged and nongeotagged) online. In this section, we will briefly mention some popular OSINT gathering tools for gathering different kinds of public information, including geolocation content, from both Internet and social media platforms.

- *Creepy* (`https://www.geocreepy.com`): This is a geolocation OSINT tool to gather geolocation information from Twitter, Instagram, Google+, and Flickr.

- *Oryon OSINT Browser* (`https://sourceforge.net/projects/oryon-osint-browser`): This contains scores of OSINT links to different services for public information discovery; it also comes equipped with privacy-enhanced features to protect your identity while conducting your OSINT search.

- *Maltego* (`https://spreadsecurity.github.io/2016/09/03/open-source-intelligence-with-maltego.html`): This is a data mining tool with GUI used to gather open source intelligence; it visualizes the results and finds interconnection between them.

- *Spider Foot* (`www.spiderfoot.net`): This is an automated OSINT tool that queries more than 100 open data sources to find information about the target.

Country Profile Information

These websites offer brief overviews and statistics about different countries throughout the world. Such overviews include information about a country's geography, history, politics, economy, international relations, culture, travel, military, health, education, and other topics.

The following are the most popular suppliers of country profile information:

- *The World Factbook* (`https://www.cia.gov/library/publications/the-world-factbook/index.html`): This is a reference resource published by the Central Intelligence Agency (CIA); it provides information on the history, population, government, economy, energy, geography, communications, transportation, military, and transnational issues for 267 world entities.

- *BBC Country Profiles* (`http://news.bbc.co.uk/2/hi/country_profiles/default.stm`): This is a guide to the history, politics, and economic backgrounds of countries and territories, as well as background on key institutions. It also includes archived contents of the BBC service.

Transport Tracking

With the advancement of communication technology, most vehicles and public/private transportation are location aware, meaning they come with a GPS or other satellite tracking system sensor to identify its current location. Tracking systems offer a comprehensive picture of the subject vehicle location in addition to other information about it such as vehicle name (if applicable), type, cargo, destination, owner, and many other technical details. Many free services online facilitate access to tracking information about land vehicles, ships, and airplanes; such information can prove extremely useful during any type of online investigation, especially when knowing that many sites also list previous tracking records of vehicles, ships, and vessels in its public databases.

Air Movements

The following services track air flights (cargo, private, and traveler airplanes). Some sites even offer a payment subscription to track military jets! Here is the list:

- *Flight Aware* (`https://uk.flightaware.com`): This company is considered the largest flight-tracking data company in the world; it offers its flight-tracking service free of charge for both private and commercial air traffic. FlightAware aggregates its data sources from air control systems in 55 countries in addition to ground stations in more than 150 countries. Using this service, you can search for flights by origin and destination airport or track a specific flight by using flight number or flight company. Private flights can also be tracked using this service. When tracking a specific flight, you can see the upcoming next flights and past flights. To see the entire flight history, you need to pay a subscription fee.

- *Flight Radar 24* (`https://www.flightradar24.com`; see Figure 7-11): This site offers an international real-time civilian flight-tracking service. It tracks more than 150,000 flights per day and has the ability to track specific types of military jets (like Russian and NATO jets) in some regions. Business subscribers can remove their private jets from public view, so it is essential to use more than one tracking service when investigating a specific target.

Figure 7-11. *Flightradar24 offers comprehensive details about each flight, including departure and arrival airports, flight route, schedule, estimated departure and arrival time, current flight speed and distance, and airplane type and model. Other details are locked for paid subscriptions.*

- *Air Cargo Tracker* (`www.track-trace.com/aircargo`): This tracks air cargo for 190 airlines; you need to supply the air cargo number to track the plane. The site also lists airline codes, airline prefixes, and airport codes.

- *Radar Box 24* (`https://www.radarbox24.com/`): This is an international airplane tracker. The free account shows basic flight information; you need to pay to unlock the full features.

- *PlaneFinder* (`https://planefinder.net`): This offers international plane tracking. The free account shows good information about each flight.

> **Note!**   The World Aircrafts Database (`www.planemapper.com/aircrafts`)
> holds information about international airline companies along with the planes
> (plane type and technical information) registered to them. The same site contains
> detailed information about each airline company worldwide.

Maritime Movements

The following services track ship movements around the globe.

- *Marine Traffic* (`https://www.marinetraffic.com`): This is the main
  marine-tracking site. Using this site, you can track any ship in the
  world. The site has a huge database of ship details and past tracking.
  To locate a ship, you can either search for its name using the site
  search facility or simply browse the live map to see all the available
  ships. To see specific ships details, click a ship on the map (ships
  appear as arrows on the live map). You can click the Vessel Details
  button (see Figure 7-12) to see complete information about this
  ship such as the name, MMSI number, IMO number, flag, weight,
  vessel type, dimensions, year built, latest position, vessel name
  history (if the ship changed its name, previous names and flags will
  appear here), and more. All this information is available with the free
  account (actually, I did not even register to view it). Paid accounts
  give more information, especially in relation to a customized map
  view, past tracking, and voyage history.

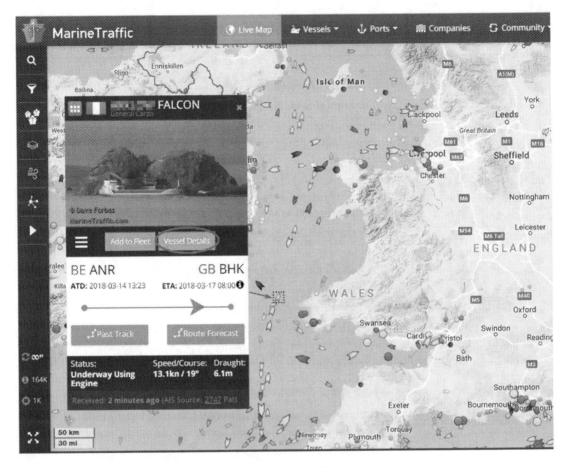

Figure 7-12. *Tracking ships using Marine Traffic website*

- *Container Tracking* (www.track-trace.com/container): This tracks
  containers for 125 companies; you need to supply the container
  number only.

- *Vessel Finder* (https://www.vesselfinder.com): This is a ship-
  tracking service.

- *Cruise Mapper* (www.cruisemapper.com): This tracks cruises and
  gives detailed information about each one, in addition to their
  current and past locations.

- *Ship Finder* (http://shipfinder.co): This tracks ships and gives
  detailed information about tracking vessels.

Note!   The following are other services that can be useful when tracking vessel information online:

- Container prefix list (`www.prefixlist.com`)

- The international identification codes of container owners (`https://www.bic-code.org/bic-codes/`)

- International port code (`www.infodriveindia.com/TradeResources/Port.aspx`)

Vehicles and Railway

The following sites give tracking information about land vehicles and railways movements:

- *ASM* (`https://asm.transitdocs.com`): This offers real-time train tracking across the United States.

- *Train Time* (`https://traintimes.org.uk/map/tube`): This offers a live map of London underground trains.

- *Aprs* (`https://aprs.fi`): This shows real-time information collected from the Automatic Position Reporting System Internet Network.

- *Spoorkaart* (`http://spoorkaart.mwnn.nl`): This is a train tracker for the Netherlands.

- *Junatkartalla* (`https://junatkartalla.vr.fi/?lang=en-US Track`): This tracks trains in real time across Finland.

- *Travic : transit visualization client* (`http://tracker.geops.ch/?z=11&s=1&x=529282.4572&y=6853173.3731&l=transport`): This offers live tracking of public transport (bus, trams, trains) in the Netherlands.

- *GotoBus* (`https://www.gotobus.com/track-bus-status`): This is a bus-tracking system that tracks buses in selected regions around the globe for the bus companies that are engaged in this service (United States, Mexico, Europe, and Canada).

- *Germany Train Route Maps* (`www.apps-bahn.de/bin/livemap/query-livemap.exe/dn?L=vs_livefahrplan&livemap`): This offers route maps for Germany.

Note!   To see a comparison of traffic signs in different countries, go to `https://ipfs.io/ipfs/QmXoypizjW3WknFiJnKLwHCnL72vedxjQkDDP1mXWo6uco/wiki/Comparison_of_MUTCD-influenced_traffic_signs.html`. Such information can be useful when investigating some images that contain traffic signs. This can help to determine the country of origin—and maybe the location—of the subject image.

Package Tracking

Package tracking is useful to track shipments across the entire world. If your OSINT work requires investigating a package sent via land or air, you can use the following links to find more information about it:

- *After Ship* (`https://www.aftership.com/couriers Track 447`): This tracks couriers worldwide. Just enter the package number, and it will automatically detect the courier company.

- *Tracking EX* (`https://www.trackingex.com`): This tracks 235 couriers.

- *17 Track* (`https://www.17track.net/en`): This is a package-tracking service.

- *Package trackr* (`https://www.packagetrackr.com`): This tracks global couriers and visualizes the delivery path with Google Maps.

- *Boxoh* (`www.boxoh.com`): This is a package-tracking service for USPS, UPS, FedEx, and DHL/AirBorne.

- *Canada Post* (`https://www.canadapost.ca/cpotools/apps/track/personal/findByTrackNumber?execution=e1s1`): This tracks packages in Canada.

- *Royal Mail* (`https://www.royalmail.com/track-your-item#`): This tracks royal mail delivery.

Note!   Track on the Map (`www.trackonthemap.com`) lets people follow your location online. You need a GPS-aware device—like a smartphone—for this to work.

Webcams

There are many sites offering free access to public webcams around the world. The following are the most popular ones:

- *World Web Cam Search* (`http://world-webcams.nsspot.net`): This displays available webcams from around the world using Google Maps.

- *Earth Cam* (`https://www.earthcam.com`): This is a live streaming webcam from different places around the globe.

- *Fisgonia* (`www.fisgonia.com`): This is a visual representation of a webcam—using Google Maps—from different locations around the globe. You can filter the cameras according to different categories such as airports, train stations, animals, traffic, universities, and so on, and you can specify the country using Google Maps.

- *World Cam* (`https://worldcam.eu`): This lists webcams in different places globally and offers information about the location such as their location on maps and weather information about the target area.

- *UM Weather* (`http://cirrus.sprl.umich.edu/wxnet/wxcam.php`): This lists hundreds of weather cameras across North America.

- *Opentopia* (`www.opentopia.com/hiddencam.php`): This lists publicly accessible webcams from different places around the world.

- *Mila* (`https://www.livefromiceland.is/webcams/geysir`): This is a live webcam from Iceland.

As we mentioned in Chapter 4, Google can also be used to locate publicly accessible webcams online. The best place to make such a search is the Google Hacking Database (GHDB) at `https://www.exploit-db.com/google-hacking-database13/`.

Digital File Metadata

We already covered in Chapter 2 how to investigate the metadata of digital files (such as images, videos, Microsoft Office files, and PDF). Some digital files—especially geotagged images and videos—can contain GPS coordinates. Investigating such files is easy; all you need to do is copy the GPS coordinates and use the services in this chapter to locate the address on a map of the subject photo or video.

Summary

Most user online activities can be associated with geolocation information. Locating information online through location-based searches can narrow down the results returned and make your investigation more focused.

In the next chapter, we will talk about something different from everything already mentioned. You will learn how to use different tools and techniques to gather intelligence—mostly technical information—about target IT infrastructure and websites.

CHAPTER 8

Technical Footprinting

Footprinting is the first task that hackers—both black and white hats—do before initiating their attacks against computerized systems. It is the act of using different tools and techniques to acquire as much information as they can before attacking the target. In the previous chapters, we covered how to use a wide array of tools and techniques to collect data online about different entities (such as people and organizations). However, we did not cover how to investigate a target's own web pages and network to acquire technical information.

In Chapter 1, we defined OSINT as referring to all information that is publicly available. This means OSINT sources are distinguished from other forms of intelligence in being legally accessible by the public without breaching any privacy or copyright laws. This legal definition also applies to technical footprinting when identifying a target's IT technologies, services, and networks.

In Chapter 1, we differentiated between three types of information gathering: passive, semipassive, and active. In this chapter, we are concentrating on the passive reconnaissance techniques only, as the other two methods may have a legal implication if applied without proper permission. Thus, you cannot consider them as belonging to the OSINT-gathering scope.

In passive reconnaissance, the target will know nothing about your information-gathering activities. You will not send any packets of data to target servers. Instead, you will browse the target website like any regular Internet visitor to look for interesting information. The amount of information gathered in this way is limited to what is presented on the target website. In semipassive reconnaissance, you are sending limited traffic to the target server. However, this traffic will not launch any alarm by the security systems implemented by the target organization's network (firewall and IDS) because this traffic will resemble any regular Internet traffic behavior.

© Nihad A. Hassan, Rami Hijazi 2018
N. A. Hassan and R. Hijazi, *Open Source Intelligence Methods and Tools*,
https://doi.org/10.1007/978-1-4842-3213-2_8

Both passive reconnaissance and semipassive reconnaissance are allowed by law in major countries (without obtaining a permit), although some countries may also consider some sorts of semipassive activities as a kind of illegal footprinting.

Note!   Active reconnaissance involves interacting directly with the target system; you can achieve this in various ways. For example, you can use social engineering techniques to acquire information from a target's help desk.

By doing passive reconnaissance, you can gather some useful technical information such as identifying the target organization's IP addresses, extracting domain name information, identifying its subdomain names, and identifying the IT devices and technologies in use. In addition, you can collect traditional types of information (for example, employee names and e-mails and document metadata) from the target website that can be used to profile target employees.

Investigate the Target Website

The first place you need to go when beginning your technical footprinting is the targeted company's web pages. Investigating a company's website will give you excessive amounts of useful information from a security perspective. The following are just some examples:

- Company address
- Branch office locations
- Key employees
- Open vacancies and job offers (job offers may reveal technologies used in the company)
- E-mail schema (by looking at staff e-mail addresses)
- Phone numbers
- Partner companies—or any company with a close business relationship
- Open hours and holidays

- News about target organization (merger or acquisition news)

- Technology used in building the target website

- E-mail system used (many organizations use open source technology like Horde and Roundcube)

- IT technologies (hardware and software) used by target organization

- VPN provider (if any)

- Digital files (such as PDF files and spreadsheets) and metadata (some organizations even post their inventory list, including IT equipment, on their websites)

- Privacy or security policy that lists IT security controls (for example, such documents may contain a password creation policy)

- Information about the organization's employees

Web pages are composed of HTML code, so it is advisable to begin there. You can view the HTML source to see whether the developers left any useful information in the HTML comments. You need also to check the head section of the HTML source code for attached documents such as CSS and JavaScript files. These files may also contain comments by their developers.

Note!   To view the HTML source code of any web page using Firefox, right-click the target page and select View Page Source. You can find useful information within HTML comment tags that look like this: <!-- this is a comment -->.

Many companies outsource their website design to foreign companies. Discovering this issue from the HTML source code will make the outsourced company part of your investigation endeavor.

Note!   Firefox has a built-in utility for aiding web developers. The Firefox Developer Tools are a set of web development tools that can be used to analyze the HTML source code of web pages. To launch the tool, press Ctrl+Shift+I or simply go to the Tools menu, select Web Developer, and then select Developer Toolbar.

Investigate the Robots.txt File

Web robots—also known as *crawlers* or *spiders*—are used by search engines to scan the Web automatically to discover new content. They are used by all search engines such as Google and Yahoo to index web contents. Web site owners use the robots.txt file in their website root directory to give instructions to web robots on what pages they want to include or exclude during the crawling process. When a robot reads Disallow: in the robots.txt file, it will ignore the file path after it. For intelligence purposes, checking this file will reveal what the website owner wants to hide from the public. To view the robots.txt file of any website, type in your browser address bar the target domain name followed by a forward slash and then robots.txt. See Figure 8-1 for a sample robots.txt file for the Apress.com domain name.

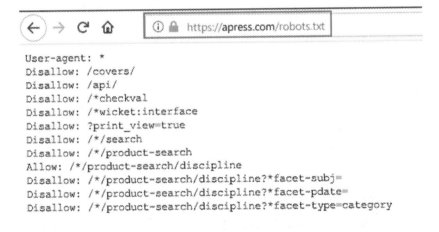

Figure 8-1. *Sample robots.txt file showing what pages are allowed to be crawled by web robots*

Note!   RobotsDisallowed is a project on GitHub (https://github.com/danielmiessler/RobotsDisallowed) that harvests the "Disallow" directories from the robots.txt files of the world's top websites (taken from an Alexa 100K global ranking).

Mirror the Target Website

Sometimes it is more convenient—when reviewing the HTML code—to download the entire target website for offline viewing/parsing, and there are automated tools for performing this task. The following are the most popular:

- *HTTrack* (`https://www.httrack.com`): Here you can copy a website for offline view.

- *GNU Wget* (`www.gnu.org/software/wget`): Here you can retrieve files using the HTTP, HTTPS, FTP, and FTPS Internet protocols.

- *BlackWidow* (`www.softbytelabs.com/en/BlackWidow`): Here you can download a complete site or part of it. You can also download any kind of files including YouTube videos embedded within a site.

Extract the Links

A target website can be linked with other applications, web technologies, and related websites. Dumping its links will reveal such connections and give the URLs of other resources (such as CSS and JavaScript files) and domains connected with it. There are many online services to extract the URLs, images, scripts, iframes, and embeds of target websites. The following are the most popular (use more than one service as they do not return the same results):

- *Link Extractor* (`www.webtoolhub.com/tn561364-link-extractor.aspx`): You can export the results to an Excel file.

- *Free URL Extractor* (`www.bulkdachecker.com/url-extractor`): Extract Links from URL/Domain (e.g. Links, images, scripts and Embeds).

- *Link Gopher* (`https://sites.google.com/site/linkgopher`): This is a Firefox add-on that extracts all the links from web pages, including embedded ones, and displays them in a new web page.

Note!   To see where a target website URL redirects to, use the following service: `http://redirectdetective.com`.

Check the Target Website's Backlinks

You should also consider checking all backlinks to a target organization's domain, as some linked websites may reveal useful information about the target. To see all linked websites to a specific domain name, type the following into Google: **site:* darknessgate. com** (there should be a space between the asterisk and the domain name).

This will return all sites that link to www.DarknessGate.com. To refine the search and return only the results from other domain names, exclude all links to the target domain from itself (see Figure 8-2).

Figure 8-2. *Finding backlinks to a specific domain name using Google advanced operators*

Monitor Website Updates

You should monitor web updates of the target website regularly. Of course, it is not convenient to monitor a website with hundreds of pages, so there are tools to automate this task. A popular tool for this is WebSite-Watcher (http://aignes.com/index.htm), which is a commercial program. This software will monitor web pages, forums, and RSS feeds for new postings and replies (even the password-protected pages) and report the changes.

Check the Website's Archived Contents

OSINT investigators should remember that the Web is always changing. Organizations update their websites regularly, and past versions of the target website may leak important information. Therefore, make sure to take a look at the previous versions of the target website using the Wayback Machine (www.archive.org).

Note!   To discover who is hosting any website, go to https://www.whoishostingthis.com.

Identify the Technologies Used

There are different ways to discover the type of technology used in a target organization. For instance, job postings offered on the target organization's site—and on other specialized job websites—are a valuable source of information (you can find the type of skills needed, required IT certifications, past experience with specific products/vendors), and from that you can easily identify the type of IT infrastructure, the OS, and other software used.

Tip!   If a target organization has more than one branch office, the type of skills needed—as listed in job posts—for a specific branch could be an indicator of the activities taking place in that branch.

To identify the technologies used to build a target website, there are many online services and tools available for this task. The most popular service is Built With (`https://builtwith.com`). To use this service, enter the target domain name to view its technology profile and relationship profile. The technology profile will show detailed information about target websites such as analytics and tracking codes, widgets, website languages, whether it is optimized for mobile views, content delivery network (CDN), JavaScript libraries, advertising networks, e-mail services, name server provider, SSL certificate, web server type, encoding, and document information. A relationship profile view offers important information about the target domain; it shows the historical usage of identifiers (such as Google AdSense identifiers) that are shared with other websites. By knowing this information, you can uncover which websites are also controlled by the same company/individual (see Figure 8-3).

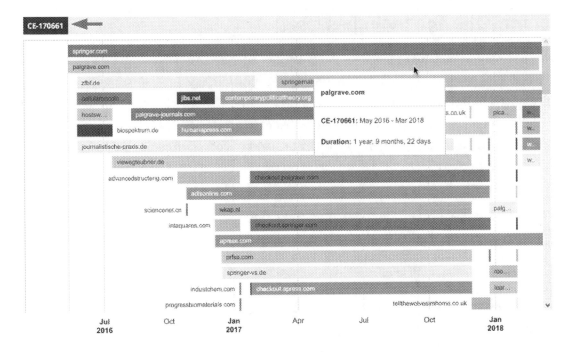

Figure 8-3. *Investigating the relationship profile of Apress.com shows CrazyEgg's tag usage and history (diagram generated by* `https://builtwith.com`*)*

Another tool to identify the web technologies used on target websites is Wappalyzer (`https://www.wappalyzer.com`). You can install it as an add-on to your Firefox or Chrome browser to investigate the technologies used on any website you visit.

Identifying the key technologies used—both software and hardware—will help you do some focused research to identify any vulnerabilities in the target organization's software, identify product-specific defects, and identify application-specific configuration problems. In the coming section, we will demonstrate how to identify a target OS server using an online tool.

Note!   To find domains sharing the same Google Analytics ID, go to `https://dnslytics.com/reverse-analytics`.

Note!   A lot of IT equipment (such as routers, managed switches, firewall solutions, servers, access controls, Internet surveillance camera, and even software packages) comes preconfigured with a default username and password. If the IT person who installs such devices forgets to update/remove the default credentials, such devices are vulnerable. The following sites list hundreds of IT equipment's default credentials:

- *CIRT* (https://cirt.net/passwords)

- *Default Password* (https://default-password.info)

- *Default Password Lookup* (www.fortypoundhead.com/tools_dpw.asp)

- *Router Passwords* (http://routerpasswords.com)

- *Open Sez Me!* (http://open-sez.me)

- *Hashes* (https://hashes.org)

To identify zero-day vulnerabilities of any software, remote services, or applications, including client-side exploits, check the following sites:

- *Exploit Database* (https://www.exploit-db.com)

- *Packet Storm* (https://packetstormsecurity.com)

- *Security Focus* (www.securityfocus.com/bid)

- *National Vulnerability Database* (https://nvd.nist.gov)

- *CVE Details* (https://www.cvedetails.com)

- *CVE* (http://cve.mitre.org)

- *0day* (http://0day.today)

- *Secunia Research* (https://secuniaresearch.flexerasoftware.com/community/research)

Web Scraping Tools

There are automated tools that can help you to collect various types of information from the target website easily. Such tools are known as *web scraping* tools or *web data extraction* tools. Imagine you want to collect e-mails from a big website (with thousands of pages). Doing this manually would be a daunting task, but when using automated tools, you can do it with a single click.

theHarvester

theHarvester (`https://github.com/laramies/theHarvester`) is a tool for gathering subdomain names, e-mail addresses, virtual hosts, open ports/banners, and employee names from different public sources such as Google, Bing, LinkedIn, Twitter, Yahoo, pgp, and more. The search conducted using this tool is passive, meaning that the target will not notice any reconnaissance activities from your side.

theharvester comes preinstalled on Kali Linux. However, you can install it on any Linux-based OS by entering the following command in terminal:

```
apt-get theharvester
```

To collect the target organization's e-mails, open the program and type the following:

```
theharvester -d springer.com -b all -l 500 -f results.txt
```

theharvester is used to execute the tool, and these are some options:

- `-d` specifies the domain to search or the company name.
- `-b` specifies a data source such as `google`, `googleCSE`, `bing`, `bingapi`, `pgp`, `linkedin`, `google-profiles`, `jigsaw`, `twitter`, `googleplus`, and `all`.
- `-l` limits the number of results to work with.
- `f-` saves the results into an HTML or XML file.

In the previous script, we are asking the tool to pull results from all data sources and to limit the result to 500 results. Also, the generated results should be saved in a file named `results.txt` in the same working directory (see Figure 8-4).

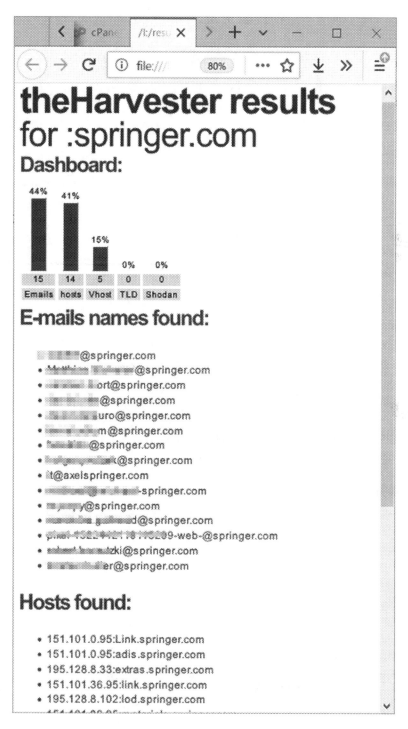

Figure 8-4. *Scraping e-mail addresses from the target domain name of Springer. com using theHarvester. The tool also resolves the target domain name into its IP address and discovers many virtual hosts related to the target domain name.*

The previous example is the simplest usage of this tool; we were able to collect target e-mail addresses in addition to discovering many subdomain names of the target main domain. This search also discovers virtual hosts (meaning multiple websites hosted on the same server). After getting some target e-mail addresses, you can use the techniques in previous chapters to build a profile for each one.

Web Data Extractor

Web Data Extractor (`www.webextractor.com`) is a commercial program that collects various types of data including URLs, phone and fax numbers, e-mail addresses, and meta tag information and body text.

Email Extractor

Email Extractor (`https://www.email-extractor.io`) is a Chrome add-on that extracts all e-mails from currently visited web pages.

Investigating the company domain name is the second task after the initial web page exploration. Different types of searches can be conducted on domain names. Let's start by finding the WHOIS information of the target domain.

Investigate the Target Website's File Metadata

When browsing a target company's website, you may encounter different types of files posted on it, such as files advertising products in JPEG or PDF format, spreadsheets containing product catalogs, and others. These files must be downloaded and investigated offline to extract their metadata. We already covered metadata in Chapter 2. In this section, we will list additional tools to analyze metadata in digital files:

- *Metagoofil* (`https://code.google.com/archive/p/metagoofil`): You can extract the metadata of public documents from a target company's website.

- *OOMetaExtractor* (`https://archive.codeplex.com/?p=oometaextractor`): You can extract an OpenOffice document's metadata.

- *Fingerprinting Organizations with Collected Archives* (`https://www.elevenpaths.com/labstools/foca/index.html`): This is a metadata analysis tool; it harvests public files from the Internet using three search engines: Google, Bing, and DuckDuckGo. Then you can search them for metadata and hidden information.

Website Certification Search

To show cryptographic certifications associated with any domain name, use these search services:

- *Censys* (`https://censys.io`)
- *Certificate Search* (`https://crt.sh`)

Website Statistics and Analytics Tools

Website statistics tools provide useful marketing, technical, and historical information about any domain name. You need to supply the target domain name only, and a detailed report is generated. The following are the most popular tools in this area:

- *Alexa* (`https://www.alexa.com/siteinfo`): Offers rich websites statistics and analytical info.

- *Moon Search* (`http://moonsearch.com`): Offers websites analytical services and Backlinks checker service.

- *Spy On Web* (`www.spyonweb.com`): Collect different information about target domain name like its IP address and used DNS server.

- *W3bin* (`https://w3bin.com`): Here you can find out who hosts a specific website.

- *Visual Site Mapper* (`www.visualsitemapper.com`): This tool shows outgoing and incoming links to a target website.

- *Site Liner* (`www.siteliner.com`): This tool shows duplicate content and related domain names.

- *Clear Web Stats* (`https://www.clearwebstats.com`): This tool shows detailed technical information about any domain name.

- *Website Outlook* (`www.websiteoutlook.com`): Different website statistics tools like social popularity, keyword analysis and website technical information.

- *Informer* (`http://website.informer.com`): This tool shows statistical information about websites.

- *Security Headers* (`https://securityheaders.io`): Here you can analyze HTTP response headers of target websites.

Website Reputation Checker Tools

There are many organizations that offer free online services to check whether a specific website is malicious. Some of these sites also offer historical information about a target website. The following are the various web reputation analysis services:

- *Threat Miner* (`https://www.threatminer.org/index.php`): This site offers domain threat intelligence analysis.

- *Urlquery* (`http://urlquery.net`): This is an online service to detect and analyze web-based malware.

- *URLVoid* (`www.urlvoid.com`): This is a website reputation checker tool.

- *Threat Crowd* (`https://www.threatcrowd.org`): This is a search engine for threats.

- *Reputation Authority* (`www.reputationauthority.org/index.php`): Here you can check a domain name's behavior score.

- *Sucuri SiteCheck* (`https://sitecheck.sucuri.net`): This is a website malware and security scanner. It will also show a list of links and list of scripts included within the target website.

- *Joe Sandbox* (`https://www.joesandbox.com`): This service detects and analyzes potential malicious files and URLs.

- *Safe Browsing* (`https://developers.google.com/safe-browsing/?csw=1`): This site offers APIs to access the Google Safe Browsing lists of unsafe web resources.

- *abuse.ch ZeuS Domain Blocklist* (`https://zeustracker.abuse.ch/blocklist.php?download=domainblocklist`): This is a blacklist of domain names.

- *Malware Domain Blacklist* (`http://mirror1.malwaredomains.com/files/domains.txt`): Holds a list of domains that are known to be used to spread malware online.

- *MalwareURL* (`https://www.malwareurl.com/index.php`): You can check a suspicious website or IP address here.

- *Scumware* (`https://www.scumware.org`): This is a list of malicious websites.

Note!   To see a list of websites that have been hacked before, go to `http://zone-h.org/archive` and search for the target domain name. If there is a previous hack, it will show you the hacked page (which replaces the original main home page), the hacker team responsible of this hack if available, and the date/time when the hack took place.

Passive Technical Reconnaissance Activities

Conducting passive reconnaissance activities for technical information means you are trying to identify subdomains, IP addresses, doing DNS footprinting, and getting WHOIS information of the target domain.

WHOIS Lookup

With a WHOIS lookup, you can find out who registered the target domain name in addition to other useful information such as the domain name owner and personal information, billing contact, and technical contact address (see Figure 8-5). This information is public and required to be so by the ICANN organization responsible for overseeing the domain name system. WHOIS information about each domain is stored within public central databases called WHOIS databases. These databases can be queried to fetch detailed information about any registered domain name. Please note that some domain registrants may opt to make their domain registration information private. (This service is called something different by each domain register and require paying additional fee, but the most common terms are *domain privacy* or *WHOIS protection*.) In these cases, the personal information of the domain registrant will be hidden in the WHOIS databases.

```
Domain Name: DARKNESSGATE.COM
Registry Domain ID: 1765860924_DOMAIN_COM-VRSN
Registrar WHOIS Server: whois.enom.com
Registrar URL: www.enom.com
Updated Date: 2017-12-12T23:50:05.00Z
Creation Date: 2012-12-12T16:51:31.00Z
Registrar Registration Expiration Date: 2018-12-12T16:51:00.00Z
Registrar: ENOM, INC.
Registrar IANA ID: 48
Domain Status: clientTransferProhibited
https://www.icann.org/epp#clientTransferProhibited
Registry Registrant ID:
Registrant Name: NIHAD HASSAN
Registrant Organization: DARKNESSGATE
```

Figure 8-5. *Partial WHOIS report about the DarknessGate.com domain name retrieved from* `https://whois.icann.org`

Numerous sites offer WHOIS information. However, the main one responsible for delivering this service is ICANN. ICANN and its local regional Internet registries manage the allocation and registration of IP addresses and domain names for the entire world.

- *ICANN* (`https://whois.icann.org/en`): This is the head organization responsible for coordinating the Internet DNS and IP addresses.

- *AFRINIC* (`https://www.afrinic.net`): This is responsible for the Africa region.

- *APNIC* (`https://www.apnic.net`): This is responsible for the Asia-Pacific region.

- *LACNIC* (`www.lacnic.net`): This is responsible for the Latin American and the Caribbean.

Many other online services give more information about registered domain names, listed here:

- *Domain History* (`www.domainhistory.net`): This shows archived domain name information.

- *Whoisology* (`https://whoisology.com/#advanced`): This is a domain name ownership archive.

- *Robtext* (`https://www.robtex.com`): This contains various information about domain names.

- *Who* (`https://who.is`): This offers a WHOIS search for domain name, website, and IP tools.

- *Operative Framework* (`https://github.com/graniet/operative-framework`): Here you can find all domains registered by the same e-mail address.

- *URL Scan* (`https://urlscan.io`): This shows different information about the target website such as IP detail, subdomains, domain trees, links, certificates, and technologies used to build it.

Now, after finding out who is responsible for the target domain name, you can begin discovering how the target company organizes its Internet resources through web hosts and subdomains.

Subdomain Discovery

A subdomain is a web address created under the current domain name address. It is usually used by website administrators to organize their content online. For example, `www.darknessgate.com` can use the subdomain `http://shop.darknessagte.com` for shopping and the subdomain `http://blog.darknessgate.com` for housing a blog.

Many website administrators may create subdomains to test new technology before applying it to the main site. Such sites are insecure because they are used in the development stage and could be left open to attack. Discovering such insecure subdomains can provide important information about the target company (for example, it may reveal the website code or leak documents forgotten on the server).

There are many tools/techniques for subdomain discovery. The following are the most popular ones.

Using Google Search Operator

Use *site:target.com -inurl:www* and Google will show all the related subdomain names of the target. For example, typing **site:yahoo.com -inurl:www** will show all the subdomains of the target domain name yahoo.com using the Google search page (see Figure 8-6).

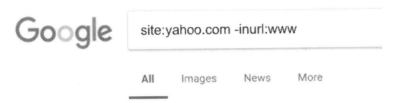

Figure 8-6. *Using Google advanced search operators for subdomain name discovery*

Using VirusTotal.com

The VirusTotal service checks suspicious files and URLs for malicious code. This service can be used for subdomain discovery. Go to `https://www.virustotal.com/#/home/search` (make sure to select the Search tab if it is not already selected). Enter the target domain name and press Enter. Scroll to the end of the page to find the "Observed Subdomains" section (see Figure 8-7).

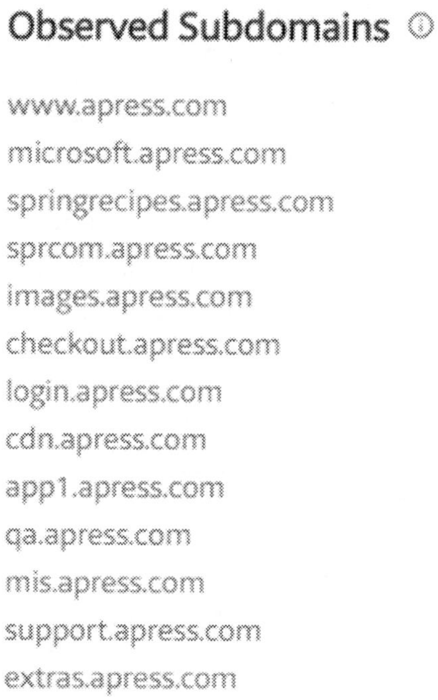

Observed Subdomains ⓘ

www.apress.com

microsoft.apress.com

springrecipes.apress.com

sprcom.apress.com

images.apress.com

checkout.apress.com

login.apress.com

cdn.apress.com

app1.apress.com

qa.apress.com

mis.apress.com

support.apress.com

extras.apress.com

Figure 8-7. VirusTotal showing the "Observed Subdomains" section for Apress.com

DNSdumpster

With DNSdumpster (`https://dnsdumpster.com`), you can find domain name information about subdomains, DNS servers, and MX records.

Here are other tools and services for subdomain discovery:

- *Dnsmap* (`https://tools.kali.org/information-gathering/dnsmapComes`): This is preinstalled on Linux Kali. It performs subdomain name discovery and shows the associated IP addresses for each subdomain name found.

- *Certificate Search* (`https://crt.sh`): This service also discovers subdomain names of the target domain.

- *Gobuster* (`https://github.com/OJ/gobuster`): This site discovers subdomains and files/directories on target websites. This tool is used as an active reconnaissance technique to collect information.

- *Bluto* (`https://github.com/darryllane/Bluto`): Here you can gather subdomain names passively via Netcraft.

- *PenTest Tools* (`https://pentest-tools.com/information-gathering/find-subdomains-of-domain`): Here you can discover subdomain names, find virtual hosts, and do website reconnaissance and metadata extraction from a target website.

- *Sublist3r* (`https://github.com/aboul3la/Sublist3r`): Here you can discover subdomain names using both passive and active reconnaissance techniques.

Tip!   Use more than one service for subdomain discovery because some services may return partial results based on their discovery method.

DNS Reconnaissance

After gathering information about the WHOIS records and target subdomain names, you can acquire more passive information about the target domain. In this section, we will list passive reconnaissance techniques to gather information regarding the DNS servers and the DNS records. The next stage is port scanning and other active reconnaissance techniques, which are considered outside our book's scope of OSINT-gathering activities.

Route Mapping

To determine the path to the target network, you need to use the `tracert` command. Please note that when information goes through networks, it does not follow the same path every time; it passes through different routers, firewalls, and other computing devices before reaching its destination. For high-value websites, the `tracert` command will be disabled, but it does not hurt to test it for your target website. There are many tools to perform tracerouting. On the Windows OS, open a command line prompt and type **tracert** followed by the target domain name (see Figure 8-8).

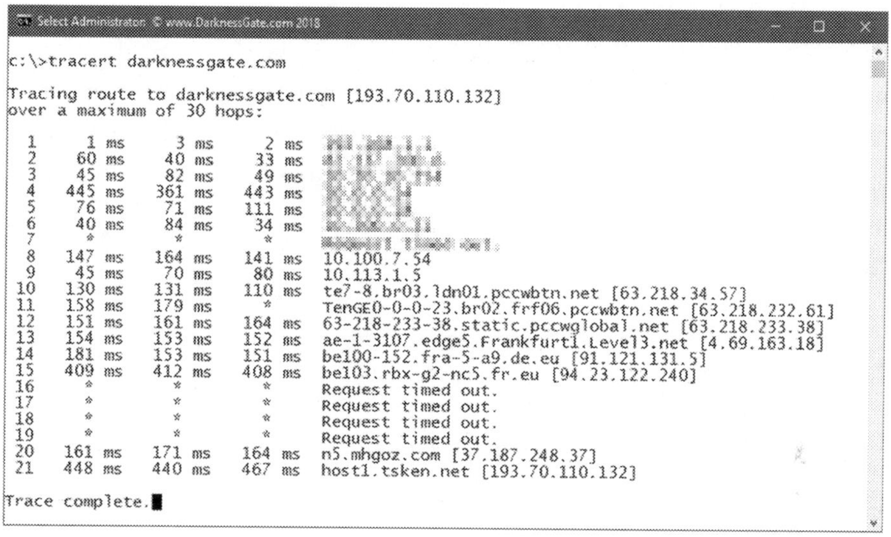
Select Administrator: © www.DarknessGate.com 2018
c:\>tracert darknessgate.com
Tracing route to darknessgate.com [193.70.110.132]
over a maximum of 30 hops:
1 1 ms 3 ms 2 ms
2 60 ms 40 ms 33 ms
3 45 ms 82 ms 49 ms
4 445 ms 361 ms 443 ms
5 76 ms 71 ms 111 ms
6 40 ms 84 ms 34 ms
7 * * *
8 147 ms 164 ms 141 ms 10.100.7.54
9 45 ms 70 ms 80 ms 10.113.1.5
10 130 ms 131 ms 110 ms te7-8.br03.ldn01.pccwbtn.net [63.218.34.57]
11 158 ms 179 ms * TenGE0-0-0-23.br02.frf06.pccwbtn.net [63.218.232.61]
12 151 ms 161 ms 164 ms 63-218-233-38.static.pccwglobal.net [63.218.233.38]
13 154 ms 153 ms 152 ms ae-1-3107.edge5.Frankfurt1.Level3.net [4.69.163.18]
14 181 ms 153 ms 151 ms be100-152.fra-5-a9.de.eu [91.121.131.5]
15 409 ms 412 ms 408 ms be103.rbx-g2-nc5.fr.eu [94.23.122.240]
16 * * * Request timed out.
17 * * * Request timed out.
18 * * * Request timed out.
19 * * * Request timed out.
20 161 ms 171 ms 164 ms n5.mhgoz.com [37.187.248.37]
21 448 ms 440 ms 467 ms host1.tsken.net [193.70.110.132]
Trace complete.

Figure 8-8. *Performing tracert on the target website*

Common DNS Record Types

Before collecting information from the target DNS, you need to know the main DNS record types. The domain name system has many records associated with it. Each one gives a different set of information about the related domain name. These are the most common DNS records:

- **A** is usually used to map hostnames to an IP address of the host. It is used for IPv4 records.
- **AAAA** is the same as record type **A** but used for IPv6 records.
- **CNAME** is the canonical name record. This record is often called an *alias record* because it maps an alias to the canonical name.
- **MX** is the mail exchange record. It maps domain names to its mail server responsible for delivering messages for that domain.
- **NS** is the name server record. It handles queries regarding different services related to the main domain name.
- **TXT** is the text record. It associates arbitrary text with a domain name.

nslookup Command

This command helps you discover various DNS information about the target domain name in addition to its resolved IP address. The command is available on both Windows and Linux. Let's begin by finding the A record of the target domain name (see Figure 8-9).

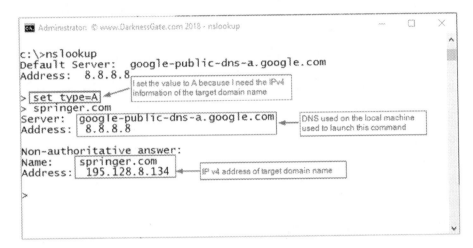

Figure 8-9. *Finding the A record of the target domain name using nslookup*

To see the MX records (mail server records) associated with the target domain name, type the command shown in Figure 8-10.

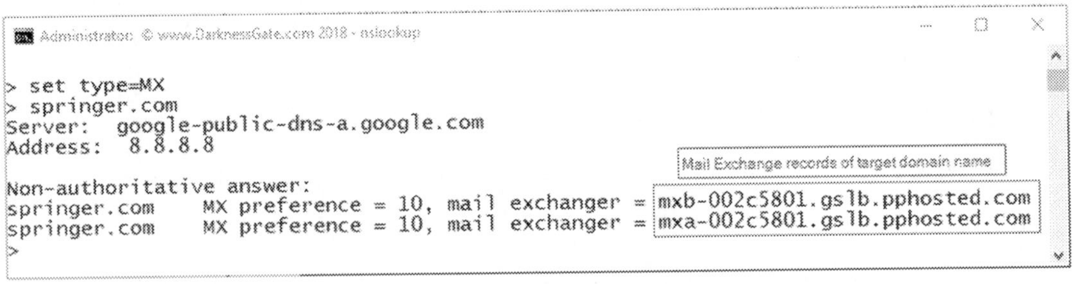

Figure 8-10. *Showing MX records with a target domain name*

In the same way, you can extract the IP address from any mail exchange server of the target domain name by typing **set type=a** and then entering the mail server address to resolve it into an IP address (see Figure 8-11).

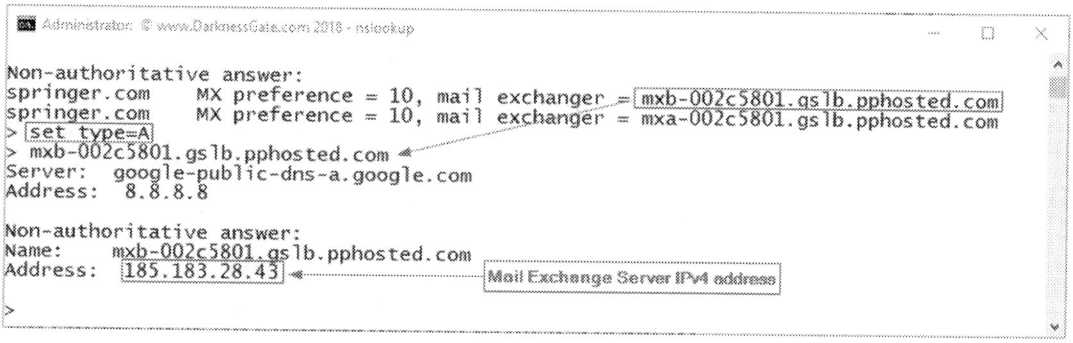

Figure 8-11. *Resolving the mail exchange server into an IPv4 number*

By knowing the mail exchange server IP address, you can further implement IP searching techniques on this IP address to locate more information about it, as you will see next.

You can use `nslookup` in the same way as using web tools; let's practice it using the MXtoolbox website.

Go to `https://mxtoolbox.com` and enter the target domain name in the search box. The site gives DNS information about a target domain name such as DNS lookup, MX lookup, WHOIS lookup, Sender Policy Framework (SPF) lookup, and DNS propagation. All this information is shown in a graphical user interface. An important feature of this site is that it gives you the authoritative name server of the target domain name (see Figure 8-12). Authoritative means the DNS server is the one that holds the actual DNS records (A, CNAME, MX, and so on) for the target domain name. Please note that during our previous `nslookup` tests, we were receiving a "nonauthoritative answer" when querying the target domain name. This because we are receiving a response from a cached version or from a local DNS server (your ISP's DNS server).

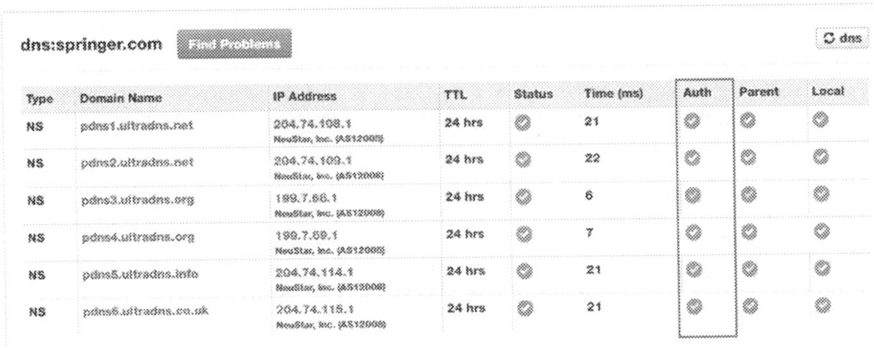

Figure 8-12. *Authoritative name server of the target domain name*

The following are other useful websites that offer DNS and web search tools:

- *W3DT* (https://w3dt.net): This offers various DNS lookup services and other network and Internet web-based tools.

- *DNS Stuff* (https://www.dnsstuff.com/tools): This offers various DNS, networking, and e-mail analysis tools.

Netcraft

Netcraft is a popular security scanner site that gives detailed security information about any website. To use it, go to https://searchdns.netcraft.com, enter the target domain name in the text box, and click the lookup button (see Figure 8-13). Netcraft will generate a detailed security report about the target website that includes the following (and more):

- Network information (IPv6, domain register, name server, DNS admin contact, hosting company, and more)

- Hosting history record

- Sender Policy Framework (SPF)

- Domain-based message authentication, reporting, and conformance record

- Web trackers associated with this site such as social sharing widgets, JavaScript files, and images

- Site technology and advertising networks

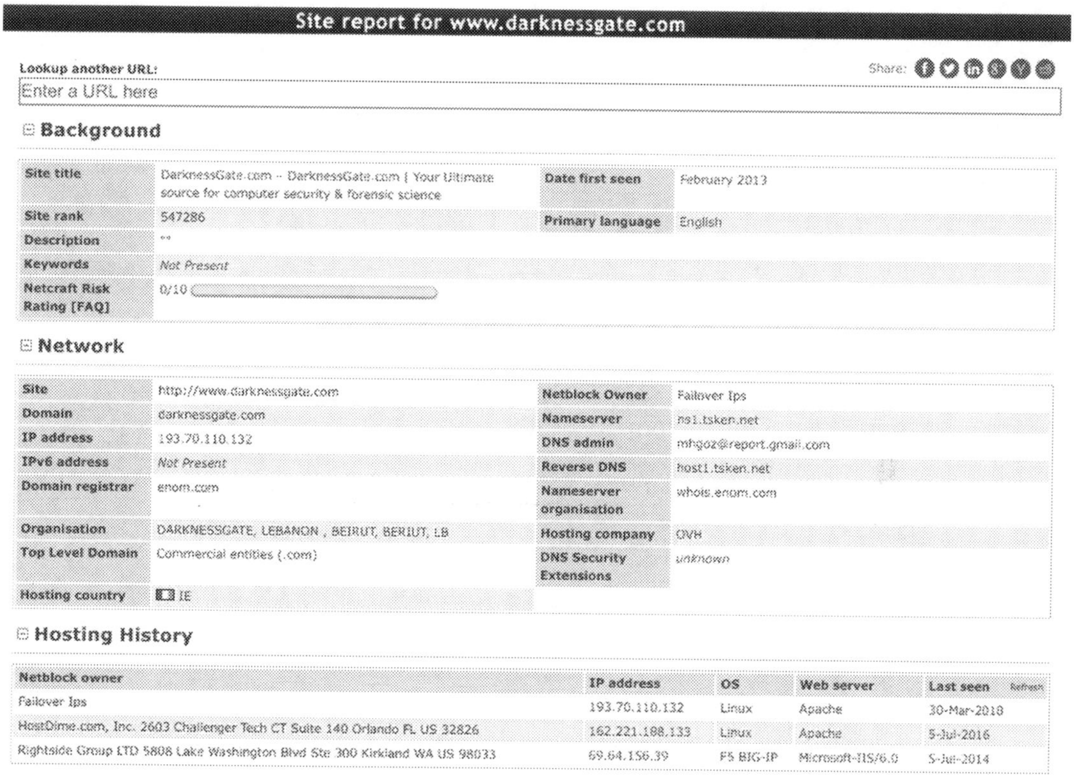

Figure 8-13. *Netcraft gives detailed security information about any website*

IP Address Tracking

In Chapter 2, we thoroughly covered the concept of IP addresses and how they can be used to track users online across various websites. In this section, we will list the most popular—and free of charge—tools that can help you to find more information about any IP address or domain name.

Here are tools for IP geolocation information:

- *IPverse* (http://ipverse.net): This shows the IPv4 and IPv6 address block lists by country code.

- *IP2Location* (www.ip2location.com/demo.aspx): This is a free IP location service.

- *Ipfingerprints* (www.ipfingerprints.com): This shows the IP address geographical location finder.

- *DB-IP* (https://db-ip.com): This shows the IP geolocation and network intelligence.

- *IPINTEL* (https://ipintel.io): This shows the IP address on a map and shows the ISP.

- *IP Location* (https://www.iplocation.net): This shows IP geolocation data.

- *UTrace* (http://en.utrace.de): Locate IP address and domain names.

Here are tools to gain information about the Internet Protocol (IP):

- *Onyphe* (https://www.onyphe.io).

- *CIDR REPORT for IPv4* (www.cidr-report.org/as2.0).

- *IP to ASN* (https://iptoasn.com): This shows the IP address to the ASN database updated hourly.

- *Reverse DNS Lookup* (https://hackertarget.com/reverse-dns-lookup): This shows reverse DNS entries for a target IP address.

- *Reverse IP lookup* (https://dnslytics.com/reverse-ip).

- *Same IP* (www.sameip.org): This shows sites hosted on the same IP address.

- *CIDR REPORT for IPv6* (www.cidr-report.org/v6).

- *IP Address Tools* (www.ipvoid.com).

- *ExoneraTor* (https://exonerator.torproject.org): Here you can check whether a particular IP address was used as a Tor relay before.

Here are tools to find out information about the Border Gateway Protocol (BGP):

- *BGP4* (www.bgp4.as/tools).

- *Hurricane Electric BGP Toolkit* (https://bgp.he.net).

- *BGP Ranking* (http://bgpranking.circl.lu).

- *BGP Stream* (https://bgpstream.com).

Here are tools to find out information about blacklist IP addresses:

- *Block List* (`www.blocklist.de/en/index.html`): Here you can report abused IP addresses to their server operators to stop the attacks or the compromised system.

- *FireHOL* (`http://iplists.firehol.org`): Here you can collect cybercrime IP feeds to create a blacklist of IP addresses that can be used on various networking devices to block malicious access/websites.

- *Directory of Malicious IPs* (`https://www.projecthoneypot.org/list_of_ips.php`): Directory of Malicious IPs.

Summary

Gathering technical information about a target website and network system is known as *technical footprinting*. During this book we focused on passive reconnaissance techniques, as the essence of OSINT gathering is concerned with acquiring publicly available information that does not need a permit in order to collect it. In this chapter, we covered tools and techniques that can be used to acquire OSINT intelligence about the target's website and network infrastructure passively.

In the next chapter, we will talk about the future and how the widespread use of the Internet, mobile communications, and social media platforms will impact the future of OSINT-gathering techniques.

CHAPTER 9

What's Next?

OSINT has become the preferred information-gathering method for intelligence agencies around the world. Traditionally, intelligence services relied on other channels to acquire information with varying degrees of reliability and usefulness; however, as computing technology continues to advance and the Internet and social networks are even more widely accessible around the globe, intelligence services have shifted a large percentage of their intelligence-gathering activities into the OSINT scope. Some intelligence experts estimate that more than 90 percent of intelligence information is coming now from OSINT sources.

OSINT is not limited to intelligence services, law enforcement, and military agencies. OSINT has become an integral component in the decision-making process for governments, business corporations, UN agencies, nongovernmental organizations, academia, the media, and civil societies such as citizen advocacy groups and labor unions. Nowadays, corporations use OSINT to investigate internal leakages, collect competitor intelligence, and predict trends in foreign markets. OSINT is also used by black hat hackers and criminal organizations to explore data that could be used to better attack or socially engineer a target.

Where Will OSINT Go Next?

The information age has resulted in an explosive amount of potential intelligence sources and will shape the future of OSINT gathering. In the intelligence arena, it is predicted that the practice of harvesting online data to counter terrorism and solve crime will increase. In addition, OSINT will continue to offer a cheap method to acquire intelligence about any community around the globe. For example, many studies show that recent protests in Arab countries were predicted by western security services after analyzing Arabic users' behaviors on social platforms at that time.

© Nihad A. Hassan, Rami Hijazi 2018
N. A. Hassan and R. Hijazi, *Open Source Intelligence Methods and Tools*,
https://doi.org/10.1007/978-1-4842-3213-2_9

In the civil area, businesses will be more willing to develop their own OSINT capabilities to gain competitive advantages and to secure their investments in an ever-changing world. Large organizations will work to have their own OSINT teams, while commercial OSINT providers will continue to offer their services to small and medium corporations that cannot afford to have an independent OSINT-gathering department.

Note!   Many corporations already use OSINT for risk prediction, which they call *competitive intelligence* or *business intelligence.*

From an information security perspective, OSINT gathering will continue to be a stepping stone for most penetration testing assessments to evaluate system weaknesses and work to fix them quickly. Organizations will work to integrate their OSINT intelligence into an organization's overall cyber-defense strategy to protect their assets and to strength their security posture.

The main obstacle against OSINT gathering is the mass volume of data that needs to be processed. Indeed, the huge advancements in mobile computing and the increased speed of the Internet will make people more willing to post a considerable volume of data to the Internet. This tremendous stream of public data will make analyzing it extremely time-consuming. Governments and giant corporations are continually testing new technologies to overcome this. Investments in analytic technology have become a priority by many governments and giant IT corporations as it will lead to processing huge volumes of data in order to turn it into data that can be queried and modeled to build conclusions quickly.

Note!   Data generated from Internet of Things (IoT) devices is also considered a major challenge. In the near future, it is expected that we will have billions of working IoT devices. The resulting data/metadata from these devices is huge and requires sophisticated analytical tools to gain useful intelligence from them.

Another challenge to OSINT gathering is the predicted growth of "fake news" online. Currently major social networking platforms like Facebook and Twitter face a real challenge to counter such activities. New algorithms—and usage policies—should be developed to verify news sources automatically before considering them valid OSINT sources.

Advancements in computing technology will certainly lead to creating efficient algorithms to handle the massive volume of data and to separate the irrelevant data from the target data. The advances in artificial intelligence and machine learning technologies will again transform OSINT in the coming years.

OSINT Process

During this book, we did not explicitly talk about the process—or specific flow of steps—that should be followed to gather OSINT. The OSINT-gathering activities can take place in no particular order according to each case or purpose. However, the flow of chapters in this book can also considered a good way to organize your OSITN searching activities.

In general, there are five main stages for any OSINT-gathering activity, as explained here:

1. *Identify the sources*: You identify the sources where you want to collect this data (e.g., the Internet, newspapers, magazines, commercial databases, and so on).

2. *Harvest the data*: You use different tools and techniques to gather data from the target sources; bear in mind that you should follow passive techniques to gather this data.

3. *Process and verify the data*: You process the gathered data and verify uncertain data from the data from more than one source if possible. You should also identify current and outdated data and exclude the irrelevant data from further analysis.

4. *Analyze the data*: You analyze the data and try to find connections between it to formulate a complete picture about the target.

5. *Deliver the results*: You present a report of your findings to the relevant party. This step is important and usually overlooked by many OSINT gatherers. It is necessary to present your key findings in an easy-to-understand format for any end user.

Final Words

To conclude, we think the future of OSINT is extremely bright! Both public and private organizations will work to integrate OSINT gathering into their overall decision-making processes. New industries will be eager to exploit the huge data resulting from the information revolution to support their business strategies and intelligence.

We hope this book was successful in shedding light on this important concept that have been widely used since the dawn of history under different names.

Index

© Nihad A. Hassan, Rami Hijazi 2018
N. A. Hassan and R. Hijazi, *Open Source Intelligence Methods and Tools,*
https://doi.org/10.1007/978-1-4842-3213-2

G